First

AMERICA IS WORTH SAVING

Other Works of Theodore Dreiser

THEODORE
DREISER

America

Is Worth

Saving

MODERN AGE BOOKS
NEW YORK

TABLE OF CONTENTS

AMERICA IS WORTH SAVING

CHAPTER ONE

Does the World Move?

IT DOES. Believe it or not. There may have been a period in which more exciting, disturbing, distressing, and straining things or developments were taking place, but no one who is alive today remembers them. You may have lived twenty, thirty, forty, sixty, or a hundred years ago, but you never saw the time in which more crashings and rumblings and upbuildings and downfallings, physically and mentally, were under way, or afloat, as we say. Such doings! My goodness! Or, my God! Not a day goes by and hasn't since I've been alive in which I haven't seen or heard of the most startling things taking place—the telephone, the electric light, the trolley car, the cheap sewing machine, the typewriter, ice-cream soda, Barnum's circus bringing Africa to America in gold-tinted cages, the Pullman car, the skyscraper, railroad-car refrigeration, the victrola, the Mergenthaler linotype, the binder and reaper, the thirty-two-share plow, the motor car, the airplane, the moving picture, radio, good roads, insulin—the Associated Press, the cheap magazine, birth control, the subway, the bus—in sum, everything as fast as they could come and as they continue to come. Consider uranium 235.

I have not mentioned the great wars, or the chemical and physical blessings that have also in some instances proved horrors. But they're in my mind. In fact, for the United States at least, and for the world when it gets around to it, scarcity has disappeared, as our vast unsalable and stored or destroyed supplies show. And, of course, plenty is at hand if we care, or are permitted, to distribute it. The only thing that hasn't changed, I want you to note, is the physical poverty of the

majority as opposed to the physical comfort and ease of the minority
which, as you know, has not changed, although now it can be if we
wish to play fair. And that is one thing which in the face of all the
invention and scientific discoveries making for plenty as against scarcity,
and leisure as against human slavery, has surprised me. For in the
midst of these devices which appeared to me to be for man's increasing
comfort and entertainment, as well as his intellectual and physical
improvement, I still discovered, as I went along, that in the main the
majority of men, women, and children in America and elsewhere
weren't any better housed, clothed, or fed than they were when I was
a child. In the earlier days men didn't appear to see, hear, or know so
much so quickly as they do now, but amid all this change today people
certainly did appear to enjoy hearing about, or looking at, or being
permitted to share in some small way at least some of these newfangled
pleasures or comforts.

But as in earlier times and as has been the case with the growth
of other lands, Titans began to appear here in America—our robber barons, or brigands of finance (as you choose). And, as in
the past and in other parts of the earth, these Titans seizing, holding, and controlling vast areas of land, vast rights in connection
with the resources of the earth and the transportation of them—coal,
iron, copper, oil, gold, gas, electricity, the railroads—not to mention
forms of communication: the telephone, telegraph, express. Great
giants these were—Vanderbilt, Gould, Sage, Morgan, Rockefeller, Car-
negie; the Crockers, Armours, Huntingtons, Fairs, and who not else.
And each setting aside for himself and his affairs not only the labors
but the returns or profits on the labors of men and women and children
—slaves, even, in the South: that is to say, returning to each as little
as possible in wages for what he did, and reserving for himself, in the
form of profits or taxes on what the masses were forced to have or use
or consume, all that could by any trickery or force be retained. In fact,
the labor-saving and plenty-supplying inventions were at once looked
upon as devices to be seized—that is, patented and controlled by individuals or small groups who had no more idea of improving the condition of the many than they had of giving all that they had to the poor.
Their thought, if any, was just the other way round: to seize and hold
these things in order to set themselves apart as rich men—multi-

millionaires—and by reason of that contrast to obtain a feeling of individual distinction and worth-whileness, which otherwise, in so far as they themselves were concerned, they could not feel.

Wealth! The envy of the have-nots pulsing like a pleasant cooling breeze upon those who, *materially,* have everything. No thought of the inventor or discoverer of any of these important devices as being anyone of importance. No thought of the scientist, the thinker, the artist, the poet as being anything of import. Galileo, for instance. Shakespeare, S. F. B. Morse, Alexander Bell, Edison, Marconi—pooh! Poor men. Dunces really. Creatures willing to devote years to perfecting a great device such as the airplane, the submarine, the dynamo or the cloud chamber or Geiger counter—and without profit. A mere living. Lunatics, of course. Fools. But compensated for in this best of all possible worlds by individuals who know enough to seize on the devices of the same—the savings or labors of every struggling mortal—and keep them packed in banks, rent them out for exorbitant interest, and so become truly great. And, of course, remain great.

And so in America, as well as other places in the world, the spectacle of sordid poverty: slavery in the south, vast slums in the newest and youngest of our great world cities—children wasting in our mills and our fields—miners digging in the earth for coal, for iron, copper, silver, lead—and for wages that barely kept a roof over their heads, a fire in their stoves, and a minimum of food on their tables. And this, mind you, in the face of this downpour of inventions and labor-saving devices, which in the eyes of most of their inventors were looked upon and intended for the betterment and comfort of all.

And yet now look!

Most of these inventions have been with us for so long—very, very many of them as long as a hundred years!

The cotton gin! The spinning jenny! The sewing machine! The typewriter! And yet about us millions of men and women unemployed —nine millions at the fewest. And no work in sight—not even with war to aid. And millions more on half- or one-third time pay. And the dole! And suicides. And cries to the effect that the incompetent should be allowed to die—not the rich incompetent but the poor incompetent. There is a distinction to be made here, as you should know.

And yet as I said in my opening word—the world does move. *It does!*

Don't forget that a war was fought in this country to free slaves—and that right in the midst of all this grabbing. Also the labor union appeared, and ever more and more of these amazing inventions which I have listed above. Also the agronomist with his science of agriculture —his vitamins—making not only two blades to grow where one grew before but seventy-five or a hundred. And machines that, Aladdin-like, turn sand or rock into silk—endless silk of all colors; or cyclotron-wise split atoms into bismuth or magnesia or lithium. But every such achievement or discovery making more and more fantastic the spectacle of poverty amid plenty—millions of jobless men, for instance, walking among warehouses stuffed with food or clothing that cannot be sold for want of money which the want of work to do creates. And these same banks previously referred to stuffed with gold which cannot be invested for want of projects which employ men—cannot even be loaned. And yet these men—their wives and children—starving! And dying—or being sent into wars where they will conveniently die—and so, no more pester about them. Not one squawk in a transport-load.

But—I repeat again—the world does move. It rotates around the sun. And the significance of that remark lies in the fact that for tens of thousands of years before written history began, and for more than six thousand years after that, the world was busily rotating on its axis and moving around the sun, but our ancestors who lived on it were positive that it was flat and static. And that the sun circled about it. What they thought did not in any way alter the fact which we now know. *Under torture* Galileo, who like all wise men after him was called an atheistic disrupter merely for discovering the truth that existed, denied that the world moved. Afterward, out of hearing of his inquisitors, he whispered the most famous of all stage asides:

"But it does move."

To suggest that there is any doubt about that today is to qualify for the psychopathic ward. And yet a great deal of our muddled thinking about the present jam is due to failure to keep this truth in mind: to seeing our world as a flat and static checkerboard on which yesterday, today, and tomorrow, men play the same game with the same checkers —with the same possibilities of success or failure depending merely on the cunning and strength of the players. The fact is that the board, the checkers, and the players never stop changing.

How do we know that? Not because natural truth changes but because the field of truth which we have discovered is constantly widening. It is one kind of game when man lives in trees and is only conscious of the need to get from nature those things he must have to remain alive. It is another kind of game when he learns how he can assist nature by fire, by husbandry, by implements of stone and clay and wood and iron, and so begins to be able to accumulate wealth. At that stage, since one man can produce more than he himself needs to live, the stronger man gets the idea of making his weaker brethren produce while he just consumes. It isn't a "wicked" idea but a perfectly natural one. Anyhow it is a fact that it occurs—men and some insects do that very thing—the slave-owning ants, for instance.

However, the game changes again when man begins really to master nature, so that a single person can produce tenfold, fiftyfold, a hundredfold what he himself needs, although each produces in one specialized field. The emphasis now shifts to methods of exchange between the different kinds of producers, so that each may get a little of each kind of product. For this purpose money has to be invented, and in course of time money becomes a whole industry in itself. Gold and silver and paper which man cannot consume, originally introduced only to fill the needs of exchange, take on an intrinsic value. More and more men are able to live—to retain and direct, if they cannot personally consume, lions' shares of what others produce—without ever producing a single thing that is consumable.

Yet here again is no abstract "wickedness" in the man who lives thus. He acts as it is natural for him to act in that particular stage of the development of knowledge. He and others like him—imitations of him—continue to do so until knowledge advances to a higher stage yet, which no force on earth can stop it from doing: until the great mass of producing people, realizing that they now know how to produce plenty for all instead of for just a few, insist on reorganizing the checkerboard and bringing distribution up to the efficient level reached by production.

This constant change, this forward movement, is like the boiling of water. During the time that the water is heating, the illusion of a static world is produced—and again quite naturally, the men who profit under the existing rules do all they can to foster that illusion. But although nothing is done to the stove, and the heat under the kettle remains the same, there comes a point where the water is suddenly changed into steam. Thus at intervals in the process of boiling and reboiling, which is human progress, there are points at which a complete change in kind takes place—the water becoming steam and blowing off the lid. That change is known by a word which is made artificially ugly by those who profiteer by existing conditions, but which is really no more ugly than, and just as inevitable as, "boiling" is in the world of kettles: *Revolution*.

A revolution is an event which respectable checker-players of the period view with horror and try vainly to exorcise with mystic spells, but which—that is, the changes effected by it—soon becomes acceptable to all—even later is canonized as something holy—in order, once again, to chain down progress and keep the world from moving any further. To make the less fortunate accept this static idea of the world, soothsayers are employed. Thus our American Revolution produces its "Daughters," a well-meaning group of ladies whom Upton Sinclair has justly dubbed the "Daughters of No More American Revolutions." But the world, like the kettle, cannot possibly be prevented from boiling up again except by turning off the heat. And that cannot be done because the heat is imbedded in nature itself: it is the insatiable appetite for truth and more truth. Whether we like it or not—and personally I do, and I hope you do—that appetite is as eternal as the appetite for food.

Do we agree thus far? If not, I don't believe we can make any headway in this attempt to puzzle out the tangle we are in. I do not advance any startling new theory brewed in my own head. I merely go to history, our common source-book of truth, and set down what I find there.

It does move! At every stage in our discovery of truth the game nature orders us to play, so that we may have life and have it more abundantly, has been different—has faced us with different problems requiring different kinds of action on our part—has made us different. We can learn from history the nature of the eternal process in the midst of which we are born. We *cannot* learn from our ancestors' ways of solving their problems exactly how we can solve our problems. We know just how the empires of Genghis Khan and conquistador

Spain and Napoleon crumbled, and how the dominion of semi-feudal England over colonial America was thrown off. But that doesn't tell us how to deal with Adolf Hitler, for man has moved far ahead in his knowledge of his basic problems, and that new knowledge makes it a new world.

Let's try to avoid abstractions. Let's not seek our solution in the idea that this system is "bad," that system "good." Each new way of life that has come along has been necessary and inevitable at the time it came. Men are motivated by their material and spiritual needs: they act to satisfy them. What was good and necessary a century ago cannot be wholly good and necessary today, though some or much of it may remain good.

From the beginning of time there has always been conflict. In religious terms it is called the conflict between good and evil. What is it in practical terms? It is the conflict between those who, being on top of the heap, are interested in trying to stop the world from moving; and those who, being at or near the bottom of the heap, are interested in giving head-room to the movement and accelerating it. The first group accuses the second of trying to interfere with "order," but the truth is just the other way about. *It is the defenders of things as they are who interfere with order,* because *the natural order of things is movement.*

For our part, let us not accuse, let us try to explain.

"It does move."

If we agree with Galileo we have somewhere to go from and somewhere to go.

CHAPTER TWO

Scarcity and Plenty

POVERTY IN the midst of plenty—the great paradox of our day."
How many hundreds of times in the past decade have we read
and heard those words? They have been recited so often, and with so
little visible effect on the allegedly "free" actions of *homo sapiens,*
that they have become just another catch-phrase, like "Yes, We Have
No Bananas." Indeed, that famous song of the decade before the depression, the decade of false "prosperity," might have been written as
a theme-song for the bedlam 'thirties.

We seem incapable of doing anything about such an obvious ab-
surdity as this poverty amid plenty. As a people we are fascinated by
the possibilities of general plenty and streamlined comfort opened up
by recent scientific discoveries. We stand in line for hours to gain
entry to the "world of the future" exhibits at our great fairs. But, to
judge by the amount of elementary thinking we have done about the
implications of such exhibits, they are just an amusing game to us
and not a reality. We have become so used to living in a gigantic
paradox that paradox is already accepted as the normal state of affairs.

We watch, for instance, research men demonstrate runless nylon
stockings, television, newspapers printed by radio, the tubing of light
upstairs and downstairs and around corners through "glass" made from
coal, the cooking of food without a stove by making the steel particles
in a frying pan rub against each other. It has been a good show, and
Mrs. America goes home to cook her family's meager supper on the
old gas range by the light from a filament bulb. After dinner she
settles down with the newspaper which has been printed downtown

and brought by a boy on a bicycle. She reads about how much of man's created wealth has been destroyed by high explosive that day, how much food has been plowed under or thrown into the sea, how many millions of her own people are on relief, and how many hundreds of millions of Europeans face starvation—and the good news that Brazil's problem of "surplus" coffee has at last been solved by a method of making wallboard out of coffee beans.

Then Mrs. America dons her best stockings, which are most likely of silk but may be of nylon, to go forth and dance or visit friends. It doesn't much matter of which material the stockings are, because in either case they are subject to runs.

How many Mrs. Americas stop to notice the paradoxes they have encountered in this brief period? And of those who do notice them, how many consider the implications of them?

The boy has brought the newspaper on the bicycle, the food is cooked on a gas range, the light comes from bulbs, there is no television, because it "does not pay" to modernize when millions of dollars are invested in the out-of-date articles. The people are idle because it "does not pay" to let them work; food is destroyed because it "does not pay" to give it to people to eat—any more than it pays to put out runless stockings. If runless stockings were available, the stocking industry would be "ruined," and therefore months of grueling research have had to be put in by experts to destroy the value of the thing they created.

"Young men," the demonstrator at the Fair reassures us, "need not fear that the day of opportunity is over, with nothing more to be invented and no new industries to be developed." Beautiful and consoling! But again the paradox: every new thing they invent lessens the "opportunities" in terms of jobs by increased mechanization of production and living amenities. Every new invention creates new paradoxes, for since purchasing power is distributed only for work done, and the inventions make less work by the human element necessary, the more we can produce the less we can consume. And this is true of not only America but of all countries everywhere, because in many countries labor is so plentiful as to be rewarded with only six cents or less a day. Still the labor-saving machines are being introduced, and greater starvation follows, for the cheapest thing in life is human labor.

If this can be discarded and humanity be reduced to a minimum in numbers, so much the better. The comfortable few will have fewer of the miserable to fear or to annoy them.

"The trouble," in those familiar words which we do not think of putting a strait-jacket on anyone for saying, "is that we have too much."

We in America produce 92 per cent of the world's natural gas, not counting the speeches of Senators and Congressmen on Saving Democracy.

We produce 60 per cent of its crude oil, 50 per cent of its lead, copper, zinc, asbestos, corn, and cotton; 88 per cent of its nickel, 82 per cent of its sulphur, 43 per cent of its chemicals, 90 per cent of its movies, 66 per cent of its silver. We possess 69 per cent of the known coal reserves in the world, 53 per cent of the world's telephones, and 81 per cent of its automobiles.

Our people are only 8 per cent of the world's population, and that is what we have. We can also point, though perhaps with less pride, to the 70 per cent of the world's gold which has been taken from holes in the ground in Africa, Russia, Australia, and elsewhere and put into another hole in the ground in Kentucky. There is nothing we can do with it except to fill teeth, but our diet in this rich land is so lacking in essential elements that most of our teeth do need filling.

The income from this vast wealth we have so divided that the man who produces most, particularly of the things everyone most needs, receives least. A quarter of our people are farmers and they receive 11 per cent of the income—and a good deal of that is paid them for not growing things or for destroying what they grow. Forty-one per cent of all our families live on an average of $758 a year. Eight million families, according to the government, "continually face starvation" while another eleven million are "fighting poverty." Only ten million families have enough or more than enough of the essentials of life, and few of those have any security for the future.

About nine million men and women who want to produce the things they and their neighbors need are described as "surplus labor." They are not allowed to work and must go hungry and in rags with their "surplus" families.

Of the two million children we bear annually, nearly half find themselves in families on relief. More of our employable people are un-employed than the total number of workers on our farms. Last year ten thousand men and women waited twenty-four hours for six hundred jobs in Cleveland, and four thousand women and girls waited in line all day in New York for twelve available jobs at eighteen dollars a week.

Meanwhile we have so much "surplus" food and clothing material that one of our main national problems is where to put it. Last May there were 615,000,000 pounds of "surplus" pork, more than 100,000,000 pounds of "surplus" butter, 62,000,000 pounds of "surplus" beef, 237,-000,000 pounds of "surplus" lamb, mutton, and mutton lard, and 86,000,000 pounds of "surplus" poultry in our cold storage vaults. Astronomical millions of bales of cotton are on hand, and in the South Negro and white sharecroppers grow more cotton up to the very doors of their pigsty "homes"—until they are incapacitated for work by influenza, pneumonia, and other ills resulting from their lack of cotton clothing, cotton bedding, cotton towels, and cotton carpets. When and if they get back on their cotton-sock-less feet, having suffered great inconvenience from the lack of cotton handkerchiefs—not to mention the complete absence of doctors and medicines—they may if they are lucky just be in time to get out the plow and earn a pittance in the fall cotton-destroying season.

In California nature's mountain ranges are rapidly being rivaled by the man-made mountains of "surplus" oranges and potatoes which we carefully spray with poison so that the hungry may not eat. And this year one-third of the California lettuce crop, of which our progress in artificial irrigation and agricultural technique has produced a disastrous abundance, is being destroyed to preserve for the American people the liberty to have rickets, scurvy, and pellagra.

The gasoline situation is equally critical. We have on hand four barrels of "surplus" gas for every car in the country, and now experts are alarming us with the information that cars could be run on natural gas, billions of cubic feet of which are blown off into the air every year.

"Surplus" cash accumulates, too. The banks are so stuffed with it that they can only pay you a grudging 1½ per cent on your savings. The great insurance companies pay out in benefits only 6½ per cent of the insurance written, and one company alone now controls five billion dollars and can't find any place to invest it.

Many are the humble victims of this unfortunate "surplus" condition, but when they need medical care they find that hospital beds have been caught by the "surplus" infection. For every two hospital beds in our country that are occupied, one bed is unoccupied and six people need hospitalization who can't afford it.

What, the little man striving to retain his sanity asks, can be the meaning of this word "surplus"? How can there be a "surplus" when millions are in dire need of these things?

The answer is that our system of distribution is geared to an economy of scarcity—and since we have discovered how to abolish scarcity, we must artificially preserve it.

We worship an abstraction called "value," which has no meaning except there be scarcity. That can be seen applying also to men and women in the sex and social worlds. The fewer of either in a given realm or area, the more valuable. Like cattle or fruit or grains at market, the greater the supply the less the cost or value. Where beautiful women are plentiful, as in Hollywood, their value falls—if the demand is for beauty.

In the broad economic realm it is as if we have been riding along on a horse and the horse has died of old age. A new streamlined car stands available to us to continue the journey, but we have become accustomed to feeding our steed oats and we suspect the reliability of anything fed by gasoline. So we are going to the most complicated and lunatic lengths to reconstruct the motor of the car so that it will run on oats.

The intrepid horsemen who have brought us thus far pin some of their hopes on exports. But our cotton exports today are less than half, our wheat exports only one-eighth, of what they were twenty-five years ago. A dozen years ago we exported four times as much lard as we do now. Up to fifteen years ago we exported 56,684,000 bushels of corn—and today we actually import more than we export.

Why? Because all over the world people are learning how to produce these things by modern methods themselves—and we have sold them the machinery to do it with. That is one aspect of the manner in which a system that has become an anachronism, and has developed contradictions within itself, cuts its own throat.

"Increase purchasing power at home" is now the cry—and obviously that is the answer. But how, unless the whole distributive system is changed to bring it in line with 1940 technology? Our horsemen, set against feeding the car gasoline because good old oats has brought them what they have and has acquired sanctity, say that it can be done by absorbing more and more people in salesmanship and distribution as technical discoveries eliminate them from production—and by new industries taking up the "surplus" labor of the old. Even if events had shown the former to be practicable—and they have shown the reverse, for unemployment continues to rise—it holds up the ideal for America of becoming a nation of clerks. (We are almost that now.) The electrical industry illustrates the fallacy of the second suggestion. Of all electrical appliances sold to American households in 1939, according to *Barron's Financial Weekly,* 97 per cent were invented before 1920. More new electrical gadgets have been discovered in the last twenty years than ever before—but either they are not on the market or, if they are, we cannot buy them.

So the steady advance of the machine throws each day more thousands into the "surplus" category. At Grand Coulee Dam, where more concrete is being mixed than on any other job ever undertaken, the super-modern mixing plant takes exactly four men to run it. On the farm, ground can be plowed and aërated, hops and corn can be picked, beans can be threshed, cotton can be hoed and picked, beets can be seeded, harvested, topped, and loaded—all by machinery. In Illinois has been developed a system of farming in circles, with a tractor attached to a drum in the center of the circle, and this system even eliminates the driver of the tractor. At the Chicago's World Fair a tractor driven by radio power was exhibited. Machines can dig seven thousand feet of ditch in one day, and perfect vegetables can be grown in crocks without any soil at all. In one mine in northern Minnesota machines can produce in less than two weeks more ore than the total volume of the Great Egyptian Pyramid, which took a hundred thousand men twenty years to build. Knitting robots can produce unlimited quantities of woolen garments in an unlimited variety of patterns.

Power-driven drums haul in the giant fishnets formerly handled by men in the salmon industry. Huge presses stamp out automobile tops, doors, and fenders in a single motion, starting and stopping by the action of a photo-electric cell as a single worker advances and retreats. Ninety-six machines with three men to mind them produce rayon all the way from viscose solution to yarn in five minutes—a job previously requiring eighty-five hours. A chemical welding process for making cotton cloth eliminates the necessity of spinning and weaving.

And so, after only ten years, in the auto industry one man working one hour produces 37 per cent more. In the tire industry one man now does in six hours what it took six men eight or ten hours to do in 1920. In the tobacco industry production has risen 54 per cent since 1925, while employment has fallen 39 per cent. In the petroleum industry production rose 13 per cent from 1929 to 1937, and employment fell 11 per cent. Bottle-blowing machines, dial telephones, and canned music in theatres displaced thousands overnight.

And now this problem is to be "solved" by producing things which not only add not a penny to real wealth, but are designed to destroy what the world already has. There is a "boom" in the aircraft industry. But there, too, technical progress inexorably marches on. A method has been discovered of making airplanes—much better airplanes—from plastic materials in ovens, eliminating the old method with its metal and rivets. We are staggered by the President's call for 50,000 planes— and yet by using only 555 ovens that number could easily be turned out in a month!

But don't worry. They won't be. The industry is bloated with orders for the old type of planes, and millions of dollars are invested in existing factories and equipment, and profits must always come before "patriotism."

There is our America in the year of disgrace 1940. "Poverty in the midst of plenty." But even so it is not our exclusive disease. Rather it is the situation at which the whole civilized world has arrived. The only difference is that here, and here alone, Plenty already *is*. We have it, here and now. As far as what we have and what we know is concerned, poverty is already abolished.

And yet when we have said that, we have still said nothing. Consider the new discoveries that are being made as to methods of production and sources of energy to run what should be our mechanical slaves, and the imagination staggers. George R. Harrison in *The Technology Review* points out that on any piece of desert ten miles long and twenty miles wide enough energy is lavished by the sun to satisfy all the present power needs of the United States. We know the power is there and that it can be harnessed. We merely have not discovered yet how to harness it efficiently.

There is immense power in volcanoes and in the ocean, and we are beginning to discover how to harness that. Knowledge of the life-force itself begins to dawn with the new-found ability to distinguish between ordinary and "heavy" carbon: fats, carbohydrates, and proteins are among the 300,000 substances which stem from a skeleton of carbon atoms. We can split the atom, and we know that every uranium atom smashed releases 175,000,000 electron volts of energy, so that an eight-pound bomb of uranium would drive the *Queen Mary* across the Atlantic, a job which now takes 6,300 tons of fuel oil. And yet as I write this a poorly dressed but intelligent man knocks at my door to ask me if I can give him a day's work or a little change!

The only thing we do not yet know is how to store all that energy. And yet plants and animals, including the human animal, are struggling everywhere for a bare subsistence. Meanwhile our big business men quarrel as to who shall control the present insignificant power plants.

It is indeed difficult to think in terms of these possibilities, of this astounding new world to the borders of which we have come.

Like any other mechanism, man can only endure so much. He can carry what is called a peak load—so much heat, so much cold, so much weight, so much wakefulness, so much undernourishment, so much continuous brain-work. Beyond that he breaks. So that we can sympathize with L. V. Heilbrunn of the University of Pennsylvania when he complains that "the human mind doesn't seem capable of making sense out of the huge mass of scientific publication that there is today."

We Americans try to dodge the implications of the main paradox by placing ourselves in another paradox. While on the one hand reveling in the prospect that science puts before us, we still glorify the ancient American myth of frontier days. Our country was built up, we say, by tough men and women who endured hardship to build for themselves and for posterity. The new generation is softened by too much luxury and needs the old fiber. We point with pride, if we have achieved wealth and comfort, to our early vicissitudes and the stalwart manner in which we endured them. "Young man," we say sententiously to our sons, "go in there and fight. Go out and get a job and win through, as we did. That's the American way."

Very fine, very noble. But the world moves. It really does. America moves—too fast, perhaps. Won't we ever get that into our concrete skulls?

We may wonder—we do wonder—how the stuff of character that we admire will be built in the Americans of tomorrow, under conditions of plenty which the world has never known and has had no chance to study in practice. We may wonder what nature will have to say about the ending of our age-long battle against scarcity of food and clothing and housing. But wonder as we may—and this whole question is decidedly one for us to study right now—we have no choice but to go forward to the inevitable social implications of our technology. If we were to destroy all the machines that face us with this problem, our sons would only start over and build them up again, and the same problem would face their sons. That is exactly what we are asking for, when we speak of "too much luxury" at this present stage, which is almost barbarian in comparison with the known possibilities: we are asking for destruction of the machines. And that is just as sensible as asking the sun to go down under the horizon and stay there.

Yes—it is difficult to make one's mind grasp the implications of modern discovery. But not so difficult, I think, as it is for Mr. Morgan and Mr. Dupont and Mr. Rockefeller and Mr. Ford to make their minds grasp the billions they possess. That is absolutely impossible. And it is for the sacredness of those ducks' eggs on a piece of paper, and the right to add more ducks' eggs, that the whole country is toiling and suffering today.

It's idle to bewail the difficulty of it. It has to be grasped, and grappled with. It has to be, because nature gave us stomachs and bid us fill them —and in obeying her we have arrived where we have arrived.

CHAPTER THREE

Europe and Its Entanglements

B UT NOW, in the midst of this fantastic maladjustment of our own country, we are being told that we should forget our troubles at home and go to Europe to help the people over there out of a hole.

What kind of mess is it, over there in Europe, in which the great brains of America seek to interfere?

Just what is this "civilization as we know it" for which England claims to be fighting? Has any civilization been thus far manifested in Europe which is for us worth knowing? Why rush into this marriage of blood without first checking up to see that our suitor is of sound stock?

Let us go back a century or so and acquaint ourselves with the ancestry of "civilization as we know it." Let's be snobs about it. It's our turn to be. The English have played the role long enough to our summer-stock ingénue.

We glance back to the year 1815—just an hour ago in the infinitudes of history—and watch the Great Powers build the foundation of modern Europe at the Congress of Vienna.

Napoleon, the phoenix of military brigandage risen from the flames of the French Revolution, has been smashed. His rival brigands, the smooth and cultured aristocrats of Austria, Russia, Prussia, and England, meet to dance and sip champagne through the night and divide the spoils through the day.

You are not to forget, though, that in the smashing of Napoleon there have also been smashed for the time being all the justifiable desires of the pre-Napoleonic French people, who were taxed and starved by pre-revolution French and European royalty into their truly great and terrible revolution—for which, today, they and not their pre-revolutionary torturers, the royalty of France and Europe, are blamed.

None of the peoples truly concerned in this recherché territorial turkey-dinner at Vienna is democratically represented, although peoples' movements for liberty and democracy are trying to surge up everywhere. The Gentlemen at the table are interested jointly in preserving wealth and power for those who have it, in every country. This is Metternich's International, the first great International of Privilege. The vulgar throngs' claims to bread and security are a common menace.

When the bird is carved up, the Gentlemen agree to meet once a year to swap ideas on how democracy can be struck down wherever it raises its ugly head, just as it has been struck down by their combined efforts after the revolution in France. This is called "preserving the tranquillity of Europe." Austria, Prussia, and Russia call it a "Holy Alliance" guided by "the precepts of Justice, Christian Charity, and Peace." It must be holy because the Pope of Rome blesses it.

All they are in fact doing is sitting down to dinner on the lid of the simmering kettle of social progress, which the revolution in industrial and transport techniques is bringing to the boil. At the same time each of the Powers, unable to keep its eyes off its neighbor's platter, seeks to elbow its way into the seat commanding the gravy. So there is a dual struggle going on.

Now we skip to the halfway mark of the nineteenth century and observe the kettles on the European cookstove coming to the boil.

Here is Germany. . . .

A crazy-quilt of kingdoms and duchies with nothing in common but a language. Napoleon has done Prussia's rulers the good turn of demonstrating how this lack of unity and of national consciousness cramps their style in the great inter-fraternal dogfight—for predatory wars must have willing cannon fodder. The people are encouraged to get together, and the first thing Prussia's king knows, they are demanding, of all things, a written constitution. The only possible answer to this is bullets. The people expose their dead, wreathed in laurel, outside the royal palace, and cry to the king to take off his hat. The king remembers what happened to Louis XVI of France in 1793. He obeys.

Here is Italy. . . .

Divided and ruled by foreign bluebloods and by the Vatican. A similar wave of unifying nationalist fervor sweeps the people. Sardinia's king, smart enough to see he must give the people something or lose all, comes out on top. The water boils, a step forward is taken, the Pope flees. But the International of Privilege is still on the job. A new set of alien tyrants is shipped in from France and Austria to keep the people submissive and divided. The Pope is slightly renovated and reinstalled.

Spain. . . .

In 1820 the people of this once-great empire compel their Bourbon ruler to give them a democratic constitution. The International cracks down, abolishes it by force of arms—though it can't suppress the rebellion in Spain's American colonies. In neighboring Portugal the International sits firmly on the lid all the way through to 1910, when Manuel, the last royal tyrant, flees to England.

France. . . .

Under this kettle, atop which the International has restored the Bourbons, the fire is very hot after 1789. By 1830 the people of Paris are out on the streets behind pavingstone barricades, and Charles X of France flees to England. Now the International tries putting in a Bourbon with a cockade in his hat instead of a Bourbon without a cockade. But he's still a Bourbon, and in 1848 the barricades go up again. The last Bourbon flees to England.

Still the International sits there—and the first act of the "Constitutional Assembly" is an attack on the common people. More barricades. With ten thousand Paris workingmen dead or wounded, and thousands more imprisoned and deported, the lid is clamped down again, this time under a new Bonaparte whom the International has been keeping on ice *in England,* training him for his duties as a special constable in the suppression of the English Chartists.

And now what has happened to the crafty Metternich himself? The Austrian aristocrat, besides having organized the International of Privilege, has a pretty warm kettle to sit on at home. A feudal social order fetters for the subjects of Austria's empire all possible advance in line with the advance of knowledge. They rise in Vienna—and Metternich, disguised as a human being, flees to England.

By this time we can see that the headquarters of the International have shifted from Vienna to London, now the asylum and nursery of tyrants. And light begins to be thrown on the realities of European "democracy," no matter how thin it is sliced or with what spicy sauces it is served.

For England is supposed to be leading the movement from dictatorship to the new conception of the people ruling their own destinies. And indeed, so far as the common people are concerned, that is correct. It implies no special virtue in the English as compared with the continentals. It is a simple and necessary result of England's being an island, and therefore able to ward off invaders and do all her fighting for swag and privilege abroad—or preferably, to get others to do it for her (the most ancient and honorable of British customs). England itself remains peaceful and can concentrate on building up trade, industry, and international banking.

For us, this is the most important part of the picture to see clearly. Already at this point, a century or so ago, there are two Englands: "the two Nations," as England's own Prime Minister, Disraeli, called them. Inevitably, under prolonged peaceful conditions, the forms of democracy for the masses are expanding. The rulers of England are not yielding to the pressure any more graciously, any less violently, than elsewhere. They shoot first and talk afterward—ask any Irishman. For many decades yet they will yield nothing in their colonies, for the colonies are mere outlets for capital and sources of raw material for home industries, and their people can still be controlled by feudal methods. But with a head-start over their continental brothers they are first to understand that, at home, there must be a safety valve for the steam. The real England that is a power in world affairs—then as now—is the City of London. It is becoming the round-bellied merchant and banker of two hemispheres. As far as mankind as a whole is concerned, more than half the weight on the lid of the kettle consists of the British money aristocracy.

And so, under this powerful leadership, the war of the International of Privilege against the people of Europe proceeds alongside of the dog-fights among the International's members.

With Bismarck, the blood-and-iron Prussian, a new force rises to upset the balance of power within the International. Bismarck unifies Germany, injects it with nationalistic fervor for a place in the sun: a place for the privileged of Germany, though the German people must fight and die for it, fooled into thinking it is for them.

Bismarck is an unco-operative fellow. He wants to sit on the kettle but he wants to push the rest of the brothers out of reach of the gravy, and remove what is already on their platters. He is also something new in international diplomacy, the soul of which has always been lies and trickery. He bamboozles the brethren as to his intentions by frequently telling the truth. (That, together with an ironclad skepticism about all idealistic phrases, is the most useful lesson learned by Hitler from his illustrious predecessor.)

In a blitzkrieg against the great empire of Austria, Bismarck appropriates its prerogative of having the first pickings from the German people. Then he turns on his French colleagues, grabs off Alsace and Lorraine in 1870. But he hasn't forgotten his fraternal duties as a member of the International. When, after the fall of Paris, the armed people of that city set up a popular government, he stands by to help the French defenders of privilege re-establish "law and order" in a huge massacre of men, women, and children. (You noticed that, when Germany again threatened Paris in 1940, the two hundred families of France yielded up the city without a struggle. They knew by experience what to expect if they put arms in the hands of the people—and their duty to the Wealth International, the European Sixty Families, we Americans might call them, as always came first.)

So now two great new powers are in existence—Germany and Italy. It looks like some of the boys are going to have to do with less turkey.

England is still the grand high mogul of the International of Privilege. Her "balance of power" policy—to keep the continental brothers squabbling among each other so that none shall be powerful enough to threaten her—remains unchanged. But where France was formerly the most probable threat, Germany has now stepped in.

Bismarck is still proving very difficult and hard to manage. He has organized Russia and Austria into a new Holy Alliance—even less holy, if possible, than the previous one—to occupy the strategic position on the lid of the continental kettle and to grab off any further wings and legs that may be going.

Time has moved on. The rabble are becoming educated in the facts of life, what with railroads, the telegraph, popular newspapers, cheap books. The game of snatch and grab has to be played under new guises.

To the delight of the millions, who "only" want life, liberty, and the pursuit of happiness, a "Peace Conference" is called in 1899 at The Hague, and again in 1907. It seems that some way out is to be sought from Europe's eternal wars, for which the millions pay and pay and pay in blood and the money they need for food, clothing, and houses.

The conferences are a farce from the beginning, and for a very simple reason. To get peace there must be disarmament. But the International is divided into Haves and Have-Nots and Not-Enoughs, and disarmament would mean that no one could any longer challenge the existing division of the turkey.

England, with a heaped plate, is willing to reduce armies so long as she can have her navy and enough weapons to keep her colonial minions quiet. She is therefore able to appear in the guise of a sort of haloed angel, the enlightened and benevolent defender of civilization— as she knows it. Millions of simple-minded Americans fall for this, hook, line, and sinker—and still today are accepting the British wig and false mustache as the genuine article.

But the German brothers want some of the Haves' turkey. The kindly Englanders, chief among the Haves, cannot consider such a thing, since they have convinced themselves that their backward subjects love being ruled by them and it would hence be a crime to hand them over to the brutal Germans.

To none of the "Peace, It's Wonderful" delegates does it even occur that the colonial and subject peoples might rule themselves.

These, then, are the achievements of the "Peace Conferences": a code of genteel rules for the conduct of war, which everyone knows will immediately be broken when war starts; and an international Court of Arbitration to which, of course, no one will appeal except when it suits him. And even while the gentlemen confer on "peace," wars break out everywhere: between Russia and Japan, between Italy and Turkey, and in the Balkans.

It is on the Balkans that the German brothers now have their predatory eyes fixed. The Balkans are the great and glorious and supreme mess of the European madhouse. In the Austrian Empire, Czechs,

Serbs, Croats, Slovaks, Poles, Ruthenians, Slovenes, and Jews have for generations been oppressed by the charming gentry of "Gay Vienna"—and, egged on by Vienna so as to make Austrian domination easy, have fought among themselves.

Other Balkan peoples—Bulgars, Greeks, Armenians, Albanians, Montenegrins, Rumanians, and inhabitants about Cyrene—are beginning to stir under the decaying heel of Turkey.

Here is something that all the boys of the International are interested in: a hodgepodge of backward peoples speaking a score of languages, each people so small that no three of them combined could make a significant opponent—but with two decaying imperialisms in the saddle.

The Tsar of Russia wants a window with a view over the Mediterranean, and sees his chance to cut off a fat slice of Turkey white meat. For Bismarck and Kaiser Wilhelm II, who carries on where old Blood-and-Iron left off, the Balkans are a duck-soup setup for expansion eastward.

And the English branch of the International? Not for themselves does it love the Balkans, but because it is milking billions of pounds out of India and has to keep others from horning in. The British navy, and control of Egypt and Suez, maintain the sea route to India. But the unprincipled Germans have wrung from Turkey's Sultan a concession for a new all-land route: a Berlin-Bagdad railway. The swine!

In the enlightened times at which we have now arrived on our journey, predatory intentions have to be disguised behind a veritable jungle of moralistic false beards. So we observe a wave of horror sweeping "civilization" at the treatment of Balkan Christians by the infidel Turks, though there is in reality little if any difference between it and the treatment of infidel Hindus by Christian Englishmen. As you would expect, the English contingent lead the horror chorus—although we Americans, always eager to view injustice with alarm as long as it happens enough thousands of miles from America, weigh in with a shrill and piercing soprano.

But behind the whiskers the privileged gentry of England are really playing the same old game. They didn't want powerful Russia to take the Dardanelles from weak Turkey, and for the Sultan's sweet sake they stopped, if not defeated, Russia in the Crimean War—subsequently to which the Sultan was allowed to continue oppressing his Balkan minorities under the most distinguished auspices. And with the dawn of the twentieth century the English are found intriguing first with one Balkan group and then with another, not for "humanity" but in order to head off Kaiser Wilhelm's drive to the East. Turkey being driven out of the Balkans is one thing; Kaiser Bill stepping in is quite another.

In 1912, Bulgaria, Greece, Serbia, and Montenegro make successful war on Turkey and then convene to divvy up—in London. Somehow they can't agree, and in 1913 Bulgaria is at war with her three erstwhile allies. A year later an Archduke—one of several German aristocrats who have got their elbows in the Balkan gravy—is shot at Sarajevo, and the lid of the whole bubbling stew blows right off. The boys of the International are at it again—this time in a big way.

The first World War ends, as you know, with all the people on earth—except the forty-million-odd who have been blown to bits or slowly killed by famine and disease—determined to stop the insanity of war once and for all. Man's mastery over nature, according to President Wilson, has now advanced to a point where the stage is set for a period of peace and plenty for all.

The Fourteen Points! Remember? But, though it seems incredible that the International, after such a fabulous and futile slaughter, can still stand in the way, it so does—as you can also remember. It still can think of nothing but the necessity to get more turkey than it can possibly eat.

By this time long experience has taught the International high skill in placating the people with the outward forms of justice and democracy, while in reality giving up no more than an inch of their privilege and taking back two inches somewhere else. So now the long-suffering human baby gets a comforter to suck on called the League of Nations, which "outlaws war." The rules for this remarkable hunt-the-slipper game take a long time to draw up, and before they are completed new wars have started all over the place. From then until now there has hardly been a day when war was not going on somewhere.

And what does the League do? Nothing! Why? Because it has exactly as much foundation under it as the old Hague Court of Arbitration—that is, none at all. It is like an elaborately furnished apartment on the third floor without any first and second floors underneath. A peace group run by the International of Privilege is like a vegetarian movement with headquarters in a slaughterhouse. The Haves are menaced by the Have-Nots and the Not-Enoughs, and all are menaced by the people's demand for real democracy. The culminating point of the farce is the Disarmament Conference in London, which breaks up in complete disorder when Russia timidly puts forward a proposal: that the countries represented should disarm.

So we find diplomats, the servants of international privilege, bargaining at back doors and gambling with human lives more shamelessly than ever now that the League has solemnly abolished secret diplomacy. The only change from before the great 1914–1918 catastrophe is that now it takes a stronger perfume of fine idealist phrases to drown out the stench. With incantations about "sacred responsibilities" the Haves hold on to what they have got while the Have-Nots scheme to take it from them. And whenever the people try to obtain control of their own affairs, seeking to smash the chains the Wealth International fastens upon progress, other enmities are forgotten and foreign branches of the International fraternally intervene, just as before. They do it in Finland, helping Mannerheim to overthrow the people's government and kill off some thirty thousand of the eighty thousand he throws into concentration camps. They do it in Spain, in 1936–1938, only they call it "non-intervention." In Germany, the Weimar Republic is deliberately smashed by France and England (read Pierre van Paassen's unforgettable account of how that was done)—who thereby create their own enemy of 1939 and ensure a new war rather than let the German people have democracy. They try it over a period of years by different techniques in Russia, but for the first time in history the intervention doesn't come off.

Why? Because the kettles of Europe—the Russian one first—are coming to full boil. The water changes to steam. The days of the International are numbered—by the simple force of unfolding truth. The world, by the fundamental order of its being, moves on.

Before we pass on let us see what is the charge against the International of Privilege?

Not wickedness. Forget that.

The charge is gross inefficiency. That and nothing more. The rest are side issues.

The charge is failure to develop and distribute the wealth that exists in the earth, and which we know how to get and use. And not only failure to do it, but the use of every manner of violence to keep others, the true representatives of the people who need this wealth, from doing the job the International doesn't do.

We shall observe this inefficiency as we go along—in England, all through Europe, in India, in Africa, and in America.

That is the charge against the International. And that is its death knell.

CHAPTER FOUR

Has America a "Save-the-World" Complex?

O N APRIL 2, 1917, President Wilson rose in an atmosphere charged with emotion and released this downpour of noble words over the heads of the United States Congress:

It is a fearful thing to lead this great people into war, into the most terrible and disastrous of all wars, civilization itself seeming to be in the balance. But the right is more precious than peace, and we shall fight for the things we have always carried nearest our hearts—for democracy, for the right of those who submit to authority to have a voice in their own government: for the rights and liberties of small nations, for the universal dominion of right by such a concert of free peoples as shall bring peace and safety to all nations and make the world itself at last free.

Twenty-three years later Captain Eddie Rickenbacker, who was called upon to kill others for right and democracy and liberty and peace but had the good fortune not to get killed by the rival claimants to heavenly authority, wrote:

The close of the World War and subsequent events have brought about the disillusionment and realization that the winner and the loser of such a conflict must suffer the consequences alike.

There are millions still unemployed; billions of dollars are being paid in additional taxes; hospitals are still filled with thousands of veterans, wrecked mentally and physically, all of them once the flower of American manhood.

The cost to the world approximated $250,000,000,000. With this staggering sum we could have built homes costing $2,500 each on 5-acre lots costing $100 an acre. We could have equipped each of those homes with a thousand dollars' worth of furniture and given such a home to every family in Russia, Italy, France, Belgium, Germany, Wales, Scotland, Ireland, England, Australia, Holland and the U.S.A.

In those lands we could have given to every community of 40,000 people or more a $2,000,000 library, a $3,000,000 hospital, and a $10,000,000 university. And if we could have invested the balance that would have been left in a way that would have brought a rate of 5% annually, there would have been sufficient to pay an annual salary of $1,000 each to 125,000 school teachers and 125,000 nurses.

Directly and indirectly, Rickenbacker adds, America has borne approximately one-fifth of the total cost of the first World War. Had we stayed clear of it, as few deny now that we should have done, we could have paid for one-fifth of the above program with the money it cost us. We could have had all those furnished homes and libraries and hospitals and universities in our own country, and there would still have been a few billions over for reconstruction aid in Europe.

We could have—if Americans hadn't had then, as they have always had and still have despite such a costly and painful lesson, a Save-the-World complex.

We are a peculiar and perverse-seeming people. Balzac said that the death by famine or plague of millions of Chinese was as nothing for the average Western citizen compared with the headache of someone in his own household. That has been more or less true everywhere except in the United States of America, where the exact opposite is the case. Our hearts bleed for the Chinese. We have enjoyed this sensation so much that we long supplied Japan with the iron to torture the Chinese a little more, and the oil to take Japanese planes to the altitudes from which it can most effectively be hurled. This makes our hearts bleed more gushingly than ever. We reach down into our patched jeans and are overcome with the sense of our benevolence.

It is for beautiful abstract words that we prefer to perform our national Salvation Act—words like Democracy and Christianity. The thought of all the heathens in benighted tropical lands gives us insomnia, and the forcing of our beliefs upon them we regard as nothing less than our duty. Few things have shocked America more than the return from the Marquesas Islands of Herman Melville, the great American novelist of a hundred years ago, shamelessly proclaiming that he had not only done nothing to save the Marquesans but actually admired their way of life. Had Melville set to work to raise a fund for a Salvation expeditionary force he would have been a hero, and his fellow-citizens would have denied themselves to contribute. But we did not want an author, we wanted a missionary; and we killed Melville as a writer by treating him as a social leper.

Last year alone we spent over $20,000,000 on missions to make the poor savages Christian. It was reported at the Missions Conference of North America in June that thirteen million Christians had been baptized, in China and elsewhere. Upon this remarkable achievement as it concerns China, Pearl S. Buck has commented:

Christ has not become a part of the Chinese life. . . . We can have no assurance that if we withdrew from China today there would be any more permanent record left of our religious presence these 150 years than is left there of the old Nestorian church—a wind-blown, obliterated tablet upon desert land.

That was highly un-American of Mrs. Buck. It is not our national custom to probe deeply into the errors and miseries that arouse our pity—to attack the causes at the roots with a view to permanent improvement. We rush in precipitately with money and with our sons and daughters, and draw up the balance sheet much later, if at all, to find that we have bought nothing except salve for our conscience.

We were the only people in the world willing to go to war to end slavery. Hundreds of thousands of our men died for that noble cause —and today we examine the "freed" South and see the Negroes slightly less illiterate, but in basic needs as badly off as they were before the Civil War: without clothing and food, without a vote, without civil liberties, living in pigsties. No matter: "theoretically," slavery has been abolished.

For more than a century we have crusaded against the Demon Rum —with money, with "Face on the Barroom Floor" propaganda, with axes, with the lifetime devotion of well-meaning men and women, and finally with laws. We are proud to have "abolished the corner saloon." In its place we, still the thirstiest people on earth, have three chromium-plated "cocktail bars" in every block.

Our best people have "saved" art. In 1866 it was reported in *The*

New York Times that three thousand "artists" in Belgium alone were living on wealthy American patrons, who purchased caricatures of celebrated paintings sold as originals. If we ever had a good artist here he had to go to Europe to be "discovered" by Americans.

Our Billy Sundays and Moodys and Sankeys "saved" millions of American sinners for the Lord, and their successors, the Aimee Mac-Phersons, are still at it. Nevertheless America still holds the unchallenged laurels as the world's leading criminal nation.

We whimpered with horror at the tales of Turkish atrocities in Armenia, and especially at the goings-on in Turkish harems, and sent emissaries to save Turkey's womenfolk from worse than death. At the very same period the vast red light districts in our own country were passing almost unnoticed. St. Louis, when I was in the newspaper business there, had four lines of houses a mile and a quarter long which were all brothels. In Pittsburgh, where churches were particularly numerous, and where just then the miserably underpaid miners striking for a living wage were being shot down in cold blood, it was the same. Idealistic Americans of those cities gave their all for the unfortunate females of Turkey.

Smart people soon began to get wise to the potentialities of the American Salvation Racket. The English caught on to it long ago and exploited it for all they were worth. If people were starving in a British colony, and there were rumblings of revolt, England didn't have to do anything about it. It was easier and cheaper to get America's Salvationeers on the job. In China the English fostered the opium trade for their own profit, manufacturing addicts by the million, while at the same time piously welcoming American missionaries sent to save the addicts from themselves.

In America thousands of leeches burrowed their heads into the racket, promoting themselves excellent incomes as collectors of Salvation money. The shrewd editor of a religious paper lifts that publication from nothing to several hundred thousand circulation by exploiting Salvationeers. All he has to do when the growth begins to lag is to find a new famine or massacre or epidemic—not in America, of course —or send a reporter to describe the distressing conditions of the savages in Africa. A week after the crusade is launched, a mountain of letters containing cash and checks is piled on the long editorial tables—and wholesalers are doubling their orders for his paper.

There was just one thing Americans were not ready to save—the financially oppressed of our own people in America. Only in the last few years has sympathy for our own oppressed and starving begun to dawn. That is not because we are hard-hearted. We are a genuinely charitable people.

It is a simple matter of geography. Geography made England the cradle of the industrial age and of the revolt against feudalism. Geography gave Americans our pathological concern about Christianity in China, Democracy in Cuba, Democracy in Europe—great abstract causes for which we will give and fight without pausing to think who is really profiting by it, or that these things cannot be imposed from without. Geography gave us our blind spot concerning the wrongs and miseries of our own people.

How? Because the America of our fathers and grandfathers was a promised land, an undeveloped land containing riches for everyone, to which they had escaped from the wars and tyrannies of their homelands. It was so far from Europe, as distances went then, that it seemed in another world. It was so big and so new that up until quite recently, when I myself was at school, possibilities of overnight wealth for the humblest citizen still existed. There was still some undeveloped land to be had in the West. Excitement as to what fortune might easily bring to the enterprising was still in the air. No matter how badly things went, no matter what sufferings the millions in Eastern cities were already then enduring, no matter how little physical abundance the millions enjoyed, there was a strong hangover of mental abundance. Heaven was just about eight hundred miles west.

And the people who felt this mental abundance were mostly sober religious folk who had taken the Sermon on the Mount to heart. In America they had not yet known want in the European sense—poverty and degradation made almost unbearable by the sense of hopelessness. Hope there still was. But they remembered what it had been like in the old countries, or what their parents had told them it was like; and when they heard of the terrible sufferings abroad they were moved not only to pity but to a desire to give something as a thank offering for their escape to the land of hope. If they had been hard-pressed

themselves—or if, though hard-pressed, they had been without hope—
they would not have cared. In the republics of Central and South
America, with their peon traditions, nobody cared.

What we did not then realize—what we have only begun to understand in the last decade—is that the American Cinderella saga was not
a story to be indefinitely continued. So far as the vast majority were
concerned, it ended inevitably with the end of free land in the West,
when the land was all gobbled up by banks and corporations and was
only available to the poor man on a basis of more or less serfdom.
There were no longer opportunities after that for the ordinary man
and woman in the realm of producing society's basic needs. Such
opportunities as there were existed now in the realm of luxuries and
of distribution and finance. The time had come, as it had come in
every European country, when the creative man who produced things
was firmly relegated to the bottom of the social heap, while the uncreative man who sold things was laden with rich rewards.

CHAPTER FIVE

Practical Reasons for Keeping Out of War

WHILE I as well as everybody else who reads the papers, listens to the radio, talks or corresponds with his neighbors or fellow-citizens anywhere, know by now most of the reasons offered for our entering or not entering the war on the side of what was once the Allies but is now the British Empire—I favor one, to me, principal reason for not entering and that is this: that the British Empire is not a democracy and never has been and, in so far as its ruling classes are concerned (and they are at present the Empire), never will be. Not that I am rising to inform anybody that America is a democracy, in full working order at this time. As I recall it, Article 1 of the ten original amendments to our Constitution reads: "Congress shall make no law respecting an establishment of religion, or *prohibiting the free exercise thereof. . . .*" Yet just now I am thinking of Jehovah's Witnesses and their religious objection to saluting the flag, since they acknowledge and salute only God as their supreme head; also the religious objections of various sects—our American Friends or Quakers among others—and what happens to them when their conscience, in connection with their religion, causes them to object to entering the army; also of President Roosevelt's unauthorized assertion that this is a Christian nation, which decidedly it is not—as everybody and most particularly the Christians themselves know. Consider the Mormons, the Jews, the Mohammedans in this country, the Shintoists among our native Japanese, et cetera, et cetera.

The same Article also states that Congress shall make no law abridging the freedom of speech or of the press; or the right of the people peaceably to assemble and to petition the government for redress of grievances. Yet I myself along with hundreds of others in recent years have been denied the use of any hall in the city of Los Angeles because my purpose was to protest against and attack the unconstitutional and illegal procedures of the hirelings of Los Angeles business men, operating through their local Chamber of Commerce to prevent any movement or speech which tended to abolish the open shop (meaning non-union cheap labor) in southern California or elsewhere. No police protection or aid for me or any other with such a motive, from any official in southern California. As for others, you have only to think of Norman Thomas, the Socialist candidate for President in 1936 and 1940, or William Z. Foster and Earl Browder, the Communist party's candidates; and of the threats and intimidations from Mayor Hague of Jersey City—or for that matter of mayors, sheriffs, vigilantes, Chambers of Commerce, and what not else throughout our entire land.

And as for freedom of the press! We all know by now what, and who, controls the press and what it may say or may not say. As many as fifteen years ago Upton Sinclair, the distinguished American novelist and social equitist, wrote *The Brass Check* as well as *Money Writes* —two books which set forth plainly how advertising and American corporation cash directed what could be said in our papers, our schools, the pulpits of our churches, and where not else. And since then the radio and the moving pictures as well as the stage (I refer to the Federal Theater Project) have felt the restraining hand of the same forces —and continue so to feel them.

However, you are not to assume, from what I have just written, that I hold America to be as yet a totalitarian state patterned after Mr. Hitler's Germany or Mr. Mussolini's Italy—any more than I hold it to be as undemocratic and imperial as the British Empire, which now holds 500,000,000 of its world-scattered colonials as well as 29,000,000 of its natives in educationless, moneyless, and privilegeless bondage. I don't. Because of the democratic war that many of our citizens are at this moment conducting against the social usurpations of our money bund—that is, our financiers, their banks and giant corporations, and newspapers and legislators and kept police and Chambers of Commerce—it is even yet a democracy of sorts. Nonetheless, as all Americans in the comparatively moneyless walks of life know, the above forces seek by way of wage slavery and enforced mass ignorance to establish themselves as overlords of America—quite as the lords and ladies and money-stuffed merchants of the south of England have established themselves over the masses of England, and through them the worse-treated masses of the British Empire.

Yes, believe or not, a quite high percentage of our American people are still alive. By personal contact and word of mouth they are still fairly well informed as to what their national Constitution means to and for them—a government of the people, by the people, and for the people; and they are fairly well determined—a fairly large number of them at least—not to be trickily undermined and sold down the river into any national mass wage-slavery in order that any clique of sixty families, patterning itself after the English titled gentlemen, may live in luxury and snobbery at their expense. Not yet. And that is why America still maintains the skeleton form or legal outline of its Constitution, even though the utmost craft backed by 95 per cent of the usurped natural wealth of the country is now at this moment being used to destroy that Constitution and so our democratic form of life.

But there are still some steps to go. Only it is just our luck that, at the time our own would-be ruling class is becoming almost unmanageable, we should be confronted by a European war that has at this writing no more to do with the problem of democracy or civilization in Europe or the world than it has to do with the state of the inhabitants of Mars, if any.

It began, if one can accept the preponderance of all the evidence, with England and France in possession of all the swag of the last great war (the war that was to establish peace and democracy) and not only fearing the growth of the power of Messrs. Mussolini and Hitler, who threatened to make them divvy up at least a portion of their gains, but at the same time fearing much more the growth and strength of the Soviet Socialist Union—which threatened not a mere division of territory captured from Germany, but the entire social reorganization of Europe, with no loot for anybody. England and France decided to do something about it—in other words, destroy Russia. For it is Russia that the grandees of Europe, to say nothing of those of America and elsewhere, have never been able to contemplate without shivers of an icy character chasing up and down their spines—have never yet been able to look upon as either human or sane. For them there must be poverty set over against great wealth—racking and destroying individual poverty as against swaggering and bejeweled and obese wealth—or the world is headed for the rocks, or the bow-wows, or hell.

Hence, a great and twenty-four-hour-a-day fear of Russia. For it was and still is growing in population. Also it was and still is finding mines and water-power sources, to say nothing of the vast forests in the north and endless cultivable land in the south. And it was and still is building and using research laboratories to unlock such resources of nature as will make it independent of any so-called rival power anywhere, particularly rival powers in Europe which were so bent on crushing if possible this iniquitous idea of economic equality between men. Also it was and is building an army and navy.

And so, finally, an almost unending series of conferences between England and France as parties of the first part and later Herr Hitler and Doctor Mussolini as parties of the second part, with a view, as appeared very clearly later, to working out something which would not only satisfy Herr Hitler's demand for territories which he insisted were stolen from him in the great capitalistic trade war of 1914–1918 (and that was true)—but also Professor Mussolini's very sound complaint that having agreed, for a price, to enter on the side of England in 1914, said price was not delivered and he intended to collect it sometime or other. So what did England say? (It may have been France, only somehow I doubt it, France still being weak and far from the pretentious power that its friend and yet rival, England, was at the time.)

"Here," said England, "is how we will do. There is Russia, with all that land and all those mines and forests and those new laboratories and giant water power plants and what not else, but it is still a clumsy power—not nearly as well equipped technically as you Germans and Italians to say nothing of us French and English. So first, all you have to do is to get ready to fight a real war, the two of you, so that when the time comes there will be no slip-up—a real conquering and dividing war against Russia. And in order to help both of you to get ready, France and ourselves will put all our spare resources at your command. So Italy, you begin at once on Spain, which has allowed a

semi-democratic, semi-Bolshevik government to be set up—a real danger to us all. For in your ultimate war with Russia, Spain, if it is
allowed to go on, might join with her. And you, Hitler, you help
Italy as much as may be needed to make an end of that democracy.
Only, of course, we all have to be very sly about this because here is
our old democratic silly, the United States, across the Atlantic to the
west of us, and it is always good for a lot of easy money for all of us
—provided we play our cards right, make it believe that all that we
do and have done is for the good of democracy, civilization, education,
and the advancement of the poor. Meantime, we, England and France,
will pretend to do something for the other side—only in a small way
of course—occasionally slip a shipload or two of medical supplies or
food to your enemy which you can sink as they come along. And once
that war is ended successfully we can go on to bigger things.

"Meantime, Germany, you can be ready to take back the Rhine
provinces which we took from you in 1918. Also, you can settle that
Silesia problem your way, if you choose. Also you can take over
Austria and maybe that territory of Austria's that we took and gave
to Czechoslovakia. Also that corridor through Poland to Danzig. But
all this and any money that we supply you to build up your army and
air force are given on just one condition, mind you: and that is that
as soon as you are able to fight a real war, you start on Russia—
attacking her of course through Poland, with whom we will arrange
things so that you will have no trouble there. Meanwhile, we English
will see what we can be doing with the Scandinavian countries in
order that when the time comes it will be possible for us to send troops
through Finland to attack Leningrad. Also we'll have ready any warships you may need either in the Baltic, the Arctic Ocean, or the Black
Sea—for of course when the time comes, Italy, you will attack through
the Balkans, the Black Sea, and wherever else you can. And France
and ourselves (England) will naturally join you at the right time.
For all we wish to see is Russia defeated—and turned over to who-
ever wishes to conduct it sensibly as a proper International Wealth
power—a member in good and respectable standing of the International Wealth combine."

And so started the present great war for democracy and civilization
—England leading the van, America earnestly and weepingly as ever

clamoring to be allowed first place and also to pay for it all (as we will, I fear). For is there any American so dumb or blind as not to have seen with whose consent Germany retook her Rhine territory, or Silesia, or Austria or the Czechoslovakian borderland? Could France have permitted any or all of that without England's consent? Or England without a previous understanding with France *and* Germany? "Appeasement" was the safe word used all along, but "appeasement" carried a very large order with it, as all who knew anything at all at the time well knew.

Only Hitler, being the world genius that he is and an essence of ruthlessness much stronger than that distilled in England or France, proceeded, once he had gathered in all these prerequisites, to double-cross the one nation that he knew full well would, at the first opportunity it had, double-cross him—namely, England. "For why," he plainly asked himself, "make war on Russia when, and at long last, I know that I have well within my fighting grasp and can probably beat England, the chief power that wishes me ill, and so be rid of her for good? After that I can take Europe."

For with a swish or two of his army—the best equipped and trained since that of Caesar—he could and soon did invade Poland and take it. Also, as plainly he reasoned, once he made clear to Russia what it was that England and France had been planning in regard to her, through himself and Mussolini, and particularly should he be willing to give her a slice of Poland—(the exact territory that had been taken from her in 1918 by England and France)—he could come to at least a temporary but worth-while peace and trade agreement with her and so make his European labor easier. And that done, and Warsaw and Danzig and his lost corridor once more in his hands, he could as he did defy England on the continent—drive her out of there. And if then she was not willing to make terms, as likely as not he could conquer her on her own island.

And we have seen what has happened. Poland taken, a non-aggression pact with Russia. England driven out of Finland—for she built the Mannerheim line. Denmark and Norway, both of which England planned to use in her war on Russia, seized. Holland, Belgium, France, all conquered and added. England driven out of Rumania and its oil wells and wheat lands added. Also, England warred upon in the Mediterranean, and Greece and Africa and the Red Sea by Italy.

I have not the time here to go into the rest of this complicated mess which no more concerns the United States—and by that I mean the true interests of the majority of the people of the United States—than it concerns the natives of the Arctic or of Pitcairn Island. You will find it all clearly explained in a subsequent chapter which I have entitled: "Have English and American Finance Co-operated with Hitler to Destroy Democracy?" They have.

American finance and English finance have done so, and that against the best interests of the masses of their respective countries. But our American mass, like the mass of the English people, do not yet appear to know that. They do not appear to know that as between the money magnates of England, France, Germany, and America as well as those of other places in the world—Belgium, Holland, Italy—there was and still is a concerted attempt to sell them out—to sell democracy out; to end, if you please, the few and yet only feebly erected basic rights listed in our American Declaration of Independence and our American Constitution—the right of free speech, of a free press, of public assembly and protest, the right to vote and elect their own representatives and to recall them, to own property and protect themselves against excessive and destroying taxation, the right to bargain for their labor and demand a fair wage, and so on. And the reason they do not know that is that money, gradually and shrewdly assembled in the hands of a few, has by them been used *not* for the benefit of the people and the land that provided them with the opportunity of so assembling it, but, as ever in the past, for mere wanton show and display of power—power to set aside the rights and privileges of the many. And this under the very government that has generously guaranteed them the basic right to their own lives, liberties, and their pursuit of happiness.

And once more England's back to the wall with one eye glued on the Union Jack and her world-encircling possessions and the other on America as her Empire-saving money bank. And all our leading bankers, industrialists, money profiteers—they and their kept press, their radio, their legislators, lawyers, judges, politicians, and financial riff-raff dancing and piping to the same tune. For England's cry has been and still is run, run quick, America! Loan or give warships, airplanes, bombs, guns, men! Quick, quick! For *you* as well as we are in danger. We are your first line of defense. Don't forget if we go down, you go down! (As though Hitler, after so long a war as this one, and with no navy to aid him, could, instantly, build one and cross the Atlantic. And that in the face of the fact that we have definitely announced that we can't build one in less than four years. And if we can't, how can Hitler?) And all this in the face of Canada and Australia and New Zealand, South Africa, and all the rest of the British Empire intact and arming to the teeth. And her navy, according to her, still undiminished. But if so, why this rush on the part of America?

The answer is money, money, money. Get America in and make her pay for it. And so, really instanter, as you recall, money beginning to pour out of America. A sudden and most unbelievable war program—billions on billions for this and that (everything that is desired by England) where previously in America there was not a dime for anything. You don't recall, I suppose, "the whole terrible wastefulness of the New Deal from beginning to end"? No money for W.P.A.— a huge, insane, political job-seeking money debauch *that,* according to our money profiteers. And the same concerning the C.C.C. and T.V.A. and the Federal Theater Project, and the Federal Writer's Project, to say nothing of the crime of old-age pensions, the dole, the Federal Housing Project; in fact, each and every attempt to reach, and permit to live for a while, the endless masses so swiftly and inhumanely discarded by our great corporations and their banks during the preceding ten years of depression. Robbery was the cry, if you will recall. The Raw Deal! The lunatic dreams of a madman! (Dr. Roosevelt.) Whereas now when England desires our aid for its grasping and justly crumbling Empire, no expenditures on our part are too great. None. We have, literally, money to burn—to throw away.

Yet voices in plenty, throughout America—and sane ones—saying: Don't send any men to Europe—this is not our war, we didn't make it. And others insisting—this before the destroyers were traded for military bases which we should have got in exchange for England's debt to America—don't give our old destroyers to Great Britain. It is an act of war. Besides, we need them ourselves. Our navy is none too strong as it is. And if England is going to lose so easily, it will put us in the position where we will be less able—not more—to meet the numerous problems that we will have to meet whichever side wins. For certainly Italy and Japan, now that they see England in a weakened condition and France in ruin, are already moving to help themselves to world territory which England, in the days of her might, very greedily and selfishly proceeded to take and tax for her benefit—not ours. Besides, these growing powers—Germany, Italy, Japan, Russia—not only represent about one billion persons now, but they are armed and ready for a long war. And in the face of that, to say that we should join with England now and affront them in every way possible when we are not even ready and when the war was not of our making—besides pouring billions of American money into the struggle and weakening ourselves for the final fray—is too fantastic for words.

"Why not," cried one American of no important name that I know of, but certainly of sound thought, writing in the *Los Angeles Examiner* of August 26, 1940—"why not obtain naval and air bases in the French as well as British Possessions on this side of the Atlantic? Both of them owe us money, any quantity of it, and if they really believe, as they continually assert, that Democracy is truly represented by the United States, why shouldn't they give us these bases in exchange for what they owe and let us fortify them against the antidemocratic powers they are so afraid of? Then, if they lose, at least they will have a safe and powerful democratic asylum to retreat to, if they really so wish to retreat." But I noted that the answers to these suggestions were that the authors were Reds, Fifth Columnists, Radicals.

Another letter in the *Los Angeles Examiner* exclaimed, and sanely enough: "We might join"—as Mr. Roosevelt later so deliberately proceeded to do, certainly without consulting the American people—"Canada in some scheme of defense of the northern half of this Western Hemisphere. But not before impressing upon our excellent and good neighbor to the north that, if Americans are to throw their blood and treasures into the defense of Canada, that Canada cease from inviting the European war to this continent by participating in it. For," went on the writer, "if she continues so to do and we join her, automatically, when Europe proceeds to retaliate, we by having joined her will be in that war. And we should not be. We have enough to do, if we insist on enforcing the Monroe Doctrine, to take care of this Western Hemisphere without having to go abroad to do it."

A third thinker on this problem, who writes for *Uncensored,* and who follows the progress of the amazing totalitarian program in Europe, wrote on August 17, 1940:

"Are the American people convinced there is essentially something for them to fight for? Or not? Essentially this is a question of morale. It is not the kind of morale general staffs talk about or can reasonably be expected to understand. For the military martinet morale may be created by conscripting the unemployed and bellowing at them when their shoelaces are untied. If this does not instill enough morale, the commanding officer will supply more with a rousing speech about 'duty.' But the kind of morale that counts has little to do with volunteers vs. conscription or with the neatness of a soldier's cot. Adolf Hitler's legions have morale that counts. Their morale is the ghastly afterbirth of the World War, incubated in the mulch of Central Europe and nursed by megalomaniacs. It is monstrous, vindictive, destructive. But it moves and it has not yet spent itself. . . . Defense of an unsatisfactory status quo is not enough to touch off the winning spirit of a people. This week it was reported from Washington that the House Rules Committee would not even permit consideration of a bill to authorize the appropriation of $5,000,000 in subsidies to make possible the lending of $150,000,000 through the United States Housing Authority. That slum clearance might have something to do with national morale would never occur to the generals and admirals to whose press conferences reporters now flock to get inspiring words for the American people. Of the deeper kind of morale which is the basic defense need there has been virtually no discussion.

"Yet exactly what is to be defended? By what it has said and left unsaid, the Administration has aroused the suspicion that it is planning to defend the Netherlands Indies and to give the British everything short of an expeditionary force. Such plans may reflect credit on the Administration's moral impulses, but there is some doubt that they make military sense. If national security means defense of the

Western Hemisphere, how much of it should be defended? Independent experts have sketched plans to delimit hemisphere defense in terms of military realities. What the administration might mean by hemisphere defense is not clear.

"Again, how is it to be defended? Nazi victories have impressed laymen with the need for bold, imaginative military leadership. The U. S. military hierarchy has been the slave of tradition. Since brains cannot be provided by Congressional enactment, laymen can only trust that the streamlining of the U. S. high command and the planning of grand strategy along modern lines will keep pace with the needs of today."

And a fourth, Mr. Manchester Boddy, editor of the *Los Angeles News,* a daily, paints another angle when he rises to inquire (August 16, 1940), "Can either side afford to win this war now?" And he proceeds to answer, "No. Victory now would crush Germany beyond revival; it would destroy the British Empire as well. The horrible disaster that would follow an immediate victory for either side would pull the United States down in its wake, because the economy of this nation has been adjusted to war. Likewise, neither side could survive defeat. Our conclusion is that peace must come gradually step by step. For Germany, through her overwhelming ability to make war, has compelled all nations of the world to participate to some extent in the current conflict. Today the United States, because of her overwhelming ability to produce, can compel all nations of the world (now able only to destroy) to participate to some extent in effecting a world transition from war to peace.

"A steadily decreasing state of belligerency will likely be maintained while the United States—*in exchange for airplanes and war material to Great Britain and food and clothing to continental Europe*—arranges a 'step by step' peace that will save life and suffering now, and put the nations of the world on a sound peace basis. For otherwise the death and destruction that will result from a deadlocked war are as nothing compared with the certain wholesale death and chaos that would follow immediate peace."

The interesting thing about this opinion to me is the bland as well as usual assumption that, war and disaster on any scale having been manufactured anywhere, America—presumably by reason of its universally advertised Save-the-World Complex—should automatically, and without thought of the cost to the American people, rush forward and supply airplanes and war material to Great Britain and food and clothing to continental Europe!

But exactly why? Do you notice any other nation doing it or even suggesting it?

Nothing of the sort. Nothing doing. They are busy enough with their own problems, they will tell you—too busy to be acting as a Florence Nightingale or a St. Francis to all the peoples of the earth. But here in America the first thought that appears to pop into the head of anyone who hears of a European or Asiatic rumpus, more particularly a British-manufactured rumpus, is for America to give itself and "give until it hurts" of its boasted plenty. Hurry, Hurry, Hurry. Run with the ambulances, the surgical and medical supplies, the bandages, food, clothing, this and that. On the other hand, however, let the masses of America ask for a dollar or two more a week, or an increase of the wretched dole extended, or something to be done for the Okies or the share-croppers or poor whites in the South —and even where labor-saving machinery has definitely cast them out —and you hear another story. What? Thirty dollars a month instead of twenty for the aged or sick? Ten cents more on the hour or the day for skilled labor? The abolishment of child labor in the factories and fields? More than twenty-five cents a day for imported Mexicans? Why, it's a crime! It's anarchy! These Russian-paid refugees are being paid to do this! Out with all aliens! Drive them out of the country! Thumb-print them! Spy on them! Trace them! Big business is being driven out of the United States by just such tactics! The American Constitution is being undermined! The country is being ruined!

How sad it is that our underpaid workers—the nine million out of work, the twenty million who are either youths who have never been employed or persons on relief, the under-pensioned old, and the over-worked children in factories—can't go off somewhere together and start a foreign war—or advertise themselves as an international disaster! How quick their fellow-Americans would then come running! Why, the poor things! How dreadful! And so food and clothing and medicine and this and that provided in plenty.

However, to go back to this very regular international rescue suggestion of Mr. Boddy's, the same is followed by two other suggestions so typically in line with our American Save-the-World complex that they hand me a laugh. Here is the first one:

"No one wants a peace that will have to be policed by the United States. Rather it should be that kind of peace that both the central powers and Great Britain want but cannot afford at this time—because to achieve it would mean certain disaster for both sides."

So maybe we can hire some Swiss or Swedish group to undertake this delicate job—at our expense, of course.

And here is number two (both in the same column—parts of the same editorial):

"The process of emerging from the current state of world war to a condition of world peace must follow a well developed plan. In this connection our legislators in Washington could well afford to study the possibilities of a modified form of military training on a 'part time' basis—and a practical way of meeting defense and deficit costs other than through ruinous taxation."

In other words, save money at home. Do everything you can to avoid "ruinous taxation" when it comes to our own self-protective plans—but when it comes to Europe, "Airplanes and war materials for Great Britain," who will not have a dime with which to pay for them. And "food and clothing to Continental Europe."

Now, I ask you!

For crying out loud!

But don't think this is the end of this protest against our going into the war to aid England. Don't go away. There's lots more.

For instance, take our Latin American neighbors, including Mexico and Central America—which now, after one hundred years of either indifference or belittling comments as to their prospects in the world, we are finding it advisable to take over in a trade sense (imagine!), assuming Germany to be successful in the war. And we don't even speak their language—can scarcely learn it. In other words, we are preparing to buy all of their surplus products, which have hitherto gone to Europe in exchange for European goods, machinery, and supplies, and either to use these products or sell them abroad ourselves for these South Americans and so keep them quiet. Or store them here—only for how long, no one knows. For by this system, of course, we will not disturb the incomes of our investors and merchants generally who are used to a fixed profit on the things they handle and don't want it disturbed—the starving masses to the contrary notwithstanding. Yet our own barns and warehouses throughout the country are already stuffed with the very things that South America might be able to sell to us if we were in need of them. Nevertheless, South America is to agree to stop sending its products to Europe, whether we can use them or not, and take in return what we have to offer, rather than let Germany build up any connection with it—a procedure which, if it did not mean war with the successful powers of Europe, would certainly mean financial disaster for this country.

For already we are planning to spend, as I have shown, from $8,000,000,000 to $14,000,000,000 on our own defense program—and now we are to add to that what will be required by the Latin Americans. One angry wit, a member of what Mr. Roosevelt would term the Fifth Column, suggested: How would it be, if instead of storing these South American products as we would have to, we were to feed the poor South American millions, some 60 per cent of whom are living on as little as 25 cents a day?

But of course, as you know, such a suggestion is sheer treason, punishable by death, preferably in Wall Street. But to me personally this is just one more of those Save-the-World bursts, like our entering the first war to make the world safe for democracy—our scrapping one-third of our navy (circa 1922) in the Christian faith that Japan and England would duly scrap theirs. Yet now, once more and regardless of what our people think, we are being rushed to the aid of Britain to save civilization when the purpose of this war is to destroy it if possible.

For at this date and to my positive personal knowledge—I have traveled in England a number of times and followed its structure and history with the greatest of care—there is nowhere on earth a greater foe to the development, mental and physical, of the masses of the earth, than the present ruling class of England. It hates democracy—much, much more than Mr. Roosevelt ever meant it when he said that he hated war. In fact it seeks the ruin of democracies, since it believes in a small ruling class and *has,* whenever it has seen any tendency to mass development showing among the people of its possessions, proceeded to crush the same—India, South Africa, our original thirteen colonies, Canada, New Zealand. If you doubt me, stop here and read my chapter in this book, "How Democratic Is England?" And the several chapters that follow that. Then return here and pay strict attention.

England sought, as you know, or should know, to crush democracy in America—the thirteen colonies. (If you doubt that, stop and for the first time in your life read our Declaration of Independence through. You will encounter an eye-opener.) It has so limited democracy in Canada that the financial wealth of that country is now controlled by the ruling class of England, and not by Canadians—the masses there as in the first world war are ordered to entrain and die, or go to a concentration camp, as did recently the Mayor of Montreal. It has been dominant in India since 1750 or thereabouts, and has starved and murdered millions of Hindus, in order that England— its ruling class, remember—might have the money to fight such wars as this one, and the last one, and their great one with Napoleon in 1805–1815. As you know, if you know anything at all, England, using the resources of the British Empire, destroyed and murdered the Orange Free State in South Africa—a republic, don't forget—in order to take over the diamond fields of South Africa and the other riches that might lie there. That was the invasion and war of a thug and a murderer, not that of an Empire boasting its interest in civilization.

Because of the cunning of Mr. Disraeli and his interest in distinguishing himself as well as the British Empire (I am thinking of the Suez Canal—that short cut to India), England invested in Egypt as long ago as 1875. Well, there were then fifteen million helots without shoes, without anything much other than a loincloth, without schools, without agricultural implements with which to feed themselves properly, without machinery to equip factories and produce goods which might add to their economic and social prosperity; also without newspapers, without any form of a government worthy of the name. However, this is now 1940. And England, although camouflaging the reality of it, has been in there for the last sixty-five years—forty-three years more than the Communists have been in charge of Russia— yet, if you choose, you can re-recite with me the above litany on the state of Egypt, and it will be essentially as true today as it was in 1875.

In sum, today Egypt has fifteen million helots, without schools, without newspapers other than five established for the edification and current enlightenment of England's ruling class installed by England to look after her interests in Egypt; also, one university to look after the education of her representatives in Egypt and their children; also a number of factories in which the men, women, and children of so-called Egypt are permitted to work for English trade adventurers and their trade representatives for no more than ten or fifteen cents a day. And hours of labor ranging from ten to twelve for men, women, and some children. Furthermore, there is no civilized procedure by which these people may hope to lift themselves to a better social position in even the local so-called civilization which England maintains there. Need I add to this any references to other British colonies—their masses? Of course I can, for I am thinking of Zanzibar, Mauritius, Tanganyika, St. Lucia, Trinidad, Barbados, St. Kitts, St. Vincent, British Guiana, Burma, India, etc., etc. And I have been all but forgetting the betrayal by England of democratic Spain. Democratic Czechoslovakia. Democratic Russia in 1919. Social democratic Austria.

England—the British Empire—but by that I mean, always, the dominant oligarchy of wealth in the south of England—is out to bleed the world for the benefit of a tiny group. And yet every effort is being made to trick the American people into fighting to save this world for this black widow of the nations. And hence this is the first and greatest and most practical reason I can think of for our staying out.

But there are other reasons, numerous and good. I can list them for you. We are not ready and we have not been ready since the last war ended. And, although $7,000,000,000 has been spent since 1932 to bring our army and navy up to the state where it should be able to face any world developments which might threaten America (as far removed as America is from Europe), yet the U. S. A. is still not ready. For, as you know, it was just about one year ago that the mechanized army unit came to the knowledge of our army chiefs, really at the exact time that the blitzkrieg came to the knowledge of Poland! And it was just about one year ago that our army started to imitate that Teutonic unit! Imagine! However, we have now, by Congressional enactment, devoted billions more to the production of modern subtleties in the way of war—although we are immediately assured by our undemocratic American financial masters that, unless business is properly rewarded, it may lose interest in this our great protective adventure, and not produce what an army and navy need. And that is one phase of our so-called Democracy that troubles me: the extreme care that our government has to take of the exorbitant if unnecessary profits of our financial magnates—not of those (if any) of any other of our citizens.

But it is not only this that troubles me. We now have in addition conscripted millions of our men and boys—an entirely new and dangerous procedure and precedent in connection with our peacetime life. For we are not at war as you know, and need not be, if we choose. Yet once such an immense army is conscripted and trained—and the enemy still 3,500 miles away—who is to say what use will be made of it once the war is over, or at any time before that, should the American people, their workers in particular, complain of any lack of food or clothing or freedom of speech or assembly or indeed any of the other of the civil rights under our remarkable Constitution as written? For right now without any war on our part, and without this impending conscription, how badly are the workers of this country treated by our giant corporations; how small is their interest in those workers beyond the steadily decreasing few they can profitably use in connection with their steadily improving labor-saving machinery! Which raises the question, Are they to be allowed to die? Or kept in slums and hovels? Or shot down? Or what? No mention of birth control, you notice, on the part of anybody—although that might help the poor. ("Never!" cry the churches.)

However, a standing army of millions, well controlled by money and its subservient militarists and their lesser officers and subalterns, would certainly prove useful in case of home labor troubles—as useful, for instance, as are the English standing army and navy in connection with the oppressed helots of India, Africa, Egypt, and wherever the oppressed and neglected natives of the colonial Empire are numerous and dissatisfied. I notice that our principal labor leaders—Lewis, Bridges, and others who seek the true welfare of American labor and its families—are nervous as to that, and refer to it continually; but how often is it even mentioned by our traitor press and radio, our moving pictures, legislators, or politicians and their subservient police and the

Chambers of Commerce of the American Manufacturers Association?

Yet with all this said, nothing that has been presented in this chapter is intended to imply that the United States should not devise and apply an adequate defense against attack from without. It should. What is implied—maybe somewhat too fiercely emphasized—is the fact that our joining up with England to defend it is nothing more nor less than joining up with a cold-blooded and cruel imperialism—not better but decidedly worse than that contemplated by the deposed Kaiser Wilhelm of the older Germany.

Say what you will of Wilhelm, he was a modern head of a modern state, which if it contemplated anything at all, contemplated social progress for all Germans, not for his particular family or group; which is more—immensely more—than can be said for the decadent group now ruling England, whose sole and wholly idiotic aim in so far as I can see is to preserve their own lunatic grandeur and social snobbery at even the expense of *their own English workers,* to say nothing of the navy- and army-dominated peoples of the rest of their Empire. And seeing that this seems to fit in so accurately with the dreams and designs of our own sixty families and their profiteer followers, who wish so ardently to be a part not of our democratic American state but rather of the noble one per cent that runs England, I say it is time that we contemplate their objectives in the clear and refuse, flatly, to share them.

Let us break with England once and for all. Let us grasp the fact that Britain's objectives are not ours and never have been. Let us, we the masses of America, assemble wherever we can and demonstrate verbally and politically—at public meeting and through the ballot box —that we understand and will never approve.

Assemble an American defensive army—yes. Fortify this northern continent in so far as defensively it can be fortified—yes. But send no money, no ships, no supplies to England. And none to Europe.

Brutal and undemocratic as well as anti-democratic plotting and conniving started this war. Let brutal and undemocratic conniving and plotting end it. For once in our national history let us refuse to be suckers; let us guard our own homeland—not England's decaying and criminal Empire.

CHAPTER SIX

Does England Love Us As We
Love England?

I HAVE ALWAYS heard it said in the humble circles wherein I
move, and I have found it to be generally true, that it takes two
to make a romance.

To this, as to all great truths, there are exceptions. Now and again
you come across a married couple in which the husband's main pastime
is kicking the wife around, or in which the wife resorts regularly to
that classical fireside weapon, the rolling pin; and the more violently
and often the boot or rolling pin is wielded, the more adoring becomes
the marital partner whose person is on the receiving end.

Such a romance—at least so it has always appeared to me to be—
is the one between England and America. The most superficial reader
of our American history cannot deny that, of all countries in the world,
England is the one that has shown the least affection for us—and consequently, one might think, deserves the least affection from us.

But no. It doesn't work that way. We are as a people what Professor
Freud calls masochistic. Our greatest thrill is being kicked in the tail
—as long as England, the object of our blind adoration, does the kicking. In fact our national motto in so far as our relation to dear old
England is concerned is: "Kick me again, daddy!" Kick me and kick
me again, please.

Before 1776 we were in much the same economic position relative
to England as India is today. England wanted the American colonies
as sources of tribute and raw materials for English industries. We were

to get as little as possible from England—at prices England dictated; and send as much as possible of all we did send to England in English ships. In order that this delightful state of affairs might continue, it was essential that America be held back from building its own industries and ships to compete with the "Motherland." By 1776 the American colonies were already £5,000,000 in the red on the ledgers in the City of London. Which somehow reminds me of how the Southern masters of our Georgia and Alabama and Mississippi turpentine camps, as well as those who in Louisiana and Texas, collect impoverished labor to proceed from crop section to crop section, first arrest and then persuade their victims to accept credit for things they need up to ten or fifteen dollars; after which they are in their service—legally bound and restrained and compelled to work until death or disease or accident or chance in some way intervenes to free them.

That condition, as all the unfortunate members of England's "family" find out in the end, could only be ended by armed uprising. And thus and so it was that our connection with England was ended. That is, England "granted" us independence after we had already taken it. The American Revolution was nothing more than good old nature adjusting human affairs to its unfolding purposes. And if you don't believe this, read the following, which I am excerpting from our Declaration of Independence, no less:

"The history of the present King of Great Britain is a history of repeated injuries and usurpations, all having in direct object the establishment of an absolute Tyranny over these States. To prove this, let Facts be submitted to a candid world.

"He has refused his Assent to Laws, the most wholesome and necessary for the public good.

"He has forbidden his Governors to pass Laws of immediate and pressing importance, unless suspended in their operation till his Assent should be obtained, and when so suspended, he has utterly neglected to attend to them.

"He has refused to pass other Laws for the accommodation of large districts of people, unless those people would relinquish the right of Representation in the Legislature, a right inestimable to them and formidable to tyrants only.

"He has called together legislative bodies at places, unusual, uncomfortable, and distant from the depository of their public Records, for the sole purpose of fatiguing them into compliance with his measures.

"He has dissolved Representative Houses repeatedly, for opposing with manly firmness his invasions on the rights of the people.

"He has refused for a long time, after such dissolutions, to cause others to be elected; whereby the Legislative powers, incapable of Annihilation, have returned to the People at large for their exercise; the State remaining in the meantime exposed to all the dangers of invasion from without, and convulsions within.

"He has endeavored to prevent the population of these States; for that purpose obstructing the Laws for Naturalization of Foreigners; refusing to pass others to encourage their migrations hither, and raising the conditions of new Appropriations of Lands.

"He has obstructed the Administration of Justice, by refusing his Assent to Laws for establishing Judiciary powers.

"He has made Judges dependent on his Will alone, for the tenure of their offices, and the amount and payment of their salaries.

"He has erected a multitude of New Offices, and sent hither swarms of Officers to harass our people, and eat out their substance.

"He has kept among us, in times of peace, Standing Armies, without the Consent of our legislatures.

"He has affected to render the Military independent of and superior to the Civil power.

"He has combined with others to subject us to a jurisdiction foreign to our constitution and unacknowledged by our laws; giving his Assent to their Acts of pretended Legislation: For quartering large bodies of armed troops among us: For protecting them by a mock Trial from punishment for any Murders which they should commit on the Inhabitants of these States: For cutting off our Trade with all parts of the world: For imposing Taxes on us without our Consent: For depriving us in many cases of the benefits of Trial by Jury: For transporting us beyond Seas to be tried for pretended offenses: For abolishing the free System of English Laws in a neighbouring Province, establishing therein an Arbitrary government, and enlarging its Boundaries so as to render it at once an example and fit instrument for introducing the same absolute rule into these Colonies: For taking away our Charters, abolishing our most valuable Laws and altering fundamentally the Forms of our Governments: For suspending our own Legislatures and declaring themselves invested with power to legislate for us in all cases whatsoever.

"He has abdicated Government here by declaring us out of his Protection and waging War against us.

"He has plundered our seas, ravished our Coasts, burnt our towns, and destroyed the lives of our people.

"He is at this time transporting large Armies of foreign Mercenaries to complete the works of death, desolation and tyranny, already begun with circumstances of cruelty and perfidy scarcely Paralleled in the most barbarous ages, and totally unworthy the Head of a civilized nation.

"He has constrained our fellow Citizens taken Captive on the high Seas to bear Arms against their Country, to become the executioners of their friends and Brethren, or to fall themselves by their Hands.

"He has excited domestic insurrections amongst us, and has endeavoured to bring on the inhabitants of our frontiers, the merciless Indian Savages, whose known rule of warfare is an undistinguished destruction of all ages, sexes and conditions. In every stage of these Oppressions We have Petitioned for Redress in the most humble terms. Our repeated Petitions have been answered only by repeated injury. A Prince, whose character is thus marked by every act which may define a Tyrant, is unfit to be the ruler of a free people."

And so will the Indian revolution come, when it does come.

Interestingly enough we thought that at that time we had obtained a complete and final divorce from England. And it was perhaps a bit of a jolt for the English at first. But they are the aptest of pupils in the school of experience, as we ought to know by now, for if they are defeated on one front, they try another; and most truly it has been said of them that they never won a war (the first world war we and France won for them) nor lost a peace. There were, as they soon decided after our apparently successful revolution, ways in which they could make America useful and subservient to them—more subtle ways of holding us in the British "family" even if the old kind of leash would no longer serve. English law, if you chance to remember, allows divorce only for infidelity, not for persistent cruelty. And they knew that, kicked as we had been and dropped about the floor, we had not been and would not be unfaithful to them. For beneath our bruises and lacerations we probably loved them too well in our heart to be done with them. And right they were, as you will see. For from that point on, just to keep our love warm, they gave us a hearty British kick every few years.

In the war of 1812 they popped down from Canada and burned our Capitol and administration buildings in Washington. I say "they," but with their usual finesse they got others to do most of the dirty work and the dying for them. In our Revolutionary War they had used some of their Bengal swag to hire cannon fodder from the Prince of Hesse-Cassel and the Duke of Brunswick. (As historian W. E. Woodward puts it: "A small amount was to be paid as compensation for those who were killed or wounded. The prince and the duke were each to receive £11,000 a year personally outside of all other subsidies. It was very nice for the prince and the duke.") In 1812 they got whole tribes of disgruntled Indians—who certainly had a perfect right to be disgruntled—to scalp, torture, and murder us. It's just an old English custom.

During our Civil War, delighted as ever to be able to weaken democratic movements by splitting them, they spared no effort to support the slaveholding secessionists. Such confidence had they in the horse their money was on—the horse of reaction which they have always backed—that they even printed stamps for the secessionists with the head of Jefferson Davis on them.

In 1893, despite the Monroe Doctrine and their own treaty with Venezuela, they wanted to carve off a piece of Venezuela. They couldn't bear to think of the poor Venezuelans going along without any democracy—and too, there was a small question of oil and lakes of asphalt, exceedingly valuable at that time. Hence they refused even to arbitrate the issue until President Cleveland surprised and pained them by threatening war.

Between 1783 and 1913 they made thirty treaties with us, and violated one in every four of them: the Definite Treaty of Peace of 1784, the Jay Treaty of 1795, the Treaty of Ghent of 1815, the Rush Bagot Agreement of 1818, the Convention Respecting Fisheries of 1819, the Convention for Indemnity of 1823, the Clayton-Bulwer Treaty of 1850, and the Treaty of Washington of 1871. Today we are being asked to fight with them for "the sacredness of treaties"—and as usual we are delighted and eager to get started.

So much for the principal kicks, up to the World War of 1914. But all the time, between kicks, they have been busy hog-tying us in a new way, just in case they should ever give us one kick too many and we should get sore.

In colonial days they had us on the leash because they had the guns and we hadn't. After our revolution they had us on another leash because they had the money and we hadn't. Again observe what the fabulous loot from India meant to English imperialism. Just when everyone needed capital to get industries going with the newly invented machines, only the Old Lady of Threadneedle Street had any ready cash. Not only could she get a long start on rivals in mechanization at home, but by judicious loans and investments in the right places could begin to dig herself into positions of control abroad where the power of the gun no longer operated.

So when the pro-English Alexander Hamilton started his United States Bank, modeled exactly on the pattern of the Bank of England, we need not be surprised to find word going around that English bankers had more than a passing interest in it. For Thomas Jefferson the United States Bank was "the most hideous evil." He saw how such an institution, under the wing of the government and yet actually controlled by a small group of wealthy individuals, meant putting in the hands of that group the power to control all production by the granting or refusing of credits at interest.

The Bank was in point of fact England's first garrison of gold in "free" America—and a more potent and less costly garrison than the Hessian detachments had been. The group controlling the Bank corresponded, as far as England was concerned, with the Zemindars and Princes of India. England really created the wealth and privilege for these, so that they should become England's allies within our gates. They were the first Fifth Columnists in America, and directly from them stem the groups of today who are leading us into the war.

After the Civil War and England's unsuccessful attempt to make America safe for slavery—a matter in which the English masses, by then becoming organized, had something to say on the other side—English bankers held nearly a billion dollars in U. S. Government bonds.

And now, following the ancient European precedent, the privileged groups in the two countries began to unite themselves by marriage. By finding themselves American heiresses as bedfellows, the landed feudal aristocracy of England who were feeling the draft from the upsurge of industrial magnates at home—the industrial development in England—got themselves the capital they needed to get their silver spoons into the industrial gravy; and at the same time they drew closer together the interests of the Wealth International's branches on either side of the Atlantic—the common interest to protect the institution of privilege against the vulgar herd of all countries.

Of course the American royal families—the old "Four Hundred"—would never have existed had the American principles of Jefferson not been tossed out of the window. In order to be let into the sacred royal circle of England they had to profess the creed of the Wealth International, which places its own perpetuation always ahead of mere old-fashioned patriotism. They had to learn how to be snobs according to the English pattern. Once they mastered the rules of etiquette, they were honored by invitations to tea at Buckingham Palace, and their daughters could even be permitted to don strange wrappings and tulle veils and drop a courtsy before the imperial throne.

Mr. and Mrs. Ordinary American were actually expected to believe—and millions did believe—that this snob marriage market proved England's affection for us. And yet of course it was nothing more or less than a new way of taking the American people's money for London's bankers, and of securely entrenching England's Fifth Column in this country.

The rules of the marriage market were very strict. If the American mate selected by an Englishman or girl was rich, everything was in order; but if not, a social crime of awful gravity had been committed. That the same is still just as true today was shown by the alarums and excursions over Edward VIII's flutter with Wally Simpson of Baltimore, which roused the venerable archbishops of England to passionate moral denunciations. Everyone knows that if Wally Simpson had happened to be a Dupont or a Morgan or a Rockefeller, and if Edward had loved her for her money instead of (the vulgar fellow!) for herself, all England would have rejoiced, with the archbishops leading the Hallelujahs—no matter how many times she had been divorced. You know that, of course—or don't you?

There has been a considerable traffic of tourists from America to England since 1918, and many visitors have come away with the impression that the English now accept us almost on their own level. That is a mere surface impression. Despite England's increasing consciousness of the fact that America exists, due largely to the movies, we remain at best a curiosity and a source of easy pickings for the "best people" over there. For every hypocritical honeyed word there is a kick to show us our place. They who talk so glibly of "defending democracy" when their empire is threatened despise us for one very simple reason: that at heart the mass of our people are, as we have always been, democratic. It is only very recently that they have recognized our existence at all except as a sucker they keep on ice across the Atlantic to help them out of a jam. Only in the last twenty years or so have their newspapers reported American events, and even now America is more sparsely covered than any two-cent country in the Balkans. Even our Presidential elections are hardly worth a line in the popular English press except when, as this year, the result is likely to affect the prospect of our once more becoming suckers for English imperialism. I have heard from Rhodes scholars who went to Oxford that, up to ten years ago anyhow, they were treated as strange zoological specimens by their young aristocratic fellow-students.

I had many revealing experiences myself with the aristocracy of England, on visits to that country. Once in the home of a wealthy London family I remarked on the ingeniousness of a toy with which the children were playing, and the lady mother said: "Yes, isn't it clever? The Germans do make wonderful toys." I picked up the toy and drew attention to the words on it: MADE IN CONNECTICUT. The lady immediately became indignant. "Why, it isn't so!" she cried. "It must be a mistake! I gave orders that all our toys must be German!" She could not bear to admit that anything so ingenious could possibly have been made by mere Americans.

On another occasion I was walking with an Englishman along a London street, and we stopped to look at the wares in a.shoestore window. I pointed to a very fine pair of shoes and said: "I'll bet those are American-made." My companion scoffed at the very idea, for it was a refined and high-class West End store, but we went inside and the assistant admitted I was right. My companion's whole day seemed ruined by the shock, but the assistant managed to calm him down by saying that he had a number of American customers and only kept American-made shoes for their special benefit.

The same attitude regularly emerges in the world of sport. The famous "sportsmanship" of the English is much in evidence when one Englishman whom they favor is beaten by another Englishman, or even sometimes by a Continental; but if an American wins, they cannot conceal their irritation and hint broadly that he must have cheated. The same holds true in the arts. Less than ten years ago the movie critic of a leading London newspaper was removed from his job largely as a result of pressure by English film producers, whose offerings he was always (and justly) comparing unfavorably with Hollywood movies. In the theatre and in their movie studios the English pursue a determined policy of excluding Americans, putting up every kind of barrier against the hiring of our actors. This is often heatedly pointed out by American theatrical circles and compared with the complete "cultural free trade" which exists on Broadway and in Hollywood. But England's only reply is still further strengthening of the barriers. They have always found that the best way to treat Americans is to kick them, and it has never failed yet. They have an outright contempt for our architecture which the rest of the world recognizes as the most progressive and characteristic of our epoch, and scorn to erect any high buildings in England and so give us credit for any original achievement. Other Europeans, Asiatics, Africans, and South Americans feel and speak differently.

To return to personalities in this connection, one Christmas season I was in England and visited the home of a certain gentleman of title, one of those spacious, peaceful country residences whose foundations are the bones of millions of Indians and Africans. The gentleman was constantly bobbing out to the hall to see what gifts and greeting cards had arrived. On about the sixth trip I heard a muffled explosion, and the gentleman came back into the room with his face scarlet. He was waving in his hand a card that had just been delivered.

"Look, my dear!" he cried to his wife. "Maria! This—this tradesman! He dares to wish us a Merry Christmas!"

The card had been sent by one of the most successful merchants in the local town. I said to myself that now I knew where I stood. If a successful "tradesman" was not allowed to wish the gentleman a Merry Christmas, that showed approximately where an American got off: about four hundred blocks back.

After the first World War, when truth began to emerge from behind the forest of manufactured propaganda, the face of England was so plain that one would have thought no American could help seeing it.

We learned by official secret documents which were uncovered that England's claim to be fighting for "democracy" had never had any vestige of truth: that England had all along had agreements to divvy up the imperialist swag for which it had really fought, and for which it got us to fight.

We learned how the privilege-defending swag-hunters in London had kept our Ambassador Page as a pet, and convinced him and the pitiful Colonel House and the even more pitiful Woodrow Wilson that there would be "domestic collapse" in the U. S. A. if we didn't enter the war. We learned later just what the tie-up was between "our" Mr. Morgan and the Palace gang over there, and how many millions the Morgan gang had made out of the blood of our sons, as revealed in the disclosures of the Nye Committee. From 1916 till the final liquidation of wartime industry in America, net corporation profits were thirty-eight billion dollars.

And so we who had been so incensed by the German propaganda in our country during the war discovered something our own privilege-defenders had known all along, and kept from us: That there had been an immense English propaganda machine here which had spent far more money, and operated on far more cynical and shameless lines, than the German propagandists. Every newspaper served us up spine-chilling tales of "Hun atrocities" in Belgium, whereas the German defense was rarely printed, and for the simple reason that our newspapers belonged to the British Fifth Columnists. Five ace American newspapermen, including Irvin Cobb and Harry Hansen, had sent a joint cable to the Associated Press, "pledging their professional personal word" that they had followed the German army through Belgium, had not seen a single instance of "unprovoked reprisal," had investigated numerous atrocity rumors and found them all groundless. It was in vain. The English Fifth Column had to give us something to heat our blood and make us indignant. Whether it bore the slightest resemblance to truth was quite unimportant.

As John T. Flynn has commented, "the British used $150,000,000 to get us into the World War and thought it money well spent." After the war Congressman Calloway revealed exactly how some of the biggest newspapers of America had been bought for England with American money. We learned of Sir Gilbert Parker's special American propaganda bureau in London with its staff of fifty-four men, its direct mailings of propaganda to over a quarter of a million influential Americans, and its export by almost every ship of noted English authors and "thinkers" to spread lies on lecture tours throughout America. The bureau had no need of an office in America. It had its own Fifth Column of Great Americans to organize the work here for it.

Yet we were surprised and shocked when we received proof of all this. But the shock didn't last long—and why should we have been surprised when essentially the same thing had been done in the Boer War? In this, perhaps the most wanton and disgraceful of all England's imperialist aggressions (if distinctions can be made in such a century-long carnival of wantonness), the natural sympathy of Americans was with the Boers. I myself as a traveling newspaperman of the time can witness to the truth of this, for I encountered the most intense expression of American feeling in regard to this everywhere. Yet there as elsewhere and at other times the English Fifth Column did its job. Our American press soft-pedaled the frightful English atrocities and told us that the highly civilized and democratic Boers were savages. The Boers implored Theodore Roosevelt to do something, and Roosevelt replied that it was impossible and he wouldn't do it anyway. History repeated itself with Franklin Roosevelt when Italy and Germany, with England's connivance, fell upon democratic Spain in 1936. England did not want democracy helped in Spain or anywhere else, and England's Fifth Column extends into our White House.

All these things are known and proved now, and yet exactly the same process is being repeated in the present war and we seem to be falling for it just as hard. John T. Flynn says that the sum already allocated for English propaganda in this war is no less than $165,000,000. Englishmen exhaling the essence of English imperialism, like Noel Coward, dramatist of Mayfair "smart sin," are wandering about spreading the poison. He arrived in Los Angeles in August and was greeted with American cheers.

So you see, we love it. We eat it up. England kicks us in the pants and you can hear it nine blocks away, and all we can say in tones of husky adoration is: "Thank you! You kick so beautifully!"

Truly, love is wonderful. For how else can one explain all this?

Let us look at another phase of this England loves us, we love England complex. But first ask yourself, what, after all, has been the main real cause and issue of most wars that have been fought, butchering off plain bewildered men and women and babes by the tens of million, during the present century? The answer to that is pretty well known to all who have dug below the surface of lovely patriotic speeches. The answer is "oil." And the two great oil empires of the world are the English and the American. But not before 1914. Before that America led and England was becoming aware of her deficiency. After that, immediately after America saved England—in 1919 that is—England decided to dominate the world's oil supply—in other words, push us out of first place. And *has,* her love for us being what it is. Let us see very briefly how the English oil magnates—who have more control than anyone else over England's government and its policy—have shown their love for America in this field of oil.

The great English oil monopoly is Royal Dutch Shell (the "Dutch" is there more or less by courtesy, since the Dutch Empire with its oil-rich Indies only exists by virtue of English naval power). The Napoleon of this concern—Napoleon indeed of the world's oil, as you will see—was the late Henri Deterding, the Dutchman who became English and was knighted by England for his services. Royal Dutch Shell, starting with control of the Dutch East and West Indies oil, came to control vast oil wealth in Russia, Rumania, Egypt, Sarawak, Venezuela, Argentina, Mexico—and the United States. It has a refinery at Curaçao, Dutch West Indies, with a capacity of 1,000 tons daily—in close proximity to the Panama Canal. The Pilgrim's Progress of Sir Henri Deterding, probably the leading helmsman of world reaction in our time, is indicated by his wives—the first of whom was Dutch, the second White Russian (after Soviet expropriation of capitalist-owned oil in Russia), and the third pro-Nazi German (Deterding has been charged with—and never denied—contributing funds to Hitler to help him into power).

After the 1919 armistice the British government set out to get control for English interests of the world's oil resources. Deterding in conjunction with the Petroleum Imperial Policy Commission arranged for British private control of Dutch Shell in peace time with quick transfer to direct government control on threat of war. At that time Lord Curzon remarked that "history would record that the Allies were borne to victory on the crest of a wave of oil"—hence Deterding's knighthood. Sir Edward Mackay Edgar, British petroleum banker, wrote that "the British position is impregnable. All the known oil fields, all the likely or probable oil fields, outside of the United States itself, are in British hands or under British management or control, or financed by British capital." That little flaw was something that could be remedied. Sir Thomas Browning remarked that "Royal Dutch Shell is more powerful and aggressive than ever was the great Standard Oil Trust of America." Deterding was, then, already controlling the most powerful organization on earth "for the production of a source of power" (quoting Lord Fisher) "which almost doubles the power of our navy whilst our potential enemies remain normal in the strength of their fleets." Rapidly British ships were being changed from coal-burning to oil-burning.

Understand what that means. It means that the much-publicized "community of interests" between England and the United States—the supposed love of England for America—is just so much eyewash. For England's world power rests mainly on oil—oil is paramount in the game of imperialism—and the United States is the one great rival on the scene. In other words, we are not only not England's greatest friend; we are, behind the eyewash and sentimentality drooled across the Atlantic, in the last analysis England's first enemy. And England

—meaning, in fact, Sir Henri Deterding—proceeded to demonstrate that fact in no uncertain manner.

Early in 1919 Deterding made the greatest addition thus far to England's oil empire by acquiring an interest in, and management of, the Mexican Eagle Oil Company. This increased Dutch Shell's production by more than 50 per cent to almost 50,000,000 barrels. Standard Oil was also bidding for the property, but the whole-hearted co-operation of the British Government with Deterding gave him an advantage in the bidding. An article in *World's Work* in 1920, describing this deal and the extraordinary closeness it showed between Shell and the English government, went on: "The next great battle is likely to be between American oil companies on one hand and the Royal Dutch-British Government combination on the other, for control of oil supplies not of markets. It will be a battle between nationalities rather than between companies."

The battlegrounds were all over the world, but the most important was right here in the United States—I almost said in "our" United States but the events that followed showed it certainly was not "ours" and was not even Mr. Rockefeller's, but was, as it still apparently is, primarily the English government's. I quote now from Ludwell Denny's book *We Fight for Oil:* "So rapid was British development of wells that over half of Dutch Shell's world production was soon coming from American fields. Standard charged the alien trust" (What? Calling Englishmen "aliens"? Call out the F. B. I.!) "with pushing production here and holding back its non-American fields, deliberately to exhaust United States reserves." Standard tried to stir up the Washington government to act as effectively with and for them as the London government did for Dutch Shell. They let loose across America a flood of "British peril" propaganda—yes, this is less than two decades ago! Deterding countered it by "permitting" American investors to buy minority shares in Dutch Shell's American companies—thereby, as Denny puts it, "incidentally letting Americans furnish most of the actual capital for the British penetration of this country." Now is your soft, warm American heart beginning to grow hot with love?

At the same time side-skirmishes between the two great oil imperialisms were in progress all over the world, with England generally succeeding in knocking our brave boys to the floor in the first or second round: doing it, of course, with the usual courtly old-world charm for which we had long since learned to care. There was naturally a she-mozzle of sizable proportions concerning Russia, where the rude Bolsheviks had informed all Deterdings, Rockefellers, and similar gentry that they actually regarded Russian oil as being the property of Russia. It would be hard to say whether the Deterding or Rockefeller blood boiled more furiously over this retreat to barbarism, but the British government, with its troops "guarding" the rich Baku oil field "on behalf of the Allies" (on behalf, of course, of Deterding), went into prompt action by recognizing the anti-Soviet republics of Georgia and Azerbaijan in return for favors to come—favors to Deterding. Officially England was boycotting the Soviet. Actually Deterding, careful to guard against the possibility that the revolution might not be overthrown according to his main plan, was hard at work dickering with Moscow for a monopoly concession. Sir Austen Chamberlain later admitted quite blandly that these Deterding negotiations were going on with the British government's knowledge. And Standard Oil was doing exactly the same—also dickering for a monopoly concession. But in this particular case neither side won, for the Soviet revolution did succeed and the Soviet government proved later to have been playing up to both the rival oil empires, not with the least intention of ever giving either the desired concession but merely to get an outlet for their oil as a quick means of raising desperately-needed cash. It was the only time anyone ever got the better of Deterding, and he was so furious that later he had the British government stage a frame-up raid on the Soviet trading offices in London as an excuse for breaking off all relations. By that time hundreds of thousands of tons of Russian oil had been sold for cash in England under Deterding's imperial nose, taking away his business right on the home ground.

But elsewhere things were going along swimmingly for Deterding. The Federal Trade Commission found that cash and stock dividends of Royal Dutch subsidiaries, other than holding companies, averaged 42 per cent in the 1902–1921 period. In the 'twenties there was the international scramble for control of the Mosul oil fields in the new England-created State of Iraq. Many thousands of Englishmen had been sent into the insufferable heat of Mesopotamia in the World War to die like flies for Deterding's lust after that oil—the same oil that

Germany with its Berlin-Bagdad railway had lusted after before 1914. And England now talked in its lofty way about the necessity for "international co-operation" to exploit the oil—so there were conferences between English, American, French, and Dutch interests under the auspices of the League of Nations—which itself was merely another front for England and its imperialism. Who do you think emerged victorious in the final outcome, who got the control? Your first guess is correct. Washington announced with pathetic pride that there had been a victory for the "Open Door" policy and that all were to share in the spoils. But Denny in *We Fight for Oil* comments:

> Great Britain retains controlling interest, through Dutch Shell and Anglo Persian holding 52.50 per cent. What kind of an Open Door is that? This question is put by American oil men who say the State Department's 'Open Door Victory' gives certain Americans less than a quarter interest, whereas before Sinclair, Standard of New York and Chester had practically all.

In 1923, when the Federal Trade Commission held an inquest on the Anglo-American oil war, the picture unveiled was a gloomy one for America. Here is what they found: "The *most important instances of discrimination by foreign governments against citizens of this country* are the exclusive policies of the Governments of Great Britain and the Netherlands" (meaning England as the dominating force of Royal Dutch Shell) "in respect to the oil fields of India and the Dutch East Indies, and the 1920 San Remo Agreement of Great Britain and France covering the undeveloped oil fields of Mesopotamia and of the British and French colonies. Denial of reciprocity of treatment to citizens of this country appears to exist with respect to the petroleum industry of Australia, British Borneo, certain African colonies, British Honduras, British Guiana and Trinidad; France and French possessions; Italy, and the Netherlands and its dependencies."

As a result of this situation Congress had been forced to take more of a hand in the game, and in 1920 it had enacted a mineral leasing law for public lands, forbidding acquisition of properties by the nationals of any foreign country that denied reciprocity to Americans.

Does that sound like the worm turning? Well, listen to some details of what the American oil concerns had to face in England's Empire—and then look about you as you go around your own land for evidence of any effective obstacles to Shell and its interests in this country—and then please tell me who it is that gets off, and where.

I quote again from *We Fight for Oil:* "American and other foreign companies are prevented in effect from owning oil-producing properties in British India. The London Government has stated that 'prospecting or mining leases have been in practice granted only to British subjects or to companies controlled by British subjects.' This restriction extends to transfer of British holdings to foreigners. . . . American consular dispatches describe the British Government policy there (in India and Burma), regarding ownership and production, as 'one of entire exclusiveness.' Standard of New York informed the State Department that it was not even allowed to purchase a warehouse in Burma."

Now turn your eyes to home, sweet, home—not your home or Rockefeller's home but the King of England's home across the Atlantic.

Here is the Federal Trade Commission of 1923 reporting again:

"The Royal Dutch Shell group in February 1922 consummated a merger of the principal properties and investments of the Union Oil Company (Delaware) with its chief American subsidiaries in a new company, the Shell Union Oil Corporation. The Shell Union Oil Corporation now controls over 240,000 acres of oil lands in the United States; has about 3.5 per cent of the total output of crude petroleum, owns extensive properties in refineries, pipelines, tank-cars, and marketing equipment; and is one of the largest companies in the domestic petroleum industry."

Now again from *We Fight for Oil:*

"In the period from 1923–27 the network of trunk pipe-lines controlled by Dutch-Shell here is understood to have increased from less than 1,000 miles to 2,064 miles. Among its 1927 acquisitions was a 600-acre terminal on the Houston Ship Channel. Dutch Shell's 1926 annual report showed that 35 per cent of its total world production came from the United States."

Now from the *Literary Digest* of March 28, 1936:

"American cash—nearly $300,000,000 to date—bought bond issues to finance a separate U. S. firm, the Shell Union Oil Corporation. Approximately 60 per cent of the common stock was and is held by Royal Dutch interests."

And today? Well, drive down the street and count the Shell and

Union gas stations, just to give you some small idea. Shell Union is now the third largest oil concern in the United States following Standard of California and Texas Oil. And if you wish to follow the love-fest abroad and see how nobly England co-operates with America, consider Mexico where a new war is brewing, a mass murder of perhaps millions of innocents, merely as a consequence of the Cardenas government's bolshevik decision that Mexican oil belonged to Mexicans. England, immediately after the expropriation there, severed diplomatic relations with Mexico. That is all they can do openly because of the Monroe Doctrine—but do you think in the long run they care two straws about any Monroe Doctrine? Why should they? Is not America eating right out of their hand? There is more than one way of taking that oil back by force of arms. It always comes to arms, to mass murder, in the end. It came to that over the oil in the Chaco. Just think of those tens of thousands of Bolivian and Paraguayan wretches who had to go and kill each other in that hell, all to decide whether Deterding or Rockefeller should have the oil—for absolutely nothing else in the world. And in the end, after years of the most appalling human suffering, nothing but a stalemate and an agreement to divvy up fifty-fifty: an arrangement with which, judging by past record, England will never be content without a further effort to win control by blood. And what of the thousands of Americans who work for Shell Union? Still working for the barest livelihood on every city street corner—and destined, seemingly, in the end to go and get killed either here or there in the next stage of the eternal squabble for more and more oil. The result of it all being, as one presumes from the past, that England gets the lion's share.

Truly, love is wonderful. For how else can you explain all these wonders, these remarkable manifestations of "love" between England and the dear innocent Americans who "speak the same language"?

How wonderful it really is can be seen by a glance at the history of our reactions when others tried to give us a gentle kick. England can stop our ships by the score, seize our mail and merchandise according to fancy, tell us with whom we can and can't trade—and we touch our hat like a Devonshire yokel passing the squire's limousine in a lane. But remember "Remember the Maine!" and how we acted toward

Spain when it was even suspected—wrongly, as it turned out—that it had interfered with one American ship? For the slightest affront to ourselves or to a friend of ours we are ready to break relations with Japan or Russia, but nothing is too strong for England to get away with. It is even *lèse majesté* now to suggest that England helped Germany to arm, or that England had anything to do with building the Mannerheim Line which brought on the Russo-Finnish war. In connection with this the most liberal of the American newspapers that I read tells me that this sort of thing is bound to continue and that we need patience and understanding in the face of what will certainly appear to be unjust discriminations! Yet maybe it is right, although I hope not.

Remember the Perdicaris case? A wealthy American goes traveling in Morocco and a local chief, Rasouli, kidnaps him and holds him for ransom. All Rasouli is doing is borrowing a technique developed and perfected in America, the leading kidnaping country of the world. But Theodore Roosevelt bursts into flame and cries across the front pages of every newspaper: "PERDICARIS ALIVE OR RASOULI DEAD!" Why should some cheap Moroccan think he can get away with a thing like that? Who does he think he is—an Englishman?

And note all through our history the attitude our government has taken toward revolutionary struggles abroad. We cheered the Greek revolt against Turkey, cheered Kossuth's Hungarian revolt against the Austrian empire. When Napoleon III was overthrown in 1870 we recognized the Third Republic of France in 48 hours. In 1873 when the Spanish King was dethroned our Minister in Madrid paid his respects to the republic the following day, on State Department instructions. Why? Because England gave us the high sign that these disturbances did not affect the basic interests of the Wealth International whose headquarters were in London: or, in the words of Charles A. Beard, "in none of the revolutions was the principle of private property impugned." But we were perfectly willing, in 1880 and 1894, to sit in on the carving-up of Morocco and the Congo, cheek by jowl with England and the other great imperialisms of Europe. And for all Wilson's beautiful "Fourteen Points," we came out of the great Versailles carve-up of 1919 with no cleaner hands than anyone else, once England had kicked us into line. Our attitude toward the recent Spanish and Chinese struggles for democracy, in which England believed the principle of privilege to be impugned, completes the odorous picture.

You might think, perhaps, that if we can't feel the English kicks in our hearts we could feel them in our pockets, usually a pretty sensitive spot. But again no—don't you know that love conquers all?

During the first World War we loaned England some seven billion dollars so that His Majesty could carve himself off a few more colonies and make a bit more of the world safe for plutocracy. England's Fifth Column here fixed things so that for even the poorest of us it was almost as much as our life was worth not to contribute our savings to the noble cause. Morgan and the other Fifth Columnists who had done the job for England got their money back with interest—the boys of the International must stand together. Out of the proceeds of the first liberty loan our government handed $400,000,000 to Morgan. But the five-and-a-half-billion-odd lent by plain American suckers they kept to make armaments for the next slaughter. Certainly they have never paid it back.

Weren't we "Uncle Shylocks" when we timidly asked the English for our money back? Or don't you remember? How dared we expect his Majesty, Defender of the Faith, personal representative on earth of the Deity and exponent of civilization as well as the good and the beautiful here below, to bother himself about a little matter of squaring a debt of honor? And His Majesty with his imperial hands full defending the sacred principle of Democracy, which barbarians (an English word for anyone who tries to imitate England) were threatening all over the place! To defend this holy thing was the most delicate of tasks requiring full concentration and no noisy interruptions from across the Atlantic. The barbarians had to be made just strong enough to enslave their own people and a few other miscellaneous "peoples of whom we know nothing" (Chamberlain's reference to the Czechs), while yet not being allowed to get out of hand and infringe on England's enslaving prerogatives in the "Commonwealth of Nations."

Finally it was intimated that to stop his noise, and to give him a chance of atoning for his sin in asking for his money back, Uncle Shylock might have the honor of collaborating in this latest crusade for God and St. George. And Uncle Shylock wept tears of joy at such magnanimity, crying: "Count me in. But don't—oh, don't—let your preoccupation with the barbarians absorb you so much that you have no time left to kick me any more! Kick me again, daddy—and this time make it real hard!"

Do we love England?

Are you asking me?

And does England love us?

Are you asking me?

P.S. To bring the story up to date I quote the following from the column of Professor William Randolph Hearst on October 11, 1940:

Another thing which should make Mr. Churchill more cheerful, and more grateful too, is the enormous aid that the United States has given the British Empire.

A friend in need is a friend indeed—especially when it is the only friend a needy empire has.

We have sent the beleaguered British Empire a goodly part of our Navy recently renovated at a cost of one hundred million dollars.

We have sent her the thousands of airplanes with which she is now bombarding German docks and factories and cities.

We are sending her the food and war materials which we are denying to others, and all we get in Mr. Churchill's five thousand word report to Parliament is a single paragraph hidden away in an inconspicuous place, and not specifying whether he refers to Canada and Australia or to the United States when he says:

"If it were not for the resources of the New World which are becoming increasingly available, it would be a long time before we should be able to do much more than hold our own."

CHAPTER SEVEN

How Democratic Is England?

WHAT AMERICA stands in most desperate need of is a national psychoanalyst who will diagnose and correct our Britannia fixation.

England could not possibly have shown us more plainly that she does not stand for the things our people as a whole stand for. This is not merely a matter of the preponderance of evidence. England as an anti-democratic force in her relations with us and with all other peoples has a perfect score. Let us not still nurse this fantastic idea that England and America "speak the same language"—that they are joint custodians of the democratic principle. They do not and are not—and the reason for this chapter and the three others that succeed it is to try to persuade the American people to please count ten and find out just what we would be dying for,. before we choose to die.

You may have visited the British Pavilion at the New York World's Fair. If so, you have stood in contemplation, though possibly not in awe, of the immense figure of Britannia with its inscription: STRENGTH—PEACE—FRIENDSHIP.

Strength? Observe Prime Minister Chamberlain at Munich, gladly donating Czechoslovakia to Hitler in return for Hitler's promise not to fight England. (A story goes that he also gladly donated Danzig, the Polish Corridor, and the Ukraine for the same purpose of appeasement, but when Hitler, according to the story, asked Chamberlain to let him have his umbrella as a souvenir of that historic hour, Chamberlain replied: "Oh, no, sir, this is mine.")

Or observe the same Chamberlain flying to Rome early in 1939 to "raise his glass to His Majesty the King of Italy and Emperor of Ethiopia," while Italian submarines and planes sank British ships in the Mediterranean without evoking a protest. Or again, see the rude little yellow men later that same year removing trouser after sacred British trouser in Tientsin—while the old lion looked on in impotence. Impotent because to resist the debaggers would have been to help the immediate enemy of the debaggers, which happened also to be the enemy of the institution of privilege: democracy. Showing the whole world that it was never England the lion had roared for, but privilege. English privilege first—but privilege, native or alien.

How much do the rulers of England stand for peace, or even understand the meaning of the word? Who sabotaged the Disarmament Conference because they had to keep bombing planes to use on their colonial subjects? Who made an obscene jest out of the League of Nations? But Chamberlain could arrive home from Munich, wave before his countrymen the ludicrous piece of paper signed by Hitler, and cry: "Peace in our time!"

And friendship? We can only ask, Friendship for whom? Not for the Czechs. Not for the heroic defenders of democracy in Spain and China. Plenty of it for the Wall Street bigwigs who would sacrifice the United States for British interests. None for the great mass of Americans. None for the great mass of their own people.

What else did you see at the British Pavilion? The enormous "Court of Honor" lined with coats-of-arms of England's ennobled brigands, arranged for the delight of American snobs by a gentleman known as the Portcullis Pursuivant. And the Magna Carta, "unique symbol of the unending and world-wide struggle for liberty and freedom."

Seven and a quarter centuries after the signing of that document, the faintest of early whispers in the growing clamor against tyranny, David Lloyd George writes thus of the legislation introduced in England as keystone of the "national effort" in the present war for "civilization":

"It is thus enacted that by a ministerial decree issued in panic, the Magna Carta and the Habeas Corpus Act, time-honored bulwarks of the lives and liberties of every subject . . . can be suspended."

If you went upstairs in the British Pavilion, you saw what England's rulers are doing now for the people of England—shyly displayed in the midst of great open spaces showing, no doubt, what they are not doing. You saw a series of steps in the building of "democracy" through the ages in England, the last of which records the following triumphant achievement:

1939—SCHOOL-LEAVING AGE RAISED TO 15

Deeply as this must impress the visiting American yokel, he finds on looking up the more recent record that this year the school-leaving age was dropped again to fourteen. That means that as you read these words, in the year of our Lord and his Majesty 1940, nine out of every ten English children are getting no education at all after the age of fourteen—in order to throw them at that age on the labor market and make extra profits from the juvenile wage standard.

Onward and upward for St. George and Democracy!

But this is wartime, you say? Not a fair criterion?

Well, the theory that the way to defend democracy is to abolish it at home is curious to me. But let that pass for a moment. Let us think ourselves back a year to the time when England was not at war.

First, bear in mind that (in the words of Sir Reginald Banks, M.P., in 1929) "only in very recent times has England even pretended to be a democratic state. The great Parliamentarians of the eighteenth and early nineteenth centuries repudiated with disgust any such theory." Up to just over a century ago the government consisted almost exclusively of landed aristocracy. By 1818 fifty rich merchants, bankers, and industrialists had forced their way into the aristocrats' parliament of six hundred. Not till the beginning of this century did the Labor Party come into the field, and with it the pressure on the governing class to make some concessions to the mass of the people.

What is the setup now in the "Grandmother of Parliaments"?

Over 400 of the M.P.'s are members or representatives of the aristocracy or employing class. No less than 181 of these are company directors holding among them 775 directorships in banks, finance companies, railroads, and armament and other industries. One hundred forty-five are related to the peerage and interrelated with one another, forming the "Cousinhood," as it has been called—the real core of England's government.

Almost all of this Tory majority of more than 400, whose parliamentary stipend is $3,000 a year each, have incomes exceeding $10,000 a year—compared with just 0.5 per cent of the people they "represent" who have such an income. In the last eight years forty-three such M.P.'s have died. Thirty-three of these left estates averaging close to a million dollars each.

This phalanx of defenders of privilege make a public mockery of democracy. Many of them never trouble to attend more than an occasional debate in the Commons, though they use its luxurious facilities as a club (it has been called "the best social club in the world"), and can be seen most days entertaining their friends to tea and buttered toast on the terrace overlooking the Thames river. When a debate is finished bells sound, indicating that there is to be a vote, and those Tories who live near by in costly mansions can be seen hurrying to the House adjusting their monocles. The "whip" of their party tells them how to vote and as they stand in line to register a few of them inquire with a yawn what it is that they are voting on. They do what they are told because they owe their seats to the party machinery, and their company directorships or other perquisites to their seats (every company—particularly the shadier ones—needs an M.P. or two on its letterhead as a "front").

Once a year their party has a conference, and here is a description of a conference in 1937, by a writer in a Conservative newspaper:

Not 5 per cent of the Tory M.P.'s went to Scarborough . . . Mr. Chamberlain was only present while one speech was being delivered. That was the speech he made himself. . . . While one Tory delegate was speaking I counted 16 members of the platform party doing crossword puzzles. . . . When the less important delegates were talking, their words were lost in the tramp of feet moving out of the conference hall to the bar. . . . The Tories have a secret committee who turn down controversial resolutions submitted to them. . . . The delegates were enthusiastic to get away.

And so far we have only looked at the Lower House at Westminster. The House of Lords—imagine the anachronism in these days!—consists entirely of aristocrats, bishops, and archbishops who are not subject to election at all. It is a rare day when more than a score of these gentlemen are present in the House, and of those the majority appear to be slumbering as some lord or prelate drones along, in words and accents which to an American ear sound like utter gibberish. The Lords still have the privilege of holding up all the Commons' legislation except money bills for two years, by which time the conditions giving rise to it may have completely changed. They go into a state of hibernation as long as there is a Tory government, but they stand, sit, or lie ready to obstruct whatever reforms might be introduced in the event of a Labor government's coming to power.

In point of reality, since the Tories have a big majority of subservient M.P.'s, the Tory inner circle runs England on behalf of heavy industry and the banks just as autocratically as Hitler runs Germany. In 1939 half of the Cabinet consisted of members or relatives of the aristocracy, with titles as long as your arm. Its head, the Prime Minister, is not elected by the people but chosen by the party, and the rest of the Cabinet are chosen by him. Changes in ministers are seldom even discussed in front of the people's representatives, but are arranged privately in the drawing-rooms of Mayfair. Hence the appointment over and over again of absurd incompetents (supremely competent, however, in the care and cultivation of dividends) to fill such vital posts as the ministries for air, for labor, for defense co-ordination, for transport, for foreign affairs.

The people have absolutely nothing to do with it. Technically—for Cabinet members must be elected M.P.'s—a minister can be thrown out at a General Election by the people's refusal to put him back in Parliament, though even then the people have no say in the choice of his successor. But there's more than one way to skin a voter. One way is for the Tory oligarchy to have the King kick the M.P. for some sure Tory seat upstairs into the Lords—creating an immediate by-election in which the defeated minister can run. When Ramsay MacDonald and his son Malcolm, renegade Laborites who had been given ministries by the Tories, were both defeated at a General Election, neither gave up his ministry for a single day. "Sure thing" by-elections were arranged for them by their new above-stairs friends, and the people had the gratifying spectacle of Ramsay being elected member for the Scottish Universities, of which as a Laborite he had advocated the disfranchisement.

University Members of Parliament? But yes—the rulers of England may not believe in very much democracy—but they do believe in spreading it very thin, in the right places. A university education is, of course, the almost exclusive prerogative of the English privileged class. A perfect spot for some democracy! By all means let the graduates of the universities have an extra vote! Another feature of English democracy is that eligibility for a vote is rated by the payment of rent or the owning of property in a district. Thus a wealthy man who has graduated from Oxford, lives in London's West End, and has a business in the city, has three votes. Three cheers for Strength, Peace, and Friendship and Civilization as We Know It!

In England, just as here, the backing of a party machine is almost essential for election as the people's representative. But in England, just to make it a bit harder for the man without "standing" and "connections," candidates must put up a very large sum of money as a deposit, which they forfeit if they fail to poll one-eighth of the total votes. And here we at least have primary elections in which voters registered under a party elect its nominee, whereas in England the candidate is hand-picked by party chieftains, so that the machine becomes all-powerful.

The Tories' main concern is that the candidate should have enough money to pay his own election expenses and to give him a very decided stake in the existing privilege system. Hence the preponderance of exceptionally wealthy men representing that party.

And what about Labor? The Labor Party is the political party of the trade-union movement. British trade unions, because of the earlier industrialization of the country, underwent a century ago the repressive savagery which still goes on over here. For some time now the unions have been accepted by the Machiavellian Tories as a thoroughly respectable institution, and have been rendered practically harmless by the simple process of putting "toppers" on their leaders and inviting them to tea with the King. You have but to attend any Labor Party Conference to see how firmly the party bureaucrats now hold the rank and file membership on a leash. After throwing out unheard practically all the resolutions that mean anything at all, the Conference Fuehrers proceed to call a vote on the remaining resolutions. This is done by the "card vote" system, which means that every delegate has one vote for every thousand members he "represents." Since two trade-union czars—who do not trouble to call a meeting of their unions beforehand in order to get a mandate—possess over five hundred votes each, if those two vote the same way on a resolution it cannot be defeated even if everyone else votes against it.

As for becoming a Labor M.P., a man cannot just run for election because he happens to be an outstanding and respected fighter for the working class in his district. He cannot produce the deposit money out of his own pocket, and therefore he must be acceptable to the machine. And in order to be acceptable he must have shown over a period of years that he will always play ball with the labor czars, whose comfortable stipends—whatever they may profess—give them just as vested an interest as big business in the social order remaining unchanged.

Thus when a Labor government finally came into power in 1924 the London *Times,* leading reactionary newspaper of the world, was able to purr within a few weeks: "They have shown a real largeness of view in rising above the deep-rooted prejudices of many among their adherents . . . and acting . . . against the known wishes of their supporters." When Ramsay MacDonald completed his betrayal of labor by becoming Prime Minister of the "National" (Tory) government, he cried: "Every Duchess in Britain will want to kiss me tonight!"

By this time the mass of the English people, who had made a uniquely brave and united bid for their rights in the 1926 General Strike, only to be quite cynically sold out by their leaders, were filled with terrible disillusionment. They began to realize that all institutions of England's antique "civilization," including those they had sacrificed to build up themselves, were clogged up by that chronic constipation which overtakes human and social mechanisms alike when they reach a certain age. The tide of militancy receded and apathy set in.

While the two Labor governments did almost nothing to attack privilege, the naked privilege governments which have held power almost all the time busied themselves with legislation after legislation to sidetrack and sterilize the mounting popular demand for social justice. Civil rights of all kinds, particularly those most fundamental to the working class, have in the past two decades been slowly strangled.

by the Emergency Powers Act, the Official Secrets Act, the Trades Disputes Act, the Incitement to Disaffection Act, and finally the Public Order and Prevention of Violence Acts.

These are the achievements of the English rulers which, because they show an actual backward movement away from Democracy, you will not find boasted about at the World's Fair. Nor will you find any mention of the fact that unemployment, having soared between one and a half and nearly three millions since the first World War, still stands at almost a million now that England is supposed to be "fighting for its life" against Hitlerism. Do you know what it means to be unemployed and on the "U.A.B." relief in England? It means that you are condemned to complete idleness, since there are no government work schemes. It means that a man and wife and two babies under five must live on 30s. a week (about $7.50 at par exchange). The effect of that over a period of years is obvious. Already in 1933 General Sir Archibald Montgomery-Massingberd was complaining that "The standard of physical fitness of the nation has dropped so much that the number of men who came up for enlistment and who were turned down has become appallingly high. The rejections are much higher than ever before and they are increasing."

Nor will you find in the British Pavilion any mention of the fact that, while from 1928 to 1938 wages went up 6.5 per cent, profits went up 22 per cent in the same period. (The cost-of-living index rose from 148 to 156 between 1931 and 1938.) You will not be told that, when Sir John Orr made his survey of "Food, Health and Income" in 1936, he found half the population of England suffering from permanent malnutrition in food calories and vitamins—with the result that rickets, tuberculosis, and bronchitis are from two to three times as rife among the poor as among the well-to-do, and infant mortality in the working class and unemployed groups is 70 and over 100 per 1,000 compared with 30 in the comfortably-off minority.

You hear about the rights of "free assembly" in Hyde Park, where so many cranks talk at once that a single voice can hardly be disentangled from the general hubbub—but you don't hear about the repeated breaking-up by police violence of democratic assemblies outside labor exchanges and at other logical meeting-places for the poor. You hear about English freedom of culture, but not about the dic-

tatorship over the theater of an official appointed by the King, about
the government monopoly of radio, about the banning of movies
favorable to democracy and (almost right up to the present war) un-
favorable to Hitler. You hear about English freedom of the press,
but not about the unofficial and entirely effective censorship from
Whitehall in times of "crisis" (classic example of which is the total
suppression for weeks of any news about Edward VIII's frolic with
Wally Simpson). Nor will you be told that six Lords own virtually
the entire press of England—three of them controlling a daily circulation of over eight million in London alone—in a country of forty-five
millions. Nor about the suspension for the past twenty years of the
most elementary civil rights in the northern part of Ireland, which is
part of Great Britain.

You will see at the Fair the products of Englishmen's toil, but will
hear nothing about the conditions under which that toil is given. You
won't be told that in large sections of the country, girls under seventeen
average $3 a week and grown women $6.25, with 15 per cent of them
working more than sixty hours a week. Nor about the farmers march-
ing to London to try to stem the monopolistic tide that is driving them
to the workhouse. Nor about the farm laborers being denied a ten-
dollar-a-week minimum wage in 1939. Nor about the railwaymen, on
the eve of the war, being refused a $12.50 minimum, while huge sub-
sidies were being paid to the companies out of the people's treasury
and dividends soared.

You hear about the celebrated "British justice," but not about the
exclusion of almost all the working class from jury service by property qualifications, about the appointment from above of all judges and
magistrates, about the suppressive effect of the libel laws and the
glorious carnival they offer to blackmailers. The Poor Persons' Department for making legal aid available to the poor is pointed at with pride,
and the only point not mentioned is that this applies to courts dealing
with just 2½ per cent of working-class litigation.

But statistics paint a black-and-white picture. To convey any real
impression of "democracy" as manifested in England, one needs to
visit the country and bring back a liberal supply of that dingy gray
pigment which uniquely typifies the English scene.

The rulers of England have organized their democratic "front" with a skill which the American visitor is forced to admire. There is Hyde Park to prove that Englishmen have freedom of speech. You cannot show on paper that the government interferes with newspapers and movies, nor can you prove that the British Constitution is not democratic, since it was never written and does not exist. To demonstrate that the government is opposed to Fascism, Sir Oswald Mosley's insignificant gang of Blackshirts is allowed to function so that it can be harried every so often and the leaders jailed in time of war—while the real and significant Fascists, who merely don't label themselves as such, continue to dominate the City of London and the press and to sit in the Houses of Lords and Commons.

And nine out of ten visitors to England never see the grayness of that land in all its hideous desolation because geographically the country is so well departmentalized. Practically all of the vast tribute that is collected from the Empire flows into London and the south, where everything worth while from the pleasure-seeking tourist's point of view is concentrated. True, London itself has its miles and miles of slum desolation, but these are tucked away in the southern and eastern fringes of the city into which only the rare tourist, seeking truth rather than pleasure, will roam.

Step but a little way off the beaten trails and you begin to understand what English critics of their own society mean when they say that democracy, in any practical sense, is a hardly-known word there.

Economists speak of "the two worlds"—rich and poor. They exist here and everywhere. In our own country, as we have seen, it becomes daily more difficult to pass from the lower to the upper world as frontiers close and opportunities wither. But between our two worlds and the two worlds of England there is this fundamental difference—that here we still have faith in democracy, and hope—hope based on a tangible thing: our Constitution, the precisely specified ideals of our revolution.

In England the mass of the population are in a chill, gray lower world of hunger and ill-health and rags and sickly squawling children and bug-ridden, wretched homes. A world with a stone wall around it, a world from which the sun is shut out. As far as lifting themselves into the upper world is concerned, these people are without hope. They must live and suffer and die in that state of life wherein it has pleased nature to place them. Pallid and stunted as a result of generations of poverty, they are almost a different physical breed. If they attempt to climb the wall, they are branded by their accent just as plainly as if it were done with a hot iron on their flesh—for the upper world has a language of its own which the cleverest man from over the wall can hardly learn in a lifetime.

Go to the northern counties, to the Scottish Clydeside, to Wales, and you see these millions from whom, having not, has been taken away even that which they had. They have never seen anything but poverty and misery, and the way of life of the rich man in the south, with his Mayfair flat and green, slave-cultivated estate in the country, can be no more to them than a dream. Butter and eggs and fresh meat and vegetables and decent clothes are strangers to them; tiled bathrooms are something they see in mocking shadow on an occasional spree at the movies. They know they can never acquire these things however hard they work with hands or brain. But since man cannot suffer want indefinitely without hope in some form or other, they go on from week to week clutching penny football-pool coupons—which might conceivably bring them in a thousand pounds, but do most certainly bring added profits to the wealthy while at the same time providing a most effective opiate.

George Orwell, the English writer, thus describes one of the stately "homes" of England in the industrial north:

"Living room 10 ft. square with copper and sink. The other downstairs room the same size, probably intended as parlour but used as bedroom. Two upstairs rooms the same size as those below. Living-room very dark. Gas light estimated at 4½d. a day. Distance to lavatory 70 yards. Four beds in house for eight people—two old parents, two adult girls (the eldest aged 27), one young man and'three children. Parents have one bed, eldest son another, and remaining five people share the other two. Bugs very bad—'You can't keep 'em down when it's 'ot.' Indescribable squalor in downstairs room and smell upstairs almost unbearable."

After forcing himself to live in such a place in order to try to understand the problems of the poor, Orwell writes:

"It was not only the dirt, the smells and vile food, but the feeling of stagnant meaningless decay, of having got down into some subterranean place where people go creeping round and round, just like blackbeetles, in an endless muddle of slovened jobs and mean grievances. The most dreadful thing about people like the Brookers is the way they say the same things over and over again. It gives you the feeling that they are. not real people at all, but a kind of ghost forever rehearsing the same futile rigmarole. In the end Mrs. Brooker's self-pitying talk—always the same complaints, over and over, and always ending with the tremulous whine of 'It does seem 'ard, don't it now?'—revolted me even more than her habit of wiping her mouth with. bits of newspaper. But it is no use saying that people like the Brookers are just disgusting and try-ing to put them out of mind. For they exist in tens and hundreds of thousands. . . . The first steam engines tottered into motion, the British squares stood firm under the French guns at Waterloo, the one-eyed scoundrels of the 19th century praised God and filled their pockets; and this is where it all led—to labyrinthine slums and dark back kitchens with sickly, ageing people creeping round and round them like black-beetles. It is a kind of duty to see and smell such places now and again, especially smell them, lest you should forget that they exist."

Now it is not my intention to suggest that such living conditions are peculiar to England. What Americans, who have a man-sized beam in their own eye, need to realize is that the rulers of England, for whose "ideals" we are asked to fight and die, have it as their regular and un-ashamed policy to keep this mass of their own people ignorant and hopeless.

Hannington, the leading English authority on unemployment, writes: "The Government cannot claim that it has not had time to tackle the problem. It has been in office almost ten years, and as a study of its record shows, it has not used that period of time to raise the standards of the people, but rather to drive them still lower by methods which have ranged from direct attack to unscrupulous trickery and deception. At no time has it shown any readiness to remedy even the worst condi-tions under which the people have been suffering. It has looked on un-concerned at the plight of whole communities in the Distressed Areas, and has even placed obstacles in the way of its own Commissioners when they have attempted effective measures for improvement. Not a single concession has been made to the advantage of the workers and unemployed which has not had to be literally wrung from this Government by organized agitation and action."

If democracy is knowledge—the knowledge of necessity—then by that criterion England cannot possibly be called democratic. There is no sense of democracy among the people by and large—no feeling such as we still have here that, however far social institutions for righting injustice may wander from their original intention, they are still there and can be brought back into line by mass pressure. The General Strike of 1926 was the last flare-up of such a feeling. Today there is not even any general consciousness that democracy is important. The most depressing feature of it for the American observer is the dreadful humility of so many of the poor in England: the cringing, the touching of hats, the "yes, sirs" and "no, sirs" and "thank'ee kindly, sirs" which greet you in every section that has been infected by the decay of the ruling class. But what else can be expected when children leave school forever at fourteen? What can they learn about democracy and what it means to them at such a tender age? Even the one English child in ten who continues schooling beyond that point is carefully guarded from instruction about democracy. As Cedric Belfrage, another Englishman, writes:

"The democratic institutions of England have been there a long time and we are taught not to discuss them and consider how they might be improved, but to accept them as rocks of ages cleft for us. The great majority of us leave school, and proceed on through life, with the haziest idea or none at all as to how our national and local government and our courts of law work. Stop a hundred people in the streets of an English town and ask them what an alderman is, how a magistrate becomes a magistrate, what are the powers possessed by the House of Lords, who run the school system and how they are appointed, and a dozen more such questions, and if one or two can answer correctly you may be pardoned for calling for sal volatile. The great majority will not only not have the ghost of an idea what the answers are, but will probably call a policeman and give you in charge as a dangerous lunatic. They accept that the machinery of their democracy is 'all right,' because after all this is England. They have never had a chance to learn the first lesson of democracy, which is that the democratic machine runs only as well as the citizens make it run. Unless the citizens take an interest in it, it will cease to run and be replaced by the antiquated—

but at least efficient within its limitations—machine of self-appointed leadership from above. That can happen either abruptly, as in Germany or Italy, or by gradual and apparently painless steps. It has been happening here for years in the latter way, and our present hopeless muddle is not due to democracy, but to the almost meaningless institutions of democracy continuing to exist as a front—and also as an obstruction—to the ugly reality of dictatorship by a tiny minority."

And that is indeed the reality of England today. It is difficult for the average American to perceive it—though many Englishmen have perceived it—because the ruling-class people of England, the people "out of the top drawer" as they say over there, who use the "correct" vowel sounds and never drop an "h," are so "nice." And few Americans ever meet any other types of Englishmen.

They are extraordinarily "nice"—as individuals. Slow to warm up, perhaps, but kind and generous and decent in their personal relationships. They have no conception at all of the bestiality and treachery of which they are guilty as a class. As a class they function with the mechanical ruthlessness and innocent conscience of a small boy pulling the legs off a spider.

For a person "not of our class" they have no ill will, as long as he accepts unquestioningly the far lower standards of life to which his status entitles him. ("He gets two pounds a week, my dear—very good for someone of that class.") Class distinction has become so rooted in them that it is the whole foundation of their consciousness. When the need comes they can drop their individuality altogether and act blindly as units in the class, like a pack of ravening tigers; and then become individuals again without knowing what they have done.

I don't think I ever saw this Jekyll-and-Hyde quality of theirs more luminously illustrated than in the report of a National Union of Women's Conservative Associations conference held in London last year. A resolution against abolition of legal flogging was opposed there by Lady Astor, who said that if the ladies present had seen the cat-o'-nine-tails administered, and if they considered the statistical proof of its failure to act as a deterrent, they would "think deeply before asking for it to be enforced."

There was, according to the press report, at this point "an outburst of laughter and jeering," and the three thousand ladies present "began stamping their feet and clapping their hands." The uproar increased as others tried to speak against the resolution, and all were howled down. Roars of laughter greeted the suggestion that "reformative treatment" be tried for people convicted of assault. Cheers were reserved for a Mrs. Buller-Kitson who described the opposition as "sentimental, sickly and soft"—and for Mrs. Neville Chamberlain, who after the resolution was passed by acclamation rose to thank the ladies for "helping to foster the wonderful spirit with which our people are facing their problems." Little did they know what kind of problems they were soon to face as a result of her husband's desperate gamble to save their dividends at Munich.

One would probably not be inaccurate in picturing the typical delegate at this conference returning to her honeysuckle-fragrant country home and, somewhere on the road, leaping from her Rolls Royce to use nails and fists on some farmer beating a dog that had killed his chickens.

In closing this merely partial and preliminary examination of British Democracy, I wish to add this:

The methods used by privilege to defend itself have so accustomed Englishmen to acting on abstract ideas—such as "good form," "playing the game," "God," "The King"—that the acquaintance they once had with Reason ceased long ago. Life for them is a mass of rituals: rituals of eating, of conversation, of dress, of religion, of sport, of royalty, of law and order. The externals of these rituals have become all-important, the realities lying behind them have vanished from view. Conversation is no longer a means of expressing ideas but of hiding them. Religion is a gymnastic exercise performed in a special kind of building every seventh day. In the law courts justice is a matter of wigs and gowns and polysyllables and more gymnastics. The House of Commons takes care of "democracy." And with light hearts the Countesses, Viscounts, and Honorables go through their daily routine in the Times Court Circular of leaving London for Cannes or Le Touquet, leaving Le Touquet for the grouse season in Scotland (Britain, almost entirely "dependent" on imports for food, sets aside seven million acres of moor land for this diversion of the rich), leaving Scotland again for the opera and tiara season in London—while the royal family christen cruisers, visit exhibitions, hand out Insignia of Knights of the Order of St. John of Jerusalem.

It goes on and on—until something catches up with England and there is a war. Now a titled lady writes from London to an American friend: "It is all very terrible here, and of course we usually go away at this season, but there is nowhere to go."

True, dear lady. In building up your privileges and maintaining them —it could not otherwise have been so brilliantly done—your class hypnotized not only the lower orders but yourselves also with your tribal gods and tabus.

Now that the whole massive edifice is quaking, and in imminent danger of crashing in ruins, you have this small consolation: you will never know what hit you.

Hitler? If Hitler had never been, the job would have had to be done by someone else.

You have turned your backs on nature's law—tried to pretend that even it was not there.

And that is why there is nowhere to go.

CHAPTER EIGHT

Has England Democratized the Peoples of Its Empire?

WITH ALL this said, the true face of England—the fundamental difference between England's ideals and the ideals set forth in our Constitution and Declaration of Independence—still remains hidden.

We can only see it by looking at the British Empire. For England is essentially an imperialism, and the United States—however much the Wall Street clique try to imitate their London friends—is *essentially* a free and equal association of peoples.

Theoretically at least, one-half of the Westminster Parliament is a democratic institution as far as the people of England are concerned. But this half of the Parliament is elected by fewer than 29,000,000 people —all in England. And Westminster has sovereignty over some 500,-000,000 people, nine-tenths of whom are not represented there.

Of those disfranchised subjects of the "British Commonwealth of Nations," some 380,000,000 are in India. That is the place to look if you would see the face of England. India has had for some time a huge political party (now over five million strong) organized from all sections of the Indian people, demanding self-government and declaring itself ready to govern. But unfortunately for those demands, India happens to be "the brightest jewel in the imperial crown"—which, translated into homespun American, means the juiciest slice from the breast of the suffering human turkey that England or any other imperialism ever carved off.

Before we plunge into this most odoriferous of all messes in our contemporary world, let us once again apply the icepack of detachment to our fevered brows. It won't do our investigation any good to try to build up a personal case against the English for the present state of India. The English are no worse and equally no better than the rest of mankind: they have stomachs to line and respond with alacrity to opportunities offered for lining them, leaving till later the job of cutting morality to fit necessity. If they have committed terrible crimes in India, the average Englishman is quite unaware of it: for the Empire is a long way from home, not one Englishman in a hundred thousand has even visited any part of it, and the business of empire-building is delegated to a special class drawn from the privileged families—

> Good easy folk who know that eels are eels,
> But never pause to think how skinning feels,
> Content to know that eels are made to flay,
> And Indians formed by destiny to pay.

Nor is there the slightest doubt that if England hadn't put the Indian people in the stocks and thumbscrews, somebody else would have. Indeed, all the great struggles between England and the Continental powers during two centuries were largely concerned with the question of routes to India and the right to squeeze India for what it was worth. Insular England was the great naval power after Spain was smashed, and therefore won out.

What we are concerned with is whether England has allowed social progress to take its proper and natural course in India. What we have to show is that it has not done so, not because it enjoys oppressing Indians but because to do so and at the same time keep a hold on the imperialist swag is an impossibility. We have to show that, because of the progress of man's discovery of natural forces which neither England nor anyone else could stop, British imperialism in India is hopelessly inefficient today and on that charge stands convicted. It is not for us to sit in moral judgment, but to decide whether any kind of imperialism is worth American lives.

What did the British East India Company find when they went to work as official monopolists of the Indian eel-skinning racket? A country of primitive self-sufficient village communities based on common ownership of land, where things were produced to consume and not to sell, with a few great and populous centers of handicraft industry dotted about. A far from idyllic society, rooted as it was in abysmal ignorance and mysticism which enabled home-grown despots to treat the people as slaves and grow fat out of their poverty. But a society fitted for a land still unaware of the revolution in knowledge going on outside. This land, "at a time when the West of Europe, birthplace of the modern industrial system, was inhabited by uncivilized tribes, had been famous for the wealth of her rulers and for the high artistic skill of her craftsmen."

Nature had richly endowed India with iron, oil, coal, gold, silver, copper, lead, manganese; with "brilliant agricultural prospects" (according to Sir George Watt) excelled by few countries in the world; with water-power resources second only to those of what was then England's American colonies. All this potential wealth, but virtually none of it developed, and socially not even advanced to the point of feudalism.

The East India boys, headed by Hastings and Clive, took inventory and went to work for God, King, and Pocket with a thoroughness which roused the admiration of all imperialist competitors. No "white man's burden" theory had been evolved then, and they did not have to waste time pretending to be interested in the welfare of the Indians. They proceeded to destroy the old social structure by introducing private property in land, without bothering to replace it with a new structure corresponding with the discoveries of civilization. Their only concern was to rob the country of every penny they could lay hands on. In just three years, from 1766 to 1768, they removed to England booty to the tune of £6,311,250—importing into India in exchange goods to the value of one-tenth that amount.

The Indian despots had been pikers by comparison. The last native ruler of Bengal had taken from the peasants, in 1764, crop levies to the value of £817,000. In 1765 the East India Company raised the ante to £1,470,000; ten years later, to £2,818,000; and less than twenty years after that, to £3,400,000.

The result? Simple as any elementary sum in subtraction. Man minus food equals corpse. In 1770 ten million Bengalese starved to death. But Warren Hastings thus reassured the Company's anxious shareholders:

Notwithstanding the loss of at least one-third of the inhabitants of the province, and the consequent decrease of the cultivation, the net collections of the year 1771 exceeded even those of 1768. . . . It was naturally to be expected that the diminution of the revenue should have kept an equal pace with the other consequences of so great a calamity. That it did not was owing to its being violently kept up to its former standard.

"I may safely assert," remarked Governor-General Lord Cornwallis in 1789, "that one third of the Company's territory in Hindustan is now a jungle inhabited only by wild beasts." And Burke added: "Were we to be driven out of India this day, nothing would remain to tell that it had been possessed, during this inglorious period of our dominion, by anything better than the orangoutang or the tiger."

Such are the foundations of that "civilization as we know it"—that holy crusade for the sanctity of weak peoples—for which England would now like us to die.

This "very singular government," as Adam Smith called it—the interest of a member of which was solely "to get out of the country . . . and carry his whole fortune with him"—appeared to be killing the goose that laid the golden eggs. But nature, as usual, had a joker up her sleeve. To experimenters back home in England were being revealed the revolutionizing steam engine, power loom, spinning jenny, and other machines. These might have remained mere blueprints for years had it not been for the treasure stolen and sent home by the East India Company, which provided the capital to make the machines without delay and on a big scale. And with these machines there arose in England a new class of industrialists with new and up-to-date ideas of Indian-skinning, who became powerful enough to smash the Company's monopoly and start out on a new tack. Holding the weaker brethren down and going through their pockets was small-time stuff to the industrialists, who saw the Indians rather as slaves to produce raw materials for their machines and purchasers of what the machines could make. They saw a radiant vision of India's teeming millions all attired in Lancashire loincloths. And so the new regime of grab was ushered in—profits now being made not by taking the pants off the Indian but by forcibly putting them on him.

The industrialists took up the job of destroying the old Indian economy where the East India Company left off, and speedily completed it. British exports to India rose dizzily until in 1850 they amounted to £8,024,000—one-eighth of all British exports. The export of twist to India rose in the proportion of 1 to 5,200 in eighteen years. But the tribute England took from India rose rapidly, too. The excess of India's exports, in merchandise and treasure, over its imports was £3,300,000 in 1851. In 1901 it was £11,000,000, and the yearly average from 1931 to 1935 was £59,000,000. (This is the reality of the oft-heard argument: "Where would India be today without British capital?" England has taken far more out of India than it ever invested there.)

What was the result now? The Indian centers of the handloom fabric industry were completely ruined. "The jungle and malaria fast encroached" on depopulated Murshidabad and Dacca, which according to Clive had been "as extensive, populous and rich as the city of London" in· 1757. The Governor-General of the "brightest jewel" reported that "the misery hardly finds a parallel in the history of commerce. The bones of the cotton-weavers are bleaching the plains of India." This was one of the main causes of the Indian Mutiny of 1857, which the English, taking advantage of the people's lack of unity, put down with a savagery never surpassed by the Nazis. Men, women, and babies were tortured and burned on bonfires, and the sahibs reported that they had "enjoyed amazingly" hanging Indians from mango trees and "peppering away at niggers."

But there's no use in being sentimental about it. If "civilization as we know it" was to be built up, if the gentry of England were to have their spacious manors and parklands and jewels and luxuries, somebody had to be the goat and the Indians were it. Arid statistics show that famine killed a million Indians in the first quarter of the nineteenth century, five million in the third quarter, fifteen million (the official estimate—others say twenty-six million) in the fourth quarter. "It's the system."

For the unfortunate Indians imperialism simply meant that they must stand still or go backward while other peoples advanced. Their only function in the British imperial machine was to toil in the fields and mills and mines to produce the raw materials for English industries—hides, dyes, jute, oil, and cotton. Whereas in olden time they had at least had access to the land to produce food for themselves, now they were to work on the land of others to produce for England. And the drive for more and more profit, for getting these products of their toil at the smallest possible price, meant that no capital could be spared for improving the land and that even the primitive irrigation systems installed by Hindu and Moslem governments fell into dilapidation. Land and people were cheap: if the wealth of the soil was used up in one place, production could go on elsewhere; if the people died by millions, there were always millions more to take their place. So the peasants fell into debt, lost their land, and ended up as actual or virtual slaves. In 1858 John Bright pointed out in the House of Commons that "the single city of Manchester, in the supply of its inhabitants with the single article of water, has spent a larger sum of money than the East India Company has spent in the fourteen years from 1834 to 1848 in public works of every kind throughout the whole of its vast dominions."

How was all this grandiose grab accomplished? There are 380,000,000 Indians in India, famines notwithstanding. The last census gave 168,000 as the total number of English sahibs in the country, about 100,000 of whom—60,000 in the army, the rest in business and the civil service— represent the effective total of male adult burden-carriers. How have the 100,000, for all their bombing planes and machine guns and other instruments of "civilization," continued to dominate the 380,000,000?

Obviously by two methods. By creating a class of Indians with an interest in the imperialist system, and so making allies on the ground. And by keeping democracy from the people. Those are the stern necessities of the system and, whatever fair words may be spoken at Westminster, must last as long as imperialism lasts. From time to time some English official in a rash moment speaks the truth about it, and Joynson-Hicks did so when he said a few years ago:

We did not conquer India for the Indians. . . . We conquered India by the sword and by the sword we shall hold it. We hold it as the finest outlet for British goods.

First England made the Zemindars of India, who formerly were mere crop-levy-collectors for the old rulers, into a permanent landlord class with the right to do nothing and live on rents. The growth of this class, each member of which is interested in maintaining British rule, is shown in the Simon report on India: "In some districts the sub-infeudation has grown to astonishing proportions, as many as fifty or more intermediary interests having been created between the Zemindar at the top and the actual cultivator at the bottom."

Then the English very naturally allied themselves with the princes of the native states, which have been either artificially created or artificially maintained—a fantastic ghost of feudalism projected into modern times. The princes soon expressed undying loyalty to the great white king, or queen as the case might be, when it was pointed out that only British machine guns stood between them and the curved knives of their loving serfs. With regard to this feature of British policy, Lord Canning had one of those illuminating moments of candor in 1860:

> If we made all India into British Districts it is not in the nature of things that our Empire should last fifty years; but if we can keep up a number of Native States without political power, but as royal instruments, we should exist in India as long as our naval supremacy is maintained.

Were these native states of India—and there are 563 of them, embracing a quarter of the whole population—not buried from the sight of all but the wealthiest traveling Westerners, the notion that England stands for democracy would long ago have been laughed out of existence. The people of these benighted regions live in a state of backwardness and ignorance which can scarcely be believed, while the princes live in even more unbelievable pomp and luxury. England's king gets about one sixteen-hundredth of the national revenue of England: the Maharajahs of Kashmir and Bikanir pocket no less than one-fifth of their states' revenue, and some princes even take a third and a half. If you look at the Jamnagar budget for 1926–1927, you find that out of a revenue of £1,000,000 the Prince took £700,000, while £15,000 was spent on education and £9,000 on medical work. In many of the states slavery still flourishes openly, and the princes—acting always on the advice of a British agent in the palace—have complete and arbitrary rights over their subjects. Writes Nehru, the Indian people's leader:

> The principal news that comes from the States is of a vice-regal visit with all its pomp and ceremonial and mutually complimentary speeches, or of an extravagantly celebrated marriage or birthday of the ruler, or an agrarian rising. Special laws protect the Princes from criticism, even in British India, and within the States the mildest criticism is rigorously suppressed. Public

meetings are almost unknown, and even meetings for social purposes are often banned.

Of course no British statesman would ever dare to admit that it is England's policy to permit and encourage such a state of affairs. They like to fool themselves that their speeches about democracy and liberty are something more than hot air. They don't like to support such feudal tyranny: the point is that they have to, or lose India. For the splitting up of the main part of India with little states dotted here and there is part of their basic and necessary tactic of Divide and Rule. India started as a problem in subtraction and ended as a problem in division. If the people were not artificially divided they would get together tomorrow to demand democracy—and say it with blood.

English apologists will tell you that England's sincerest wish is to see all groups in India acting like brothers. But they can hardly expect Americans, who remember England's policy in trying to hold us down as a colony, to believe that. When Lord Elphinstone, Governor of Bombay, said in 1859 that *"Divide et impera* was the old Roman motto and it should be ours," he was enlightening the world with another of those unfortunate candid moments. The Commandant of Moradabad confirmed it when he said: "Our endeavor should be to uphold in full force the (for us fortunate) separation which exists between the different religions and races, not to endeavor to amalgamate them." Remember these deplorably tactless words next time you are told about the "unfortunate conflicts" between Hindu castes and between Hindus and Mohammedans in India.

What is the truth about these "unfortunate conflicts" between Hindus and Moslems? That nobody has yet been able to show any evidence of their existence before the English came, in the form manifested since that time. There were wars between a state ruled by a Moslem and a state ruled by a Hindu, but these were essentially not different from the wars between two "Christian" kings in Europe. Hindus and Mohammedans living in the same community do not appear to have rioted against each other. And over and over again in recent years the tendency has been shown for Hindus and Moslems to fraternize in the common fight against England. They fraternize in the unions and in political parties. In the Congress Party, which the English try to tell us is a "Hindu movement," there are many Moslems, including some of their finest leaders. As for the Moslem League, which the English encourage in every way and put forward as the voice of Indian Mohammedanism, it is a tiny fanatical group which probably would not exist at all but for official help. The present Indian constitution sets apart 480 provincial legislature seats for Moslems (most of the seats are thus earmarked for particular groups to ensure that this constitution's "democracy" won't be democratic). At the last election over seven million Moslem votes were polled, of which just 321,772 were for Moslem League candidates. The real truth of this matter is shown by such events as the Amritsar affair of 1919, when such "extraordinary scenes of fraternisation occurred" (according to the government report) that "Hindu leaders had actually been allowed to preach from the pulpit of a Mosque." This sort of thing would not do at all: "such men are dangerous." General Dyer had his troops fire on an unarmed and cornered crowd, killing 379 and wounding another 1,200—to create "a moral effect from a military point of view," as it was charmingly explained. For this gallant action Dyer was awarded a purse of £20,000 and officially congratulated in the House of Lords. Yet in 1940 the Viceroy could solemnly declare that "the only stumbling-block" to the rapid advance of Dominion Status for India was the disagreement between the tiny British-supported Moslem League and the Congress, with its five million members embracing every group in India.

You hear a great deal nowadays about this "advance to Dominion Status" and about India's new constitution. How much democracy is there in this, how much talk? With regard to "Dominion Status," this is one of those beautiful British phrases which, like the constitution of England itself, is just a phrase. Nobody has ever defined what it means. No less an authority than the London *Times* says that it "is not susceptible of definition in a precise constitutional document," having "carried so many different shades of meaning at different times," and in any case Lord Birkenhead has said that "no sane man could assign any approximate period for the date on which he could conceive India attaining Dominion Status." Added Prime Minister Baldwin: "Nobody knows what Dominion Status will be when India has responsible government, whether that date be near or distant." The only clue is Churchill's statement in 1930 that "we have no intention of casting away that most truly bright and precious jewel in the Crown of the King."

As far as tangible things are concerned, all the Indians have is the constitution which was presented to them with an air of tremendous benevolence on April Fools' Day, 1937. Under this constitution they have Indian assemblies in the various provinces, though not, of course, in the quarter of India that still remains feudal. Later on, if they are very good, they are supposed to get a Federal Assembly offering eighty-six general, open seats and one hundred twenty-five seats for nominees of the princes. Over these delightful assemblies the Governor-General will keep a fatherly eye, being equipped with the following powers among many others: to appoint or dismiss ministers, to veto legislation, to pass rejected legislation, to forbid discussion of legislation, to control the armed forces and police, to dissolve the legislature, and to suspend the constitution. The event which would make it necessary for him to suspend so convenient a "democratic" constitution is indeed difficult to imagine.

There is your "democracy" in India. Oceans, torrents of words—alluring promises for some dim future of which "no sane man could assign any approximate date"—and meantime the good old game of grab, the pauperization of the people, the barriers set up against natural progress—all so that a few decadent aristocrats in England may satisfy their petty vanities. Most Indian leaders are emphatic that this new constitution, which makes every real or artificial division among the people official and permanent, only makes matters worse than before. Gandhi, most moderate of them all, says:

Democratic Britain has set up an ingenious system in India which, when you look at it in its nakedness, is nothing but a highly organised military control. . . . The Collectors and Police may at a mere command from the Governors unseat the Ministers, arrest them and put them in a lock-up.

So much for political "democracy." In the far more important matter of direct democracy through trade unions we have an even more farcical picture. As soon as the trade-union movement began to get under way in India the Viceroy issued by decree a Public Safety Bill, and in 1929 the thirty-two main leaders of the movement, including three Englishmen and several Moslems, were arrested, charged with no illegal action but merely with "conspiracy." Their trial at Meerut was dragged out for three and a half years, during which, of course, the removal of their leaders almost paralyzed the trade unions. In 1933 the "criminals" received sentences varying from three years' rigorous imprisonment to transportation for life. The most significant feature of the trial was that during the first two years of it a "Labor" government was in power in England.

India has no democracy, and never will have under England, because imperialism and democracy are opposites. Nor will the people of England ever have effective democracy until England ceases its imperialistic oppression of weaker peoples.

The tears shed by the Chamberlains and Churchills about "poor little" Czechoslovakia and Norway and Finland are the final word in hypocrisy, however much these gentlemen may think they believe in freedom and self-determination as abstract ideas. India has challenged them to prove their words, but all the Indians get, desperate as the position of England is, are insubstantial promises. Promises were given in the last world war, in which over a million Indians participated on the strength of them. They were all broken. They had to be broken because, as Lord Rothermere says, "India is the lynch-pin of the British Empire. If we lost India, the Empire must collapse—first economically, then politically."

I read in the *Los Angeles Time* that "India's real feeling on the war issues is strongly anti-Nazi and was reflected in mid-September when there was a spontaneous pledge by native princes and other leaders to help the British." Yes, it is wonderful how loyal the native princes are: if you had such a swell racket, wouldn't you be loyal to those without whose protection you could not operate? But the Indian people have not the faintest anti-Nazi feeling. They cannot conceive, and I am equally powerless to conceive, how their lot could be any worse under Nazi rule.

What is their condition today? Here are some facts:

"The average Indian income," according to Shah and Khambata, the leading Indian economists, "is just enough either to feed two men in every three of the population, or give them all two in place of every three meals they need, on condition that they all consent to go naked, live out of doors all the year round, have no amusement or recreation, and want nothing else but food, and that the lowest, the coarsest, the least nutritious."

It is a fact, as any visitor to India will testify, that great numbers of families do indeed "live out of doors all the year round." It is difficult to walk through the streets of Bombay at night because of the people sleeping on the sidewalks. This is perhaps preferable to sleeping under a roof, considering that (according to the Bombay Labor Office) 97 per cent of the working class in that city live in one-room tenements often containing from two to eight families in one room. Here is a description of such a "home" by an Indian woman doctor who was sent by the Bombay government to investigate:

In one room on the second floor of a chawl, measuring some 15 by 12 feet, I found six families living. Six separate ovens on the floor proved this statement. On enquiry, I ascertained that the actual number of adults and children living in this room was 30. . . . Three out of six of the women who lived in this room were shortly expecting to be delivered. . . . The atmosphere at night of that room filled with smoke from six ovens and other impurities would certainly physically handicap any woman and infant both before and after delivery. . . . In the rooms in the basement of a house conditions were far worse.

The lady puts it delicately. The infantile death rate in families living under such conditions is 524 (in 1933–1934) per thousand births compared with 57 for England. The expectation of life in India, by International Labor Office figures, decreased from 24.8 years in 1921 to 23.2 years in 1931. It was 30 half a century ago. "Throughout India," said the Director of the Indian Medical Service in 1933, "disease is increasing steadily and rapidly." In 1928 Bengal's Director of Health reported that "the peasantry are in a very large proportion taking to a dietary on which even rats could not live for more than a few weeks." Thirteen million Indians are estimated to be suffering from venereal disease, six million from partial or complete blindness due to lack of food, two million from rickets. There are hospital beds for one in forty-five hundred of the population. And while the average income per Indian is estimated at between two and three cents a day, the Dundee Jute Trade Unions delegation reported that in the jute industry alone "the total gain to English shareholders in the ten years 1915 to 1924 reached the enormous total of £300 million sterling, or 90 per cent per annum of the capital."

Another point worth quoting is from the recent report of wartime conditions made by a *Collier's* magazine staff writer. It is that, with all civil rights of the most elementary kind now abolished, there is no longer any room in the jails, which are packed like sardine cans. The police, therefore, now break up meetings by smashing the kneebones of the people with sticks, so that, if they can manage to get "home," they are compelled to stay there.

Now let us take a brief tour around the quarter of the world's land surface which is the British Empire, and see how much democracy there is in the other bright jewels of the imperial crown.

In Egypt—nominally "independent," actually no more than a British colony—the people organized themselves into a mass national party, the Wafdists, similar to the Indian Congress. The Egyptian parliament became dominated by the Wafdists in 1926, so the English government promptly told their royal Egyptian Charlie McCarthy to suspend Parliament rather than let the constitution of 1923 operate. The London *Times* made a typically English comment: "The most numerous party in the state is the Wafdist. They count among their followers 90 per cent of the population . . . but it is not in any sense the true spokesman of the uncomprehending and largely illiterate Egyptian people."

The Egyptians do not have much time to become literate, even if they had the opportunity. Children under twelve work in some industries a seven-hour day, children over twelve work a nine-hour day. Ninety-five per cent of the population suffer from trachoma, an eye disease which prevents anyone from entering the United States. Four per cent of Egyptian women can read and write. In 1936 there were 1,226 British officials in Egypt taking salaries of at least $5,000,000 annually, according to the Anglo-Egyptian Chamber of Commerce. Each year England takes from Egypt $10,000,000 in dividends on private investments.

In the British West Indies the English governors are virtual dictators, no social legislation of any kind exists, and trade unions are suppressed by terror. In the four main islands exactly 5 per cent of the population have a vote, and candidates for the legislature (which has no power anyway) must have an income of at least £200 a year. From 1935 to 1938, strikes, demonstrations, and riots swept over the islands; British warships were sent five times to "restore order"; and in that process 46 were killed, 429 injured. The wages of agricultural laborers in Trinidad average from 30 to 50 cents a day. The principal English companies with Trinidad interests paid these dividends in the two years 1937–1938 and 1938–1939:

> Tate and Lyle .... 31¾ (plus 40% bonus)
> Trinidad Leaseholds 42½
> Apex (Trinidad) Oilfields 70

In 1926 the four major Trinidad oil companies, allowing for taxation and amortization, earned net profits of £1,500,000 for idlers in England —and the total wages paid in all Trinidad oil fields for that year were £473,000.

In the African colonies, conquered by England with a combination of ruthless violence and invariably broken pledges, the natives are being "educated for citizenship and partnership in the British Commonwealth of Nations." This is done by forcing the Africans off their land and making peons of them in the Englishmen's mines, so that they rarely ever see their families. Fifty-five per cent of the natives in the Southern Rhodesia mines go down as casualties from disease caused by lack of food. Almost every African has hookworm and two-thirds have malaria. The infant mortality varies from 300 per thousand in Nigeria to 400 in Kenya. The average yearly wage of an African on the tobacco plantations is thirty-three shillings, the average for English "overseers" £1,000. There are penal codes covering personal freedom of movement, freedom of speech, importation of literature and even of phonograph records. The white colonial governments have unfettered power to intern or deport natives without trial, to break up any political or industrial organization and confiscate their funds, to prohibit or summarily disperse any gathering. It is a crime to state that employers pay low wages. Taxes are very light for the whites but the natives must pay up to a third of their "incomes" in direct taxes alone. Sir Alan Pim's report on Northern Rhodesia showed that in that colony, from average family incomes of twenty-eight shillings a year, taxes of 7s. 6d. are taken.

Democracy? Everyone can vote—provided only that he has property of over £150 value and an income of over £100.

After the destruction of the highly advanced civilization of the Boers by English violence and fraud, Webster Davis, First Assistant Secretary of the Interior under McKinley, wrote from his personal observations:

When the British nation realises, as it surely will, how the inhuman partnership of Chamberlain, Rhodes and plutocrat journals has drenched the African belt in the blood of gallant British soldiers and brave Boers, when they learn how Britain's sons were left unburied upon the battlefields of South Africa as food for vultures and wild beasts, when they further realize the awful expense, already estimated at $900,000,000 to say nothing of the large number of lives lost, the awful sorrow and suffering in many a British home, they will realize how foolish their government has been and how unnecessary it was to wage war against a small handful of brave defenders of two little Republics. It is a crime against civilization, a crime against humanity, a crime against the peaceable progress of the human race.

Capital among the aristocracy grows stronger and stronger, vice and luxury are rampant upon every hand, notwithstanding these sufferers at their very doors are eating crusts moistened with their own tears; but yet they have not time to care for these, but can waste untold millions of their treasure to crush liberty, to destroy republics, and thus cast a shadow over England's history and make the name of English aristocracy a stench in the nostrils of God-fearing, liberty-loving, justice-seeking people everywhere. England is a country dying at the top . . . the home of the millionaire, whose heartless chuckle rings throughout the kingdom as he weighs his hoarded gold and clips his coupons.

Now let us travel to the parts of the Empire which have "attained Dominion status," as the saying goes.

Let us pause en route at the island of Cyprus, just to say hello to the Cypriot editors whose newspapers were suppressed in 1939 (before the war) for printing without comment remarks made by Members of Parliament at Westminster.

Again just a brief pause at Ireland. What do we need to say about Ireland in this land to which millions of Irishmen, disgusted by England's trickery and savagery in trying to keep them in subjection, have fled? We need only note how even now the traditional Divide and Rule policy is being carried on with the artificial creation of "loyal" Northern

Ireland, an official appendage of England where no civil liberties have existed since its inception. And perhaps, just to remind us of the manner of Ireland's conquest, this quotation from Justin McCarthy about the state of that land in 1603:

Holinshed says that except in the cities or towns the traveller might journey for miles without meeting man, woman, child or even beast. . . . Mr. Froude affirms that in Munster alone there had been so much devastation that 'the lowing of a cow or the sound of a plough-boy's whistle was not to be heard from Valentia to the Rock of Cashel.' It was made a boast by at least one of those engaged in ruling Ireland on behalf of the Queen that he had reduced some of the populations so deeply down that they preferred slaughter in the field to death by starvation.

The story of Eire, today one of the five "Dominions," is final proof of the fact that England is not and has never been willing, as it claims to be, to grant independent government "when they are ready for it" to Empire peoples other than those of English origin. And even to its own sons who have founded colonies, it does not "grant" independence. They get this independence, which is in any case limited, because England knows they will otherwise fight for it as we in America did, and will win as we did. But the Irish, like the Africans and Indians and Malays and West Indians, must actually fight to win anything at all. The extraordinary national conceit of the English makes them confident that no "lesser breed" can beat them in a fight.

About the aboriginal inhabitants of Australia, Canada, and New Zealand, of course, nothing is ever heard now. As a factor to be reckoned with in the big game of grab they were wiped out early, and are now becoming extinct. New Zealand had a particularly fine primitive civilization based, like the Indian, on common ownership of the land. The English dealt with that by "buying" the land with rum and firearms from the chiefs, who had no right in the world to sell it. Today the remaining New Zealand Maoris are a subject race suffering from all kinds of abuse, and it is less comical than tragic to see photographs of Maori troops arriving in England to "defend the Motherland." As for the white New Zealanders, they have officially about the same amount of democracy as the people in England. But there is this vital difference: that the control of their finance from the City of London keeps democracy just as effectively in check, if it seeks to expand beyond a limited extent, as would a colonial setup of government. England has £146,000,000 invested in New Zealand, and the result of this is interesting and instructive. New Zealand elects a Labor government; this government wishes to embark on a number of social and public-works projects; it can do this only with London's financial aid and consent. So a Labor Finance Minister visits London, and London gives him a terrific browbeating and a small loan—on condition that his government "loyally" refrain from letting democracy get out of hand.

The same more or less applies to Australia, where England has £500,000,000 invested. Australia, too, gets a Labor government, which can do just as much for Labor as the owners of the £500,000,000 allow. The result is that Australian people are inflicted with exactly the same kind of censorship and repressive legislation that the English people have been getting for the past two decades. Australia has no Bill of Rights and will never have one as long as it is a British Dominion. The unemployed—it is incredible but true that in so vast a land with exactly two persons populating each square mile there is an army of "surplus labor"—were getting in 1934 the princely sum of 6s. 6d. a week to live on. That, as a morbid Sydney journalist took the trouble to discover, was 6d. more than the maintenance cost of an inmate in the Lost Dogs' Home, 8s. 3d. less than the cost of keeping the water warm for a week for the shark in Sydney's aquarium, and 17s. 9d. less than the weekly expenditure on a prisoner in jail.

The golden chains binding Australia to Mother England are so strong that as soon as Holy War was declared last year—and this was done without consulting the Australian Parliament—the removal of all civil liberties along the lines laid down by Mother was energetically proceeded with. The Governor-General, who is sent out from England C.O.D., now has almost complete dictatorial powers, being free to demand information from anyone on any subject on pain of jail, to enter and search premises at will or whim, to arrest without warrant people who "an officer suspects are about to commit an offence." This, of course, is just the everyday peacetime state of affairs in Northern Ireland.

Canada, too, is now fighting for "democracy." Contrary to general idea, it has no legal right to keep out of one of England's wars, but automatically becomes a belligerent; it had already been put into the present war by the English Governor-General days before the Parliament "declared war." If you want to know just how much democracy Canada has and is fighting for, you have but to read the Red Book of *Defense of Canada Regulations.* Here you will find in fifty-seven fragrant pages as complete a demolition of democracy as Hitler ever dreamed of: freedom of speech and publication completely suppressed (a member of Parliament can oppose the war in the House but no paper may report it), and civil rights blown sky high. Citizens can be arrested without warrant and held without trial just as long as the Minister of Justice thinks fit (even in England the authorities are still bound eventually to show cause why citizens should be held without trial). The outmoded legal precedent that a man is innocent until proved guilty is abolished. And, perhaps the most striking challenge to Hitler, any policeman or member of the forces can on his own initiative arrest anyone he "suspects of having committed a war offense."

Has President Roosevelt seen Canada's Little Red Book? We can only presume that he has, and consequently that he approves of these lofty ideals for which England is fighting.

It is not a comforting thought for the people of America who still, despite the astounding contortions through which the word "democracy" has been put, think they know what they mean by that word.

Last June at Charlottesville Roosevelt said: "We will extend to the opponents of force the material resources of this nation, and harness and speed up those resources in order that we ourselves may have the equipment and training equal to the task in any emergency."

The equipment he mentions included, no doubt, an American Little Red Book.

CHAPTER NINE

English Critics of English Imperialism

IS ENGLAND A DEMOCRACY?

MY WORK companions were men with families endeavoring to live on seventeen shillings a week [$4.25 American money]. The poverty in their case was infinitely worse than mine. And as my Christian faith in God was utterly dependent on the complementary truth of the brotherhood of man, and demanded its practical expression, I asked what right had I, or any other Christian to live in comfort, as I had done nearly all my life, and as my class did continually, while others suffered constant economic hardship? True, as I tried to argue, they were less competent than men of my class, and on that account earned less. But then again, they were less competent because heavily handicapped from the outset as to food, quick education, and a thousand other amenities. Sophistries failed, and the sense of great injustice grew. Either these men were to be regarded as human personalities and treated as such, with equal respect, or they were not. My Christian faith said they were; in practice we denied it."

—*Hewlett Johnson*
Dean of Canterbury Cathedral
(*Present incumbent*)

"Descend where you will into the lower class, in Town or Country, by what avenue you will, by Factory Inquiries, by Revenue Returns, by Mining-Laborer Committees, by opening your own eyes and looking, the same sorrowful result discloses itself: you have to admit that the working body of this rich English Nation has sunk or is fast sinking into a state, to which, all sides of it considered, there was literally never any parallel. At Stockport Assizes, a Mother and a Father are arraigned and found guilty of poisoning three of their children, to defraud a 'burial-society' of some £3.8s. due on the death of each child . . . and the official authorities, it is whispered, hint that perhaps the case is not solitary, that perhaps you had better not probe farther into that department of things. . . . In the British land, a human Mother and Father, of white skin and professing the Christian religion, had done this thing . . . had been driven to do it . . . to escape starvation."

—*Thomas Carlyle* (*nineteenth century*)

"It was not the custom in England to confer titles on men distinguished by peaceful services; however good and great; unless occasionally, when they consisted of the accumulation of some very large amount of money."

—*Charles Dickens* (Bleak House)

"Englishmen hate liberty and equality too much to understand them. But every Englishman loves and desires a pedigree."

—*George Bernard Shaw* (*Preface to* Man and Superman)

Men of England, wherefore plough
For the lords who lay ye low?
Wherefore weave with toil and care
The rich robes the tyrants wear?

Wherefore feed and clothe and save,
From the cradle to the grave,
Those ungrateful drones who would
Drain your sweat—nay, drink your blood?

Wherefore, Bees of England, forge
Many a weapon, chain, and scourge,
That these stingless drones may spoil
The forced produce of your toil?

—*P. B. Shelley*

Ye Liberals and Conservatives,
Have pity on our Human lives,
Waste not more blood on human strife;
Until we know some way to use
This human blood we take or lose,
'Tis sin to sacrifice our life.

Let's not have war till we can make
Of this sweet life we lose or take
Some kind of pudding of man's gore;
So that the clergy in each parish
May save the lives of those that famish
Because meat's dear and times are poor.

—*W. H. Davies*

A race that binds
Its body in chains and calls them Liberty,
And calls each fresh link Progress.

—*Robert Buchanan* (Titan and Avatar)

"It is a melancholy object to those, who walk through this great town, or travel in the country, when they see the streets, the roads, and cabin-doors, crowded with beggars of the female sex, followed by three, four or six children, all in rags, and importuning every passenger for an alms. These mothers instead of being able to work for their honest livelihood, are forced to employ all their time in strolling, to beg sustenance for their helpless infants, who, as they grow up, either turn thieves for want of work, or leave their dear Native Country to fight for the Pretender in Spain, or sell themselves to the Barbadoes.

"I have been assured by a very knowing American of my acquaintance in London that a young healthy child well nursed is at a year old a most delicious, nourishing, and wholesome food, whether stewed, roasted, baked, or boiled; and I make no doubt that it will equally serve in a fricassee, or a ragout.

"I do therefore humbly offer it to public consideration, that . . . at a year old they be offered in sale to the persons of quality and fortune, through the kingdom, always advising the mother to let them suck plentifully in the last month, so as to render them plump, and fat for a good table."

—*Jonathan Swift* (*eighteenth century*)

"Neither in America nor in France have the mind and the imagination of the middle and working classes been subdued by the aristocracy as they have in England. English liberty has not been paralleled by equality; and the conditions of English political institutions maintain that submission to the aristocracy by reason of the economic system they involve."

—Harold J. Laski

"I am sure my bones would not rest in an English grave, or my clay mix with the earth of that country—I would not even feed her worms if I could help it."

—Lord Byron (Letters)

"Such conditions of destitution are without parallel in the memory of living persons. The devastation in the Welsh coalfields can only be compared with the war devastation in France."

—Neville Chamberlain (*when Minister of Health*)

WHAT HAS BEEN THE EFFECT OF IMPERIALISM ON THE MATERIALLY BENEFITED MINORITY?

"I mentally apostrophize the Christian British people. 'Ladies and Gentlemen,' I say, 'you are Christians in name, but I discern little of Christ in your ideals, your institutions, or your daily lives. You are a mercenary, self-indulgent, frivolous, boastful, blood-guilty mob of heathen. I like you very much, but that is what you are. And it is you —*you* who call men "Infidels." You ridiculous creatures, what do you mean by it?'"

—Robert Blatchford

"Our inequality materializes our upper class, vulgarizes our middle class, brutalizes our lower class."

—Matthew Arnold

"When I review my impressions of the average English citizen, impressions based on many years' study, what kind of man do I see? I see one divorced from nature, but unreclaimed by Art; instructed, but not educated; assimilative, but incapable of thought. Trained in the tenets of a religion in which he does not believe—for he sees it flatly contradicted in every relation of life—he dimly feels that it is prudent to conceal under a mask of piety the atheism he is hardly intelligent enough to avow. . . . Charity, chastity, self-abnegation, contempt of the world and its prizes—these are the words on which he has been fed from his childhood upward. And words they have remained, for neither has he anywhere seen them practiced by others, nor has it ever occurred to him to practice them himself. Their influence, while it is strong enough to make him a chronic hypocrite, is not so strong as to show him the hypocrite he is."

—*G. Lowes Dickinson*

ENGLAND AND ITS COLONIES: HAS IT BENEFITED ITS COLONIAL PEOPLE?

India

"We have no right to seize Sind (India), yet we shall do so, and a very advantageous, useful, humane piece of rascality it will be."

—*Sir Charles Napier* (*nineteenth century commander of British forces in India*)

"The chiefs were fleeced and treated unfairly, but it is needless to pursue further the unpleasant subject."

—*Oxford History of India*

"The Hindus had been accustomed to live under tyranny, but never under tyranny like this."

—*Lord Macaulay*

"A system [English imperialism in India] of oppression, corruption, breach of faith, peculation and treachery."

—*Richard Brinsley Sheridan*

"I do most confidently maintain that no civilized government ever existed on the face of this earth which was more corrupt, more perfidious and more rapacious than the Government of the East India Company from 1765 to 1784."

—*Sir George Cornewall Lewis* (*in House of Commons, 1858*)

"I was in the Indian police five years, and by the end of that time I hated the imperialism I was serving with a bitterness which I probably cannot make clear. . . . It is not possible to be part of such a system without recognising it as an unjustifiable tyranny. . . . Every Anglo-Indian is haunted by a sense of guilt which he usually conceals as best he can, because there is no freedom of speech, and merely to be over-heard making a seditious remark may damage his career. All over India there are Englishmen who secretly loathe the system of which they are part. . . .

"In Burma it was a double oppression that we were committing. Not only were we hanging people and putting them in jail and so forth; we were doing it in the capacity of unwanted foreign invaders. The Burmese themselves never really recognised our jurisdiction. The thief whom we put in prison did not think of himself as a criminal justly punished, he thought of himself as the victim of a foreign conqueror. The thing that was done to him was merely a wanton meaningless cruelty."

—George Orwell

Africa

"It would be absurd to deny that European civilization, through the machinery of state and trade, has carried some considerable benefits into Africa; but the autocratic dominion of European over African has been accompanied by such horrible cruelty, exploitation, and injustice that it is difficult not to believe that the balance of good in the world would have been and would be infinitely greater, if the European and his state had never entered Africa."

—Leonard Woolf

South Africa—The Boers

"They did not resist, but yielded in protest to superior force, and from that day no Boer in South Africa has been able to trust an English promise. The manner in which we advised or allowed our representative to act was insolent in its cynicism. A treaty but a few months old was staring us in the face. Our conduct would have been entirely intolerable if we had rested simply on superior force—if we had told the Boers simply that we must have the diamond fields and intended to take them. But we poisoned the word, and we justified our action by posing before the world as the protectors of the rights of native tribes. . . . The annexation has been a swindle."

—Henry Froude (nineteenth-century historian)

Canada

"On the British side of the line, with the exception of a few favored spots where some approach to American prosperity is apparent, all seems waste and desolate. . . . The ancient city of Montreal, which is naturally the commercial capital of the Canadas, will not bear comparison in any respect with Buffalo, which is a creation of yesterday. . . . A widely scattered population, poor, and apparently unenterprising, though hardly and industrious . . . drawing little more than a rude subsistence from ill-cultivated land, and seemingly incapable of improving their condition, present the most instructive contrast to their enterprising and thriving neighbours on the American side."

—Lord Durham (report on Canada, 1839)

"No man is good enough to be another man's master."

—William Morris

WHAT IS ENGLAND'S FOREIGN POLICY?

"It is not too much to say that the foreign policy of Great Britain is primarily a struggle for profitable markets of investment. To a larger extent every year Great Britain is becoming a nation living upon tribute from abroad, and the classes who enjoy this tribute have an ever-increasing incentive to employ the public policy, the public purse, and the public force to extend the field of their private investments, and to safeguard and improve their existing investments. This is, perhaps, the most important fact in modern politics, and the obscurity in which it is wrapped constitutes the gravest danger to our State.

"What is true of Great Britain is true likewise of France, Germany, the United States, and of all countries in which modern capitalism has placed large surplus savings in the hands of a plutocracy."

—J. A. Hobson (English Liberal economist, 1902)

"It is the almost universal opinion on the Continent that the aims of British policy are to strengthen Germany so as to counter-balance French and Russian influence, to avert German Naval competition and German colonial ambitions by giving Hitler a free hand in Eastern Europe and to encourage German and Japanese aggressive designs against Soviet Russia. That is also the opinion of nearly all the Americans to whom I have spoken on the subject."

—*Robert Dell* (Manchester Guardian *correspondent at Geneva, 1935*)

"As over Ethiopia our policy is palsied by one fundamental thing. More and more it stands out over every other factor. A large section of English opinion is obsessed with a delirium tremens which sees everywhere the red rat of Bolshevism gnawing its way into its bank cellars. Hitler may arm to the teeth, bestride our trade routes, yell for colonies; no matter, this agony about their beloved bank balances blinds these people to all else. Hitler, they think, may save them from being plundered by 'the Reds.' He well may—to do it twice as effectively himself. Nothing will get done till we are cured of this ignoble paranoia."

—*Professor F. L. Lucas* (*of Cambridge University, 1937*)

"It is said that this [the Finnish campaign] was a case of aggression. Well, the British Government has met with cases of aggression before; and it has uniformly dealt with them without indignation, its conduct being unaffected by considerations of moral principles, and has been guided simply by what it has thought best suited to its own interests. . . . The contrast between its reaction to these hostilities and its habitual reaction to Fascist aggression is so glaring as to convict it—not of gross dishonesty and hypocrisy, which no longer matter—but of a deliberate intent to build up among our people a war mentality against the U.S.S.R. at the most inflammable moment in modern history.

—*D. N. Pritt, K.C., M.P.*

"Patriotism has become the last refuge of the profiteer. We have seen this on a vast scale in Italy and in Germany, where the connection between big business and the violent nationalist movements that seized power is notorious. In Japan the same process has been at work. Even in Great Britain we have a Conservative Government which upholds the interests of big business, and at the same time has embarked on an arms race and is reverting to international anarchy. It calls itself 'National,' and declares that party politics are dead, which is its mild and gentlemanly way of asserting the Fascist claim to a monopoly of government and treating political opponents as outside the pale of the nation."

> —*Major Attlee* (*Lord Privy Seal of the Churchill War Cabinet, 1935*)

"There is nothing so bad or so good that you will not find an Englishman doing it: but you will never find an Englishman in the wrong. He does everything on principle. He fights you on patriotic principles; he robs you on business principles; he enslaves you on imperial principles."

> —*G. Bernard Shaw* (The Man of Destiny)

THE BRITISH EMPIRE—WILL IT ENDURE?

"If one studies the British Empire one clearly seems to see in it the hand of God and the forging of an instrument for the carrying out of His will. . . . We have never risen to the realization of what was God's purpose in bringing the Empire into existence."

> *Archdeacon of Manchester* (*preaching on "Christ and the Empire," 1938*)

"The British Empire is on the decline. She does not know her danger, and she will not until someone kicks her from behind, for she is so apathetic. There will never be a fall such as the Roman Empire. The halfpenny press has so educated the masses that that is impossible, but England will lose her power. Until now she has been very lucky and has depended almost entirely upon her splendid seamanship. But that time has gone by, and England has so little to fall back upon. . . . We have only a certain knowledge of the Bible, a little common sense and the capacity to die well and alone."

> —*George Meredith*

"Our present parliament is obsolete: it can no more do the work of a modern State than Julius Caesar's galley could do the work of an Atlantic liner. . . . Our national dispositions may be good; but we have been badly brought up, and are full of anti-social personal ambitions and prejudices and snobberies. Had we not better teach our children to be better citizens than ourselves? We are not doing that at present. The Russians *are*. That is my last word. Think over it."

—*George Bernard Shaw* (*Preface to* The Apple Cart, *1930*)

"Everywhere now goes up the cry for national unity. Yes, but unity for what? Alliance with Germany to permit the destruction of French democracy and the dismemberment of Russia? And with Japan to pick the carcase of China? Our youth will not continue to die for that.

"Nor will they arm and die merely to repeat another victory as fruitless of good and as pregnant of evil as that of 1918 has proved to be. If we have to fight again less than three decades after the last victory, how soon after the next shall we have to fight?

"If you tell those who are to bear your arms that these new ways of peace and defence here urged are visionary and hopeless; that only the old way can defend our country, then these youngsters, looking for a moment at the 'defence' which the older way has given, may decide to go without defence; to refuse to bear your arms. And they will be right."

—*Sir Norman Angell* (*1938*)

"The menace of the Fascist Powers has grown to alarming proportions under the encouraging hand of the British National Government. Democracy has been betrayed and Fascist aggression has been encouraged in Spain, Austria, Czechoslovakia, China and elsewhere to such an extent that even the most vital interests of our own country are now jeopardized. At the same time that Government has shown itself completely incompetent to deal with domestic matters.

"Unemployment remains as bad as ever, working class standards and conditions are tending to decline and agriculture is in a state of chaos. It is not at all unlikely that within the next few weeks or months Chamberlain will announce reversal of his foreign policy upon the basis that he has tried appeasement and it has failed and that he must call on the Nation to unite behind him to fight Fascism in what will be a purely imperialistic war. When that moment comes, if public opinion is allowed to remain in its uncrystallized state, it will swing behind him with results as disastrous as those of 1914–18 for the common people of this country and Europe."

—*Sir Stafford Cripps, K.C. M.P.* (*March, 1939*)

"The record of English foreign policy may be searched in vain for a single instance in which it has been influenced, let alone determined, by a motive of a generous character, such as the support of the weak against aggression, of liberty against oppression, or of mere justice and respect for international law. . . . Whenever practical interests have not happened to coincide with equity, England has been consistently and invariably the defender of vested interests and established power, however flagrantly oppressive, aggressive, and unjust. England can always be trusted, if in nothing else, to be the determined supporter of reaction."

—*Robert Briffault*

"If the history of England be ever written by one who has the knowledge and the courage, and both qualities are equally necessary for the undertaking, the world would be more astonished than when reading the annals of Niebuhr. Generally speaking, all the great events have been distorted, most of the important causes concealed, some of the principal characters never appear, and all who figure are so misunderstood and misrepresented that the result is a complete mystification."

—*Disraeli* (Sybil)

"I believe—I stand accountant for the words to that which gave me the power of thinking and writing them—I believe that if the time and money and thought now given in England to the propagation of wholly incredible doctrines, which are no sooner uttered in one pulpit than they are repudiated in another—if this time and money and thought were given to the understanding and scattering abroad of the simplest laws of national economy, of physiology, of health and beauty, in another generation our England would be greater and mightier than she has ever been."

—*Henry Arthur Jones* (*Edwardian playwright*)

CHAPTER TEN

Has England Done More for Its People Than Fascism or Socialism?

THIS IS a heretical question. Let no one think I do not appreciate the enormity of my crime in even asking it—still more in answering it. Under present conditions of American liberty I am offering myself for public hanging, drawing, and quartering by the Dies Committee.

The new "American" code earmarks Nazism and Communism together as "alien isms," even to discuss which with attempted detachment is more heinous than for a nineteenth-century schoolgirl to discuss sex. But Imperialism, the system in implacable opposition to which our forefathers placed our Constitution, is apparently *not* an "alien ism." We are asked to be hotly in favor of it, because our Wall Street gangs are jealous of the swag England has got out of it and would like us to shed our blood to get them a slice.

However, I intend to exercise my constitutional privilege, while I still have it, of discussing this question. We need not jump into the morass of theoretical argumentation about Fascism and Communism. But if we are to get our ideas straight we must consider the results of those systems and scale "free" England down to its correct proportions in comparison. For we are told that one is white and the others black, and therefore we must all root for the white like good little children of Mr. Roosevelt. As far as I am concerned—and I believe this goes for most Americans, despite all the earnest efforts to stifle free thought— that kind of totemic mysticism simply will not do.

The comparison is no easy one to make, not only because of the prejudice that fogs the whole question over and denies the possibility that anyone examining it will be sincere, but also because of the absence of "freedom of the press," as we understand the phrase or think we understand it, in Germany and Russia. I am afraid that I know our own press and the English press too well to accuse it of being free, for I know it to be controlled by the advertising interests without which it could not exist. Freedom of the press, like democracy itself, like any kind of freedom, is a relative term. I cannot agree that everything that is claimed for Germany and Russia is a lie and everything that is claimed for England is true, merely because Nazism and Communism put up legal barriers against expression of views opposed to their social systems. I do, on the other hand, assert and know that truth exists with regard to material facts, and that eventually, no matter what steps are taken to suppress it, it must emerge for those who take the trouble to sift the evidence.

There are many things that we know definitely about Nazi Germany and Communist Russia: things that their governments either could not or did not want to conceal, or that, despite attempts at concealment, were revealed by events inevitably resulting from them.

The main point that cannot be concealed is whether those systems are efficient, by comparison with the system of privilege-"democracy" in England and the British Empire.

Let us for the sake of argument accept England's contention that virtual abolition of civil rights, such as we now find there, is necessary when fighting for civil rights. Let us examine England and Germany between 1932, the depth of the world crisis, and 1938—and make what comparisons we can in the realm of more or less undisputed facts and of statistics given in their official publications.

1. Germany deifies a thing unknown to science called "the Aryan race," and rejects liberal culture. It glories in book-burnings and pogroms, and sees no reason to conceal the decline in university students from 133,000 in 1932 to 72,000 in 1936.

The English deify the equally mystical concept of the "English Gentleman's" superiority over all other breeds. They do not burn books or permit pogroms—in England. In 1936 their proportion of university students to the total population was slightly smaller than in 1932, but slightly larger than Germany's after the cultural purge. Over 90 per cent of those students, who receive what is generally known as a liberal education, come from the upper economic tenth of the people.

2. Germany's economic system is nationally planned, but is still based on the foundation of dividend profit. The government assumes the right to tell business what it shall produce and how much, but at the same time guarantees business increasing profits. Before they came to power the Nazis cried: "Smash interest slavery!" In 1938 and 1939 the rate of interest was considerably higher in Germany than in France, Belgium, Switzerland, and Holland, the value of state and municipal bonds having risen by over 50 per cent under Hitler (*Statistisches Reichsamt* figures). The increase of millionaires from 1932 to 1937, says the German *Year Book,* was 1,266; of multi-millionaires, 180.

England's economic system is based likewise on dividend profit, but is officially a "free competitive" system. Actually all major industries are controlled by private or semi-private monopolies protected, and in many cases *set up, by the government.* From 1932 to 1937 the income garnered by coupon-clippers rose over 40 per cent.

3. Germany has abolished trade unions, as far as the right to strike is concerned, declaring that there must be "unity" between capital and labor—or else. Since the government which enforces "unity" gives all the cream to capital, it is clear what labor gets out of "unity."

England has a very large trade-union movement, the leaders of which convene to map the policy of "His Majesty's Loyal Opposition" without the formality of asking the members what they feel about things. The head of the movement is Sir Walter Citrine, who was knighted by the king for opposing with such burning loyalty.

4. Germany's wage rates (by its own statistics) have remained since 1933 at 97 per cent of the 1932 crisis rates, but because of longer working hours weekly earnings have increased. England's wage rates rose 13 per cent in the same period, with working hours about the same. The longest working week for which there was an agreement before this war was 104 hours in Germany, 60 hours in England. In Germany industrial accidents doubled in number while employment rose 50 per cent; in England accidents increased 35 per cent while employment rose

12 per cent. Figuring the rise in living cost, actual real earnings of wage workers rose 8 per cent in England, 5 per cent in Germany.

5. Social-insurance, health, pension, and other social expenditures per wage worker slightly declined in Germany (although wage deductions for these services rose steeply) and very slightly increased in England.

6. The income of wage- and salary-earning Germans relative to the income of coupon-clippers declined (in 1932–1937) by 50 per cent. In England the corresponding decline was 16 per cent. (These figures were worked out from official *Year Book* material by the statistician Jurgen Kuczynski.)

7. Germany virtually wiped out unemployment, seven million more people having jobs in 1938 than in 1932 and the remainder of the problem being solved by concentration camps and social ostracism of Jews. England had 2,745,000 unemployed in the crisis year 1932 and still had 1,791,000 in 1938.

8. In Germany, exploitation of the country's natural resources to increase both normal and synthetic production has been vastly intensified. The amount of tillable land still idle is almost nil. England has seven million acres of land set apart for millionaires' grouse-shooting (according to the London Anti-Vivisection Society), and Professor Julian Huxley says: "A doubling of the present amount of food grown in this country is not only perfectly possible, but a modest estimate of what could be achieved by applying the scientific knowledge which exists." In 1934 England imported 53 per cent of its meat, 89 per cent of its butter, 38 per cent of its eggs, 60 per cent of its fruit.

Place on the scales these main features of German and English life in "normal" times, and of course the English on the whole have the best of it. Legally they have the right to oppose the government, to get a good education, to fair trial, to give their work or withhold it, to strike for better conditions—though realities make those rights increasingly ineffective or a mere formality. English wage- and salary-earners are a little better off than the German with regard to living standards, though it is notable that of late the care taken to prevent accidents at work seems to be even less in England than in Germany.

Items 7 and 8, on the other hand, add weight to the German case, from the viewpoint of the average wage-earner and of objective efficiency. The most important of all human rights in industrial society is the right to a job, to a self-respecting place in the social structure, though to my concept of civilization both vote and job are essential. Leaving aside for a moment the anti-Semitic savagery and the concentration camps, which do not affect the majority, a wage-earner might sum up the picture by saying that Germany gives him a job, England gives him a vote. The English masses have theoretical civil rights and may vote for the nominee of one of two political machines every five years or so. The German masses have a guarantee of work under dictated conditions, provided they submit. The total of English unemployed in 1938 is probably about the same as the total "non-Aryan" and concentration-camp population of "Greater" Germany in the same year. Whether it is better to die quickly by torture or slowly by hunger—and unemployment in England means nothing less—is a question on which there will be difference of opinion.

It will be said that the Nazis have only "solved" unemployment, and "solved" the problem of idle resources, on one basis and with one object in view: war. That is perfectly true and makes it farcical to speak of this as a "solution," even if it had bettered the condition of the masses, which it has not. But it may also be said that England's government during the past few years has pursued a policy whose very inefficiency led just as inevitably to war: a muddled policy of betraying democracy everywhere and of meaningless talk about the disarmament and colonial questions which amounted to refusal to consider them. And the unemployment slack that England did succeed in taking up was eliminated in war industries—yet even then vast unemployment remains.

Consider all these points, and England still has the edge over Germany. But the more we look at it from across the Atlantic—from the point of view of our inglorious present, but standing on the battered rock of our national ideals—the more it resembles a comparison between an angry bull in a bull ring erected for entertainment and a financially erected bull ring with its accompanying toreadors and hired bull baiters—meaning thereby Germany (the bull) and the world-encircling British Empire aiming to destroy it for commercial reasons. And though it may be natural to some to prefer the entertainment bull ring and bull fighters, it is still more natural to reject both as spectacles for our sons and daughters. No sane person could offer the slightest defense for the business of torturing the bull, and again it is no defense of the bull-ring owners and their bull-fighting hirelings that the lowering of the masses' share in the national income has been *less* in England—that the people of England are starved *less*—that in England men and women work *only* a sixty-hour week. If people for whom the holders of power have no use are not deprived of their physical freedom in England, that is a poor sort of defense when the only freedom they have effectively is freedom to starve by slow stages.

The point is that a government which Americans should support (but which our present rulers can be relied on to betray, as in Spain and China) is one that *raises* the masses' share in the rising national income, *reduces* their working hours in line with the advance of technology, steadily *increases* their effective democratic rights. Those are things that England cannot claim to have been doing in the past twenty years. Nor have we Americans any right to look superior about it when we contemplate the present trend in our own land. But in the most typically American (in my sense of the word, not Mr. Dies') period of our history we did come nearer to doing those things than any European nation; and that is still the ideal firmly planted in our Constitution. It has always been and still is the only ideal worth fighting for.

But now we have to move on once again to the British Empire. It is an unreal approach to our comparison to confine it to England, which contains less than 10 per cent of the people under English rule. To fight for England is inevitably to fight for the Empire as it exists now —at least until England's rulers take the opportunity India has offered them to show a change of heart. And when we look at the Empire, what edge can we now give England over Nazi Germany?

We find anti-Semitism rampant in Palestine, anti-Hinduism rampant in India. No, of course the English are not officially anti-Semitic or anti-Hindu—it's the Arab and Moslem minorities. But try as they will, the English cannot find evidence of such rioting in Palestine before the British Mandate, or in India before the East India Company.

We find standards of living which would have been unimaginable to men in the barbarian state of development. We have already glanced at these standards in India and Africa. Here is what a doctor from the

Dutch East Indies, after a visit to Trinidad in 1935, reported to the governor of that island:

> He had twenty years' experience in the Dutch East Indies and although he had first-hand knowledge of conditions resulting from vitamin deficiencies, he had never seen such distressing conditions as existed here. . . . The Medical Officer stated that every adult above the age of 20 years was affected, and that the working life of the population was reduced by at least 50%. . . . The Medical Officer was asked whether these people were aware of the nature of the disease which crippled them, and he said they were not; they took it as a matter of course. A condition of lethargy pervaded the whole community, which was only broken on festive occasions or in times of disorder.

We find everywhere the arbitrary suppression by England of all books, newspapers, and public assemblies which the English do not like. We see attempts to redress grievances suppressed with guns and clubs in (to mention only the most recent instances) Rhodesia, South Africa, Zanzibar, Mauritius, Tanganyika, St. Lucia, Trinidad, Barbados, Jamaica, St. Kitts, St. Vincent, British Guiana, India, Burma, Palestine. Occasionally, it is true, there are official inquiries—after the shootings and beatings—into the nature of the grievances, but of what comfort are inquiries that never produce any practical results? The findings are merely reported in the English press (thereby producing the illusion of English "democracy" and "enlightenment") with editorial comment that they "give the customary distressing picture of undernourishment and disease" (*Manchester Guardian,* 1938) or that "It is disquieting to those who believed that the principle of native trusteeship was being generously carried out in the colonial Empire" (*The Economist,* 1938).

The kindly aristocrats of England—some of them—are "disquieted." So what? The "distressing picture of undernourishment and disease" continues to be as customary as before. And the final chapter is that such a soft-hearted official as the Governor of Trinidad above mentioned, who drew attention to the condition of the people, is denounced in the House of Lords and "retires" six months later "on grounds of ill-health."

Leonard Barnes, a recent English critic of English imperialism, can write in England that "it is necessary to emphasise the point that during the present century the movement of events in the colonies has on the whole been away from, not towards, self-government." But try to buy Mr. Barnes' excellent and factual book in the colonies or in India.

And we find everywhere a truly amazing picture of England's failure even to develop the known existing resources of its colonies efficiently, much less to put forward any program of industrial progress. Can it be wondered at that rising imperialist rivals like Germany, hungry for outlets for their goods and capital, cast eyes of bitter envy on old lady Britannia?

For an example of this sheer inefficiency we need look no further than the two English colonies on our own continent. British Guiana, the South American empire outpost, has remained undeveloped for one hundred thirty years under England, with unestimable water power going to waste, with only 62,000 acres of sugar where 1,620,000 acres could be developed to produce 2,500,000 tons of sugar annually. The sugar planters, according to Guy de Weever in the *Contemporary Review,* "object to introducing more laborers, fearing a rise in the standard of living!" Such a dire danger to the imperialist economy must be thwarted at any cost.

British Honduras had in 1923, according to the *Pan-American Magazine,* exactly twenty miles of metaled roads outside Belize, the capital, and two public schools under the government for a population of forty-five thousand.

In Egypt, along the banks of the Nile, there are still 1,900,000 acres which could be brought under cultivation at once by irrigation. A million villages could be supplied with water by extension of the water-pipe system. As I have already pointed out, the present living conditions of the Egyptian people are among the worst in the world.

In Australia and Canada millions of acres of land that could be developed lie idle, while even Englishmen, supposed "inheritors" of the Empire, are not allowed to settle there unless they are comparatively wealthy!

In the Gold Coast colony of Africa, England points proudly to the increase in educational expenditure from 3 to 7 per cent of the government revenue, between 1913 and 1931! It has been reckoned that if the population of the Gold Coast remained stationary, every inhabitant would be able to read and write at the current rate of progress by the year 2631.

The colonial governments almost appear to compete among each other to see which can do the least to educate the people. I quote from the report of the Education Commission which visited the West Indies in 1931:

An experienced observer of education in several parts of the world, after a recent visit to the West Indies, informed us that in his opinion, primary education in the West Indies was the least progressive of any which he had encountered in the British Empire. . . . Our general impressions, as a result of our tour, are not unlike those of the observer whom we have quoted.

The "brightest jewel," however, cannot let this claim go unchallenged. In India, illiteracy is claimed to have dropped from 94 per cent in 1911 to 92 per cent in 1931. This—if the most rigorous birth control is practiced or if there are enough famines to keep the population from rising—gives us the year of grace 2851 as the date by which all Indians will be able to read and write.

India still leads the field as a practical demonstration of English imperialist—shall I say "inefficiency," or may I say "criminal imperial repression"? As far back as 1894 Sir George Watt wrote that "with the extension of irrigation, more thorough and complete facilities of transport, improvements in methods and materials of agriculture, and the expansion of the area of cultivation . . . the productiveness of India might easily be increased by at least 50 per cent." India's water-power resources, second only to those of the United States, are just 3 per cent developed—while Switzerland, with not one-tenth of the resources, has developed them to the extent of 72 per cent. As for man-power, where labor is already so cheap and plentiful, India's population increase from 1870 to 1910 was 18.9 per cent, compared with 45.4 per cent for the whole of Europe. Yet the English will tell you quite solemnly that only birth control or famines can solve the Indian problem.

Seventy-three per cent of India's population was dependent on agriculture in 1921 (12 per cent more than in 1891). And yet the Indian economist R. K. Das estimates that 70 per cent of the area available for cultivation is wasted. In the *Indian Central Banking Inquiry Report* of 1931, A. P. MacDougall writes:

It has been stated that the soil of India is naturally poor. This is not correct. It has become poor. The great river valleys must at one time have been among the most fertile in the world. In Denmark and Germany the greater part of the land in its original state consisted of barren wastes of sand growing nothing but gorse and heather. . . . If the output were in terms of English production, the wealth of the country would be raised by £1,000,-000,000 a year. Yet England is by no means highly cultivated. This does not make any allowance for part of the land in India producing two crops per year.

It is for this land, so grotesquely mismanaged, forcibly held back from the logical implications of modern knowledge, with all its miseries piled up higher than towering Everest, that England's Prime Minister Churchill can prophesy "the dull roar and scream of carnage and confusion" if the English were to withdraw!

Churchill needs an ear specialist. The roaring and screaming—and they are not dull, at that—are going on now. And if Germany can beat England at the game of mass human torture and fabulous inefficiency, then it will have to go some. Certainly competition between the two, each using different methods but each achieving roughly the same results, has been keen.

As to whether the native peoples of colonial countries "prefer" English or Nazi rule, this unenviable choice will not in any case be left up to them. They will take what's coming, and like it, until they are strong enough to throw off all imperialists.

I have an English friend who lived for many years in Tanganyika, which England grabbed from Germany after the first world war. She knew the natives well, and when she asked them which rule they preferred, they told her after some reflection that they preferred the German.

Under both, they said, they had the same conditions to endure. But England came with a Bible in hand and democracy and false promises on its lips to enforce those conditions, while Germany simply said:

"We have the guns. You haven't. You do what we tell you and no damned nonsense. Ja?"

And the natives, at least thankful for such frankness, said:
"Ja!"

Now we come to the point where I am really asking to be hit on the head. Here is the great heresy. I am going to set down some facts and figures favorable to Russia. But please don't run out on me.

When I referred just now to Switzerland's remarkable development of its water-power resources, it is unlikely that anyone suspected me of getting a payoff from the Swiss government for that little boost. But now I am going to report on the Russian government's use of its water power, and the only question in the minds of Mr. Dies and his friends (a group apparently now including the Honorable Franklin D. Roosevelt) will be how many rubles I received. There is nothing I can do about this pathological state of mind, and I shall be waiting patiently for Hoover's F.B.I. men to call for me and put me where I can no longer record unpleasant truths.

However, I am not rising to proclaim that Russia is Utopia. I have already stated that Utopias do not exist, and I would not care for them if they did. All I intend is to quote the most reliable statistics we have —and I rate them just as reliable as those given for Germany and England—about the actual results of the regime in Russia during the past two decades, as far as the ordinary citizen of that country is concerned.

To continue this lengthy apologia, which should not be necessary if we lived in rational times: I am not suggesting that because I believe Russia has greatly increased physical and mental living standards for its masses, therefore England and America should go Communist tomorrow. I am trying to examine facts. I am advocating only that we should study these facts together with all others available—refute them if they can be refuted—see which ones have value for us and which have none, and learn from the former while rejecting the latter. Horribly un-American, I know—as un-American as Thomas Paine. But the human cranium is a funny thing and you can't stop it from seeking truth.

"Let me start with a mild quotation:

"The output of pig iron per head of population in 1938 was 145 kilograms in Great Britain, and only 87 kilograms in the USSR. In Great Britain the output of steel per head of population was 226 kilograms and of electricity 620 kilowatt hours, whereas in the USSR the output of steel per head of population was only 107 kilograms, and of electricity only 233 kilowatt hours."

Who is this speaking? Eugene Lyons? Neville Chamberlain? Herbert Hoover?

No. The gentleman's name is Josef Stalin, and the speech from which it is taken was made at the Eighteenth Communist Party Congress in Moscow, as a warning to the people against over-optimism now that Russia has become the second greatest producer of goods in the world. I quote it at the outset in order to show that Russians can be as modest as anyone else about their achievements—and also to remove all delusions that I think, or even that Stalin thinks, the average standard of living is higher in Russia than in England and America.

Let us very briefly examine what Russia has done for its people.

It made a central and all-embracing plan, industrial and agricultural and cultural, for the whole Soviet Union. The plan created, by 1938, 2,292 research institutes with a blank check to put into practical effect without delay the results of their researches. The plan is a plan to produce goods for the people, just as much of everything as they need, so that there is no possibility of "surplus," nor of that "frustration of science" (to use Professor P. M. S. Blackett's expression) which exists in England and the British Empire, where a rise in the living standard, an end of scarcity, is something to be "feared."

Groups of scientists have been sent to every corner of the Soviet Union to study production conditions and see how they can be improved. By these groups no less than 30,000 kinds of wheat have been classified, in order that the kind most suited to any given district may be discovered. The same has been done in the case of fruits, tea and coffee, vegetables, and all types of grain. Russia needs 120,000 tons of rubber every year and used to import all of it. Rubber-bearing plants yielding as much as 38 per cent of pure rubber were discovered growing wild—and this year only 20,000 tons are being imported; next year the whole rubber need will be home-grown.

The result of this work is that today peaches are being grown in the far north where the temperature drops to 40 below; and in polar latitudes "you may stand in a field where the ripe grain touches your face."

The order had gone out from the barbarous "totalitarian" government to "spread wheat north, industry east." Remember that Czarist Russia was an empire, very similar to the British Empire, with a great number of colonial peoples whose business it was merely to produce raw materials for the western Russian industries. Now it groans under this frightful "totalitarian" rule which has no interest in keeping one group of people back so that another group may go forward. There is no reason on earth why the peoples of the eastern and central Asian sections should not progress freely and normally toward industrialization. And now you begin to see, if you are willing to be open-minded about it, how truly modest Stalin was in the speech I have quoted. For he compared the per-capita production of all the U.S.S.R., all the old Czarist empire, with that of England—not with that of the British Empire. When he figured the population of his country he figured in the Kazaks, the Tadjiks, the Uzbeks, and the Kirghiz, and all the other minority groups who formerly had just the same status in relation to Russia as the Indians, the Africans, the Malays, and the West Indians now have in relation to England.

For the people of the U.S.S.R. as a whole the production of coal has been increased from 29 million tons to 137 million tons a year; of oil, from 9.2 million tons to 30.6 million (1937) ; of tractors, to a total of 558,000, with one factory turning out 40,000 a year; of machinery, to twenty-three times what it was in 1913 (1937; scheduled output for 1942, 225 per cent higher yet). Thousands of miles of new railroad have been opened, and the output of new main-line locomotives by 1942 will be over 2,000 a year. Where Czarist Russia had 6,250 miles of paved road, modern Russia has a network of them plus 80,000 miles of waterways navigable by deep-draught vessels, plus airlines covering the land. Cotton cloth production rose to 2,694 million meters in 1932 and to 3,496 million in 1938; shoe production to 94 million pairs (1932) and to 212 million pairs (1938). Wage rates rose 371.4 per cent from 1929 to 1937, while they fell 2 per cent in England and 21 per cent in Germany —and at the same time the price of bread and butter was halved, eggs were down 75 per cent, meat 63 per cent, and working hours were shorter. Rest homes of fabulous luxury were built on the Black Sea Riviera, where ordinary working people and their families now go by the hundreds of thousands without charge. Hospitals and doctors were made freely available to all, and while Germany and England reduced their university population the Russians increased theirs from 417,000 in 1932 to 542,000 in 1936—students being actually paid a wage while attending. Theaters sprang into being by the thousand; a vast movie industry was created. Where 78 per cent of the population had been illiterate under Czarism, the total number of school children rose in 1938 to 34,000,000 and illiteracy was down to 8 per cent. Books by the world's best authors were circulated in astronomical numbers (76 million copies of the works of Pushkin, Gorky, Chekhov, and Tolstoy alone, up to 1936). Newspaper circulation—without advertising— leaped from 2.7 million to 36.2 million. Crime declined precipitously and prostitution became a memory. Pogroms vanished into thin air: Russia was the first country in the world to make the mere utterance of an anti-Semitic sentence a punishable offense.

"Not a bad achievement for twenty years," you may say, "—if you can believe it."

Good friend, nobody on earth is more in favor of healthy skepticism than I am. But do you recall the tale of the naked king and the small boy who, while all the adults took their cue from the crowd and admired the king's raiment, piped up, "But the King is naked!" There really does come a time when, in spite of all the angry voices insisting that white is black, an honest man must accept the plainly obvious and at least give it credit for being gray.

I cannot testify to the decimal-point accuracy of the Russian statistics, nor can you or anyone else testify to the decimal-point accuracy of English or American statistics. I was last there in 1927–1928. But I can quote a trustworthy friend, who has traveled twice around the world and was in Russia as late as 1936, who writes me:

I did not go around Russia counting the shoes and tractors. But I have seen the new shoe and tractor factories and I am capable of forming reasonably accurate conclusions. I haven't counted the editions of Tolstoy but I have seen the bookstores, the people standing in long lines to buy as soon as a new edition is announced, and the editions exhausting themselves in a few hours. I do not know from personal observation how many people visit the Black Sea rest homes, but I have seen many thousands of them—ordinary working people—enjoying there such luxuries as their kind only dream about in England. I cannot guarantee that there is not a prostitute in the length and breadth of Russia and that not one anti-Semitic syllable is ever uttered. I can only say that I never saw the one nor heard the other—and I cannot say the same of any other country I have visited.

But perhaps you are willing to believe the statistics but remain unimpressed. "What good is all this," you may ask, "if it was all done by violence and if the people have no democracy and civil rights?"

It would take at least a whole book to discuss that, and even then those who refuse to open their minds would certainly not read it, so I will just as certainly not write it. I prefer to save breath and ink and concede to the theoreticians that the Russian trade unions have no power and that the people are slaves to a new ruling clique and have no democracy. Why argue abstractions? Perhaps it is a little strange that the Fascist and Nazi destroyers of democracy publicly spit upon it on every possible occasion while not one word has ever been officially spoken against it in Soviet Russia. Stalin must be the genius of all the ages if he can promise democracy day after day, week after week, year after year to 170,000,000 people and yet make them submit so enthusiastically to dictatorship. But let that pass—these Russians are strange and sinister folk. Stick to facts. Isn't it one fair test of democracy to see what people as a whole want and then see if they get it? If they do get it, the wish of the majority is apparently being obeyed. What people as a whole want, so far as my observation goes, is more food and more houses and more clothes and more leisure and more opportunities to use that leisure pleasantly and advantageously. The facts show that the Russians, having abolished the dividend system, are now getting these things at a faster rate of progress than has ever been recorded in history. But perhaps that doesn't prove anything, or does it? And, of course, there may well be many things in Russia that are bad and to be avoided, such as whatever it was that caused the famous purges and the attack on Finland. Granted: but are we so feebleminded, is England so feeble-minded, as to be unable to choose between good and bad? Does the whole experiment have to be labeled "poison" and avoided like cyanide, because there are chunks of grit in the mixture?

And as for violence: I look over the world—yes, including our own country—and seek in vain a land where violence is not. I don't like violence; I have met many Russians and none of them liked it. But I refuse to condemn others for the mote in their eye when there is a beam in my own.

Now you may belong to yet another school of thought, which

denies the validity of the comparison between modern Russia and the extreme backwardness of Czarist Russia, but is willing only to compare Russia today with other countries today. You argue, in this case, that the very backwardness of old Russia made a spurt after the first world war inevitable, after the fashion of nature abhorring a vacuum; and that Russia could have progressed much faster than it has—and would have done so under the dividend or imperialist system. This has become a more and more popular line of argument as the facts about Russia's material progress become more and more undeniable. It has the apparent advantage of not being subject to confirmation or refutation.

It would perhaps be rash to claim that what has been done could only have been done by Communism, and I do not claim that. One should not ignore what has happened during the same period in Turkey, where a modified form of the dividend system with a considerable degree of central planning now exists. Turkey has not advanced so fast and far as Russia, but it has less natural wealth.

Our comparison, though, is between Russia and England. And this line of argument does happen to be refutable with regard to England, by a simple and entirely scientific demonstration. We have only to look at the Russian achievement in the central Asian Republics, where conditions in 1917 were the same as conditions in British India, only more so. If we compare Kazakstan and Kirghizia and Uzbekistan and Turkmenistan and Tadjikistan and the Kara-Kalpak Republic as they are today with India as it is today, we have our scientific demonstration.

In 1936 Rabindranath Tagore, poet of India, wrote:

The chronic want of food and water, the lack of sanitation and medical help, the neglect of means of communication, the poverty of educational provision, the all-pervading spirit of depression that I have myself seen to prevail in our villages after over a hundred years of British rule make me despair of its beneficence. It is almost a crime to talk of Soviet Russia in this country, and yet I cannot but refer to the contrast it presents. I must confess to the envy with which my admiration was mixed to see the extraordinary enthusiasm and skill with which the measures for producing food, providing education and fighting against disease were being pushed forward in their vast territories. There is no separating line of mistrust or insulting distinctions between Soviet Europe and Soviet Asia. I am only comparing the state of things obtaining there and here as I have actually seen them. And I state my conclusion that what is responsible for our condition in the so-called British Empire is the yawning gulf between its dominant and subjugated sections.

Now for some more statistics:

In India the most limited social-insurance system is unknown, there is no Public Health Act, and provision for public hygiene, sanitation, and health is almost non-existent. In Soviet Asia, as in the whole Soviet Union, the health and well-being of all citizens is the concern of the government from cradle to grave, and all are entitled to free medical and maternity care, free hospitalization, holidays with pay, and old-age pensions. In the whole of Russia there has been a seventyfold increase in public-health expenditure, now amounting to fifty-three rubles per head compared with about five cents a head in India. There are already more than ten times as many hospital beds per head of population in the Soviet Union as there are in India, and the third five-year plan alone calls for doubling of the beds available in the Uzbek, Tadjik, Kazakh, and Kirghiz Republics. Smallpox deaths have steadily increased in India since 1914; in U.S.S.R. the disease is now almost negligible. For the great majority of Indian workers there are no limits to the hours of work nor to the age at which children may begin to work. For Asiatic citizens of the Soviet, as for the others, the seventeenth birthday is the first day on which they may enter industry —and then for not more than a five- or six-hour day. One year later they are full-fledged citizens with a vote, and with the right to run for public office. (Of the 1,143 deputies in the Supreme Soviet, 284 are between the ages of eighteen and thirty.)

You dismiss the Russian system with the scornful word "totalitarian"? All right, that is permitted, but is it not a little childish to look no further? Before 1917, just one-half of one per cent of the Tadjiks could read and write (compared with 6 per cent in India in 1911). By 1933 60 per cent were literate, compared with 8 per cent in India in 1931. There were 100 school pupils in 1914. In 1939 there were 328,000. Expenditure on irrigation rose from 3 million roubles to 61 million in just two years (1929–1931)—the large part of the money coming not from local taxes but from central government funds. In India the total irrigated area rose from 46.8 million acres to 50.5 million acres in twenty years (1913–1933)—and that was done with capital investment demanding over 7 per cent interest. Before 1917 Tadjikistan had no industries whatever; now it has preserving factories, silk factories, electric power stations, clothing factories, a big meat industry, a brewery and a cement factory, ten printing works, brick factories, and other industries. Where there were no modern roads at all there are now 12,000 kilometers of surfaced road. Where there were 13 doctors and 100 hospital beds there are now 440 doctors and 3,675 beds, and by 1937, 36 infant-welfare centers had sprung into being. Compare these figures with those for India and see how completely un-British it all is. How un-American it is, we know from Mr. Dies.

Look at Uzbekistan, the biggest of the central Asian Republics, and the same picture presents itself. Three to five per cent literacy before 1917, and in 1932 no fewer than 1,371,000 child and adult students out of a 5.5 million population. Industrial output more than quadrupled in twenty years, electrical output increased seven times over in only eight years. (In imperialist days, just as today in India, "the hands of the ruined handicraftsmen were cheaper than electricity.") Dozens of new industries, including 51 cotton-spinning factories and an agricultural machinery plant. Doctors increased from 128 to 2,185. In 1935, 118 Uzbek newspapers with one million circulation—and before 1917 Uzbekistan did not even have its own alphabet.

In Soviet Armenia, scene of the most frightful massacres and sordid poverty but a generation ago, the people now work harmoniously together growing their own cotton, working it in their own mills driven with their own power. From their orchards they produce 15 million cans of fruit every year.

One could quote such statistics endlessly. But the vital point is that all this was made possible only by the complete discarding of the imperialist system, which is compelled by its nature to prevent industrialization of colonial territories, to keep them poor and backward so that the "mother" country may be rich. If you dispute this as a theoretical proposition, just look at India and think again! As soon as imperialism is abolished it becomes possible and desirable to bring the backward peoples up to the level of the most advanced by allocating to them a lion's share of the budget, so that we find twice as much being spent by the Soviet Government (in 1927–1928) in Uzbekistan per head of population as in Russia proper.

The "racial minority problem" has gone with the wind: it never was a problem in reality—the problem was imperialism. The peoples of central Asia were kept ignorant and virtual slaves, and discord was sown among them in Czarist days because it paid. The system was exactly similar to that still used by England in India, artificial boundaries being drawn to cut national groups in two and foster racial hate. Now under what is being called "Soviet imperialism" (a mere phrase which has nothing to do with realities) each people is a separate unit, with its own language and culture, in a multi-national federation with common interests and objectives. "Soviet imperialism" is nothing more than a modern projection of the principles on which the United States was created from an equally varied collection of peoples. The same principle has been applied, with the same success, to the "Jewish problem," which likewise never was really a problem at all.

Perhaps the most dramatic of the recent achievements in Soviet Asia is the revolution in the condition of women. You have probably read in *Mother India* about what happens to women and little girls in India. In Russian Asia it was just the same. Girl children were married to complete strangers at the age of eight or nine, becoming nothing more than chattels who did all the work and were disciplined with a whip. Women were compelled to hide their faces behind a fantastic horsehair net or cage. After 1917 the ruthless "totalitarians" in Moscow prohibited compulsory marriage and the sale of women, and fixed the age of consent for the Asiatic republics at sixteen. In a few years the entire barbaric structure of Asiatic tradition with regard to women collapsed. Fannina Halle has described what happened on International Women's Day in 1928:

On that day . . . tens of thousands of women, huddled in *paranjas* (horsehair veils), poured like a menacing avalanche through the narrow choked streets, square and bazaars of the ancient Central Asian cities. . . . Above this silent gloomy approaching mass, still without faces or eyes, a sea of red flags floated high in the air. . . . Amidst strains of music the vast multitude, including a number of men and children, gathered round the Lenin monument, which was likewise decked with red banners and native carpets, and the women waited breathlessly for what was to come. Thundering, stinging words, but words that were new, unaccustomed and inspiriting, that moved the hearers' hearts so deeply that they called forth a real frenzy of enthusiasm. . . . They [the *paranjas*] were flung aloft into the quivering air, timidly at first, but then with ever wilder and more frenzied speed. . . . They were piled in rapidly growing heaps, drenched with paraffin, and soon the dark clouds of smoke from the burning common abjuration of a thousand-year-old convention, now become unbearable, flared up into the bright sky of the Spring day.

To conclude this very brief comparative study I can do no better than quote from one of the most courageous and honest Christians of the day in England, who recently visited Russia and compared what he saw with his own country—the Reverend Hewlett Johnson, Dean of Canterbury Cathedral. He brought home no Utopian visions, he found much to criticize, he saw a people working hard and enjoying few luxuries, but he says:

Nothing strikes the visitor to the Soviet Union more forcibly than the absence of fear. . . . No fear for maintenance at the birth of a child cripples the Soviet parents. No fear for doctors' fees, school fees, or university fees. No fear of under-work, no fear of over-work. No fear of wage reduction, in a land where none are unemployed. . . .

Our system lacks moral basis. It is only justified on the grounds that no alternative exists. It gives rise, when Christian men and women accept it and acquiesce in it, to that fatal divergence between principles and practice of Christian people, which is so damning to religion, and which found its sternest critic in Christ himself. The gap between Sunday, with its sermons on brotherhood, co-operation, seeking of others' good, and Monday, with its competitive rivalries, its veiled warfares, its concentration upon acquisition, its determination to build up one's own security, becomes so wide that many of the better men and women of today remain outside the Churches altogether. Hypocrites they will not be. The young especially, with their modern passion for sincerity, are in open revolt. . . .

Our order is neither Christian nor scientific, and I find it hard to say in which capacity, as Christian or scientist, it offends me the more. When I read, as a headline in the *Observer,* not long before the war:

POLAND'S GOOD HARVEST

SEVERE BLOW TO RECOVERY

I recalled the words of an American Professor of Agriculture after seeing ten million acres of cotton ploughed in and five million pigs slaughtered: 'If this will bring national prosperity, then I have wasted my life.' An age of science has given way to an age of frustration of science. . . .

In no sense is our economic order scientific. Still less. is it Christian. Placing a premium on selfish motives, it inflames the acquisitive instinct, and smashes human lives. While half our population is undernourished and a sixth of our children disastrously underfed—the words are those of Sir John Boyd Orr—machines, save in time of war or war scare, stand idle, and many hundreds of thousands of workers, capable of producing food, clothing, and housing in abundance, drag out a miserable existence of enforced and demoralizing idleness. . . .

Slumps and booms, unemployment and mis-employment, the dole and the multi-millionaire, the scales weighted for financiers and against the workers, frustrate society and produce strains and stresses whose logical conclusion is war. . . .

If this is strongly said, it is because it is warmly felt and needs the saying. Years serve only to increase the challenge. Hardness develops into ruthlessness and brutality. The situation worsens.

I would only add: if a system which, for all its faults, makes a determined and far from unsuccessful attempt to alter this situation is "undemocratic," then we might be pardoned for crying "Down with democracy!"

On the other hand—and I think it is more sensible—we might bestir ourselves a little and, before flinging the word "democracy" wildly around any more, find out what it means.

CHAPTER ELEVEN

What Is Democracy?

IN THE last World War, 123,000 young Americans died "for democracy." "For democracy" another 190,000 were wrecked and maimed
physically. Nobody has bothered to count how many were mentally
wrecked "for democracy."

The death score includes 965 drafted warriors who, possibly becoming
skeptical about the great cause inscribed on their banners, didn't wait
for Germans to kill them but killed themselves; and 35 who—their
skepticism taking a less negative form—had to be killed by their own
side.

We know how much democracy resulted from this human sacrifice.
But how many of the dead (the doughboys' average mental stature, we
were told, was that of an eleven-year-old child) could even have defined
the beautiful four-syllable word for which they died?

How many of us today, after that lesson and the lesson of the two
decades following, have any clear understanding of the word which
we speak and hear more than any other except "swell" and "nuts"?

Stop the next political phrase-spinner you run into, and ask him to
define "democracy." Ask the next dozen people you meet. Blow the
hot air out of their sails and pin them down to realities. Watch them
flounder—and see if any two of them have the same idea of what democracy is.

Why are we so vague about it? Not that we haven't thought a lot,
as a people, about the concept of democracy. Most of us admit one
thing: that it threatens the individual's power against the majority, and

consequently the wealth that gives him that power. Hence the poor are on the whole in favor of it and those who possess wealth are on the whole against it. But since our Constitution makes it "un-American" to be against democracy, the wealthy express their antagonism to it by means of distorted definitions of what it means. They need to make as many as possible of the poor accept those distortions. So our vagueness about democracy is not purely a matter of chance and native dumbness. There are those for whom it is desirable that we should be vague.

Definitions of democracy have been given by half the writers that ever put pen to paper. Hendrik van Loon has pirouetted through the corridors of time and discovered that democracy has never existed anywhere.

That is correct, but not surprising, because democracy is not an absolute thing and cannot therefore in an absolute sense "exist." We can observe a donkey approaching a field of carrots and can say quite positively that at a certain moment, barbed-wire fences permitting, he achieves the carrot of his desire. Not so with the human donkey approaching the carrot of democracy. This carrot appears to dangle on the end of a stick which is tied to the donkey, and as the donkey advances the carrot recedes.

When we set out to discover what democracy is, we have a big task and a long journey. All through recorded history we see this growing, quickening concept dangling ahead of man, impelling him to action. We watch philosophy unfold from Plato to John Dewey and find democracy woven into the central design of the fabric. The philosopher "pries into men's souls" to find what they believe and why—how and why their beliefs change—what their relationship to nature is and how it changes. If the forces of nature are as eternal and irresistible as Science reports, how can men organize themselves to deflect and harness the rapids, to make them his friend as well as, or instead of, his foe? To what extent is it possible for us to be masters of our fate—to be free?

A brave and daring question. One possibly based on man's ignorance of the immutability of the forces that have brought him into being. Nevertheless, since he did not make himself, it is quite possible that it is these same forces that through him, their tool or creation, are forming the question in him. Certain it is that historically it was and still remains his great dream. Most certainly it did not appear to the philosophers like an apparition out of nowhere. It came as an answer to their questionings about the injustices and shortcomings of society. Injustices had existed inevitably ever since man, coming down out of trees, and getting up on his hind legs, learned enough by aiding nature to be able to produce more than one individual could consume. Since when, whether by reason of natural law or "free will," he has become an acquisitive animal interested in making a profit from the labor of his weaker brothers. Yet, interestingly enough, he has not always remained an acquisitive animal. There have been exceptions. Buddha, Lao Tze, Christ, Confucius, Thomas Paine. Someone actually thought of the Golden Rule and the world of things as they are changed, and the dream of things-as-they-might-be broadened with that new conception of human relations.

However, when the first democratic principles began to be adopted in practice by civilized men, it wasn't because those who had the power had a sudden access of benevolence, but because injustice evoked a reaction from below—that is, resistance from below—and the alternatives were either a safety valve (that is, compromise) or an explosion. Generally the explosion came anyway in the end because the safety valve was too small. Thus "democracy" came to the Athenian state, where already by 600 B.C. land had become concentrated into a few hands and five-sixths of the tenant farmers' product was taken from them as rent, so that often they had to sell their children as slaves in order to live. To the free citizens of the state, Solon gave a democratic constitution, to save the state. But for every free citizen at the height of Athenian prosperity there were eighteen slaves, and democracy for the one in eighteen couldn't solve the contradiction of slavery which removed opportunities of working from free men.

Philosophers' dreams of "freedom" are necessarily limited by the contemporary limitations of man's power to produce abundance. So in Plato's *Republic* everything is held in common—by a select group of loftier souls, who spend their time in thought while the slaves toil to feed them. Disliking the smell of the real world, Plato solved everything by saying it was not real: that his ideal world alone was real. We cannot blame him for that because in an almost completely unmechanized age the problem of plenty for all was unsolvable.

Aristotle, servant of Philip of Macedon who conquered Athens, condescended to admit that the real world was real, and even that society gradually evolved from a lower to a higher state. But for him the kettle must simmer and never boil: changes must take place slowly and solemnly within the iron fence of things-as-they-are, otherwise known as law-and-order. He was a very wise man, but no wiser than the conditions of his time and standing allowed.

In Byzantium the corruption of slave society reached a peak, and from it the Neo-Platonists went scuttling into the Egyptian deserts, picking up a rash of oriental mysticism en route. In the deserts they indulged in an orgy of escapism such as we have among many intellectuals today. The world of the senses was a hoax, so that the dream of democracy was a fatal chimera. Man's best bet was to "turn his inward eye upward, and in the spiritual beauty of God's mind find eternal life."

But the dream went on, because the world moved on, because man's knowledge of his world grew, because hope could not die. The chain of causes and effect could not be broken.

Medieval tyrants needed instruments of war, and the engineering genius of Leonardo was born. The needs of expanding commerce gave birth to the compass, sextant, and chronometer, to the science of astronomy—to Galileo's "But it does move." Finer, more efficient tools were invented as manufacturers and merchants competed one against the other.

In the sixteenth century Thomas More, in England, revived with his *Utopia* the fashion of inventing ideal commonwealths. Conditions then were still such that no baby born had more than an outsider's chance of reaching the age of twenty-one. But just then invention was opening up the dim possibilities of an age of plenty—and as we have seen, the extent to which plenty can be distributed among men is the extent to which democracy can be envisioned.

Francis Bacon saw it coming, and in his *New Atlantis* sent out a call for scientists and philosophers to cease thinking in a vacuum and apply their minds to man's essential problem, the problem of ending want and ignorance. He might be called the first democrat.

With the Industrial Revolution in England, the Aristotelian imperialist-"democracy," the dream became clearer and bigger in the minds of

William Morris, George Bernard Shaw, and H. G. Wells. It was caught up by poets and thinkers in the new rich land of America, by Whitman, Henry George, Edward Bellamy. All these believed with Rousseau and Kant that the law of man's nature is social and that the Good is social good—that which serves the common interest. But others, the servants and beneficiaries of things-as-they-are, stood ready to distort the new and dangerous theories. Had not Darwin shown that man had evolved from the monkey through natural selection and survival of the fittest? Very well then: since it was desirable for the fittest to survive, the precept most useful to society was every man for himself and the devil take the hindmost.

That theory of rugged individualism going onward and upward forever—retained to this day by privileged persons in all lands and particularly in America—was very handy to those who sought moral justification for sitting on the kettle of progress. But it ignored, as one critic puts it, the consideration of "what happens if everybody bolts for the exits in a theater fire." It ignored the implacable and basic law of social existence. What was efficient for nature's purposes when we swung from bough to bough by our tails is no longer efficient when all of life, because of our acquired store of knowledge, is organized socially.

Questions of this kind, relating to the ancient dream of a perfect state, are of the highest importance for us to consider just now when the word "democracy" is receiving such savage mistreatment on all sides.

We begin to see, as we line up the philosophers and pass them in review, what an illusion the Perfect State always was as a fixed and absolute idea. It is always relative in the sense that everything we see or think of is relative, since what we see depends on the circumstances or position from which we see it.

The angle of our vision has widened since Plato, and that of our grandchildren will have widened still more. But what we can now perceive, and which Plato could not, is that the phenomena of nature, understanding of which is the core of our problem, are both relative and absolute at the same time. We may not know what they are, because of our imperfect vision, but we do know *that* they are. At any given stage of evolution the things that would create happiness for men are there in nature. We do not invent, we discover. Each stage we reach calls for new discoveries needed by the next stage ahead, and a kind of chemical convulsion occurs in some "inventor's" head. The possibility of going up in the air existed centuries before the first balloon ascended. Man merely had not found out about hydrogen.

The history of science and philosophy is the history of man trying to crack the shell of the unknown and lay bare the kernel. But because of the constant evolution of nature and man, by the time we crack the shell of a given nut the kernel may have already passed on to a higher stage and grown a new shell of mystery inside the old one.

Such a kernel is democracy, so that there is no such thing as an absolute Perfect State, and anyone who tells you such a state was achieved for all time in Philadelphia in 1787, in England with the Reform Bill of 1832, or in Russia in 1917, is a liar. Certainly Jefferson shows in the Declaration of Independence that he would have made no such claim. Life itself is not perfect. It is a series of evolving arrangements under natural laws. There is a lot of freedom for us in them, but the moment you smack into one of the laws—if you get burned or frozen, or try to lift too heavy a weight—you know it. No matter if you're Shakespeare or an elephant, those laws are there and they are enforced.

Nature didn't choose to hand the primary organism very much of anything, but she gave it remarkable persistence. The amoeba couldn't evolve until the earth was cool enough to provide moisture, but at that point there was a working mechanism trying to live in, for it, new surroundings. The amoeba has hunger and can, via a "phantom canal," push out energy like a foot, and move in the direction where food lies. Also away from opposition or danger. To this "phantom canal" there are no walls, and yet the amoeba travels quite straight in the direction desired, taking what it wants if it finds it, or, if not, trying another direction. It can surround something, enfold it, chemically absorb it.

What is this immaterialized energy? That we still don't know, but I call it genius of the highest order.

Perhaps more important for us is this question: "Why doesn't it— this genius—Creative Genius of Nature—create the perfect mechanism right away and skip all the long and painful eons of evolution?"

The only answer I can see is that it doesn't want to. Struggle, growth, change, contrast, along with pleasure and pain, are some of the laws of its being—its desire to put on this show called by us Life; and because of this desire on its part, and by and through these laws, it supplies us with whatever of pleasure or pain it or we know. Plainly it lives on adventure. So with man.

So in the civilized world moving toward more democracy and more freedom—or rather, more sense of freedom, since we can never be free of nature's laws—the tendency of nature has been to let the homunculus run a long struggle and see what he can get. His pleasures or his troubles arise from the fact that he always ends by wanting more than he is entitled to, which in a scarcity economy means that others must do with less than they are entitled to in order that he may have more. But from nature's point of view up to now that has been good, for by that struggle between individuals and groups the living world has developed: its pleasures, pains, surpluses, and seeming but not real deficiencies—for in nature is everything ready to be discovered. As science today knows, we need only to search and find out—enjoying life as best we can as we go.

Cruel, yes. The creative force is quite brutal in its methods. It gives Edison the power to create something new almost every day while to a man born next door it barely gives the ability to sweep a floor. It gives one woman an ugly face and body, and her cousin such beauty that men lay everything at her feet and she need not stir. It is a cruel dictatorship and at the same time a recklessly bountiful genius. It gives the opossum a score of young and the ability to feed but twelve, so that the weakest must fall from the pouch and perish. It produces as many as 500 million mackerel eggs during a spawning time on a square mile of ocean surface, and condemns 999,996 in each million to die before they live. But also it decrees that from the putrescence of death shall always come new and yet more abundant life.

The point is that out of this struggle the onward-and-upward movement has come. Hence it is absurd to say that "capitalism," the system of competitive struggle for the available turkey and gravy, is absolutely "bad" and "undemocratic." It is equally absurd to say that it is absolutely "good." It was the system best adapted to nature's unfolding purpose, and gave us as much democracy as the traffic would bear, at a certain stage of our development—just as primitive tribalism was best adapted to that purpose in ancient Polynesia before the missionaries came, in

India before the English came, and among the American Indians before we barged in. Such systems could and did persist until the people knew about other systems geared to the demands of progress—and then they were doomed.

Our present competitive system based on scarcity was as inevitable as sunrise. The champions of it are entirely right in pointing out that it has made us what we are today. But the question now is: What are we today? Does it function efficiently any longer? Do we like the reflection of ourselves in the mirror?

The question is, whether this system's displacement by something else has not, with scarcity at long last potentially ended, become as inevitable as sunset.

The best of all definitions of democracy is that it is the knowledge of necessity. Knowledge is death to the old, and new life springs from the putrescence. The advance of democracy is no more than the advance of knowledge.

In order, then, that there shall not to be plenty for all in our era, there must be ignorance on the part of most.

In order to continue suffering for the want of things that can now be produced in endless quantities, the mass of the people must remain ignorant of their existence; or at least ignorant of how to extract them from nature and, once extracted, how to distribute them so that a few cannot, for reasons of selfish display and vanity, prevent the many from sharing what is enough for all.

The extent therefore of our national ignorance of these things is the extent of our lack of democracy.

CHAPTER TWELVE

What Are the Defects of American Democracy?

IN THE past century we have multiplied our population by ten, our capacity to produce by 360, and our majority standard of living by very little—indeed, if you consider the sense of security which is of paramount importance to man, the living standard has been more an exercise in division than in multiplication.

Do you notice something wrong there?

Strange, isn't it? We have "democracy," and the answer is a lemon thrown on a garbage heap and sprayed with oil. "The will of the people."

We are proud of being a democracy and by some standards we have a right to be. The spirit and aspirations of our people are certainly democratic. We are a democracy by the charter of our origin and existence, which proclaims before the world that all men are created equal (not in ability, of course, but in rights) and that if the state obstructs the majority's rights to happiness they have the right and duty to overthrow it.

There were many signs of real democracy prior to the Constitutional Convention. Nearly fifty years before that event we were enacting laws requiring establishment of schools. "It is impossible for us to conceive the boldness of the measure which aimed at universal education through establishment of free schools," writes Horace Mann. "As a fact it had no precedent in world's history; and, as a theory, it could have been refuted and silenced by a more formidable array of argument and experience than was ever marshalled against any other institution of human origin."

Next, as I have emphasized in other places in this book, democracy has been more than an ideal. From the first it actually began to work. It became the target at which our national life was aimed. It became effective as soon as the Constitution was submitted to the representatives of the states for ratification. The document itself is unique in that for the first time in the history of the world men sat down together and drew up a constitution which was submitted to the people for signature. Written provisions assured passage of bills over a President's veto by a two-thirds majority of Congress; habeas corpus and attainder; amendment of the Constitution; no religious test as qualification for office. It is a marvelous framework for democracy. More marvelous it is that the first reaction of the people to it was to make it more democratic. They said in effect, "You have not guaranteed us our liberties. We fought for liberty. We want set down in black and white an assurance of that liberty for ourselves and posterity."

So it was that the Bill of Rights, stating explicitly the liberties of the individual, came into existence. The right set forth in the Constitution to amend that Constitution in order to extend democracy was acted upon two years later. The majority of all amendments to the Constitution since that time have been in the direction of greater democratic rights for the people.

From the first, however, there were certain barriers to democracy, which were by no means swept away by our Constitution. For instance, if today we have corporate wealth strongly entrenched behind reactionary and undemocratic laws, a hundred years ago we had slave traffic, and before that bonded servants. In other words our democracy was not a gift. It wasn't even a bargain. We fought a revolution for it. We fought a civil war for it. We even fought the first great world war under the illusion that we were fighting for it. And before that—about 1898—democratic freedom-loving Americans declared war against Spain in order to free what they had heard were the oppressed Cubans and did then and there free them. (Only, as we later found, to deliver them hog-tied into the hands of Wall Street.) Meanwhile the enemies of democracy as the mass of Americans see them—our money and special privilege group—are no sooner displaced from one position than they take up their stand in another.

To cite a few recent illustrations of what I mean: After the Supreme Court of the United States voided convictions on handbill ordinances existing in various cities, which were used almost entirely against groups promulgating ideas at variance with our "vested interests," arrests continued under new guises, such as for littering the streets. It was necessary for the Supreme Court to make a second ruling, extending and clarifying its first ruling. Freedom of communication, the court ruled —even if it happened to be the poor man's press in the form of leaflets —was superior to the cleanliness of the streets.

If liberty, and the liberty to own property, were synonymous to some people one hundred and fifty years ago, they certainly are not to most Americans today—as Herbert Hoover can well testify. In a career singularly marked by error, perhaps his greatest blunder—and one which he will not soon commit again in public print—was to interpret liberty in the old Roman sense of the liberty of the privileged classes. He reflected the opinions of the financial minority, which feels it is its inalienable right to go on piling up profits without regard for the hardship worked on the majority. According to the group for which Hoover spoke, the threat to corporate wealth is the threat to liberty, and liberty does not extend to the right of the workingman to strike against the corporations. That, we have reason to know, they define as syndicalism, and it is actionable in Hoover's State of California (as well as others) under the Criminal Syndicalism Act. This act is used in California to curb unions by big farmers, by growers' and shippers' associations.

The 1934 report of General Pelham Glassford, Federal Conciliator sent into California agricultural regions, reads: "After more than two months of observation and investigation in Imperial Valley, it is my conviction that a group of growers have exploited a 'communist' hysteria for the advancement of their own interests; that they have welcomed labor agitation, which they could brand as 'red,' as a means of sustaining supremacy by mob rule, thereby preserving what is so essential to their profits—cheap labor; that they have succeeded in drawing into their conspiracy certain county officials who have become the principal tools of their machine."

Was anything ever heard from Mr. Hoover—for that matter, from any of the corporate crowd—on the suspension of civil liberties of lettuce pickers of California, of the throttling of democracy by Governor Chandler in sending state troops into Harlan County in the absence of disorder, of the illegal barring of Negroes in Oklahoma from registering to vote?

The record of attempted exercising of civil liberties is marked with blood. It is not the man with money to hire a lawyer whose civil rights are abrogated, nor any individual who represents him who is cracked over the head when he expresses his political views. No representative of corporate wealth in America is ever held incommunicado for thirty-six hours for seeking redress of grievances. The blood is long dry on the violence that bought their liberty. They accept it complacently as their right, while denying the necessity of protecting such rights to others. Today, on the contrary, blood flows fresh and bright from the battles for free expression of agricultural workers, laundry workers, ten-cent-store clerks, waitresses, Southern mill workers, who take the place of black slaves. In sum it is a new set of obscure people, unimportant people, the lowly who do not count, who have risen and who, more and more of them, are rising up to ask for their liberties under the Bill of Rights.

The people whose rights are invaded are obscure. They are unable usually to pay for legal aid. If the press mentions their case, it is usually to libel or misrepresent. Protection of civil liberties is, however, universally available to those whose civil liberties are never invaded.

But as dark as things may look at certain times, the obscure people are liable to get their rights eventually. For you have only to dig into the history of this our American experiment to find out the reason why. It is you might say based on the fact that the mixture of peoples from all parts of Europe, Asia, and Africa, who found refuge from oppressive social conditions in their native lands, were vastly taken with not only the opportunities but the primary fellowship which ruled in the frontier areas of America, before the harsh class distinctions of Europe and elsewhere had had an opportunity of manifesting themselves here. In other words they were permitted a "taste" of what freedom from economic oppression plus the friendship or, if not that, at least the easy tolerant membership, of workers and adventurers of their own social and economic level could mean. To a degree unknown to them previously they became "sold" on the idea or possibility of democracy—its workability—false or true.

Hence if today we see the Bill of Rights trampled under foot by insolent officials, we also find various groups interested in preserving and promulgating these basic rights. I say promulgating, because a bill has just been passed in New York State—over a hundred and fifty years after the writing of the Bill of Rights—which requires exercises in all public schools in the state to teach the meaning of the Bill of Rights. Also the American Bar Association has launched an educational program providing for widespread dissemination of information concerning our constitutional liberties "to the end that violations thereof may be the better recognized and proper steps taken to prevent and correct them." Other steps in the same direction are the Civil Liberties Unit of the Department of Justice, and the Senate Civil Liberties Committee headed by LaFollette—out of whose investigation grew the LaFollette Oppressive Labor Practices Act, now pending in the House. There is also the long-established American Civil Liberties Union.

However, even today—owing in part no doubt to errors in our educational system, as well as to the gradual influence of our corporate-wealth class, anxious to maintain their financial supremacy at the expense of any or all, on our press, our pulpit, radio, moving pictures, advertising, and the perfection of the modern propaganda mechanism—many are totally ignorant of the wide latitude of their constitutional liberties, and easily allow themselves to be intimidated by arrogant officials and bullying police officers. I myself have seen men chased off the streets by armed guards without protest on the part of anyone, pickets bullied and harassed, union meetings broken up, groups with unpopular opinions dispersed—all without any indication from the people so bullied and mistreated that they were being denied their constitutional rights.

But in any program of teaching the Bill of Rights, the first to be schooled should be our officials. Our Constitution excuses no one. Officials in many parts of the country, and particularly at the behest of the corporations seeking to undermine the rights of the individual, today arrest persons for distribution of handbills—and that after the Supreme Court has upheld their rights so to do. After a second ruling extending and clarifying the right of the individual to distribute handbills, local police still made arrests. The police and departments of law claimed ignorance of decisions rendered by the highest tribunal of their land. But if ignorance of the law is no excuse for the individual, why should it be for officials? If fined or jailed for false arrests, perhaps those bodies might widen their legal horizons.

Yet, the mass of the people of the United States still believe in liberty, as they have well demonstrated. Once a case is stripped of misrepresentation and put before the people as naked fact, as was Mooney's, the people are genuinely stirred to do something. Indeed, as I have shown, we well know the capacity of the American people for indignation can be very great. However, we also know today the capacity of our American corporate wealth, now solidly unified in its purpose to control and rule America, to distort facts when the truth threatens dividends. Today as many times in the past it is to their interest to mislead the public on issues, and for a large part they have been able to do so. Setting their own narrow interpretation on liberty, they oppose to it the word *license* as appropriately descriptive of opinions differing from theirs.

Today they are ready to extend freedom of opinion only to such persons or groups as reflect their views. But the Okie, the Communist, the isolationist, the man who seeks to draft wealth along with man power, the man who opposes conscription altogether—expression of opinions by such men as these is seen as a perversion of liberty. However, in times of crisis there has always been a movement to suspend the liberties of the mass; and the excuse given now, as in the last war, is that we can preserve our liberties only by abrogating them.

In this connection I would like to quote Mr. Grenville Clark, a writer in the *Bill of Rights Review,* who curiously enough advocates, as a method of preserving our free institutions, such measures as the repeal of the Johnson Act; permission for sale at moderate cost of our most modern planes to the Allies (this was written before France's capitulation); stopping of exports of tin, rubber, and copper to Russia; doubling of our merchant ships and allowing these ships to be sold or chartered to the Allies at reasonable terms; also by beginning public discussion "as to the advisability of governmental grants to the Allies so that, when they are needed, public opinion may be formed and the Congress can act quickly." Let this question relate to outright grants, not loans. *For what is the use of piling up new debts that we know*

cannot be repaid? Which causes me, for one, to ask: Does freedom of
assemblage rest on loans or outright grants to Britain? Is the right of a
speedy trial at the mercy of the repeal of the Johnson Act? Are we in
danger of search and seizure unless we prepare public opinion for
outright grants to Britain—our non-democratic and wholly imperialist
neighbor? It is regrettable that the first issue of a splendid publication
dedicated to the extension of constitutional liberties should have included an article by one who has so little faith in the durability of democracy. I cannot but believe that democracy will outlive many Mr.
Clarks, and there is little to substantiate the doctrine that its survival
depends upon sending merchant ships to Britain, whether on tick or
for spot cash or merely for the glory of the rescue.

Charles Beard views the preservation of civil liberties as quite as important in times of stress as in a world at peace. He demands ironically,
"Why should anyone worry about civil liberties? Are not the people
who cry aloud in the name of liberty very often noisy churls who would
not practice it if they had the power of government? Are not most of
them obscure persons of such slight importance that it matters little
whether they are in jail or not?"

But, he continues, all we hold noblest and best in American civilization rests upon civil liberty. Sweep away this civil liberty, and popular
government would perish.

Before we save someone else as a measure to preserve our liberties,
let us start by preserving them at home. There is enough to save here.
In 1939 we find Mayor Hague of Jersey City censoring meetings *before*
they are held and prohibiting them on the grounds that something
might be said which would produce disorder. "With the never ending
audacity of elected persons," as Walt Whitman describes the Mayor
Hagues, that official was able to impose such undemocratic concepts on
a whole city.

But the Supreme Court of the United States—often a bulwark for
democracy although traditionally the last stronghold of vested interest
—read Mr. Hague a lesson on the Bill of Rights.

But even in a now liberal Supreme Court we find, coming from a
Justice with a long record of liberalism back of him, such decisions as
the Flag Salute ruling, requiring children to salute the flag, for the
purpose of promoting loyalty and morale. Since voluntary rather than

compulsory salute has served us well for five generations, as has been pointed out, why should it now be necessary to resort to coercion of young children, even to the extent of overriding their religious scruples?

In lower courts it has often happened that, although the Constitution states that witnesses may be sworn in either by affirmation or by swearing on the Bible, or both, testimony from persons refusing to swear on the Bible has been thrown out or discredited on that ground solely. Despite the religious freedom promised in America, we also find President Cleveland threatening to send troops into Utah unless the Mormons cease practicing polygamy.

The article of the Constitution providing for extradition of persons accused of crimes from states where captured to the state having jurisdiction over the crime, has often been broken in the name of tolerance and common sense. Governors have sometimes refused to sign extradition papers for persons who have run away from Georgia chain gangs, or who have been arrested to serve out sentences for crimes committed years before. This humane act has often been lauded by individuals, who feel that the exemplary life led by the person wanted in another state entitles him to asylum.

In Rhode Island, where the Constitution was not ratified until 1790, and then only by the narrow margin of thirty-four to thirty-two, police censorship of motion pictures goes on without effective contest.

If Rhode Island was late in ratifying, Connecticut, Massachusetts, and Georgia waited until the sesquicentennial of the Bill of Rights before they ever thought of ratifying it. This coincided with the time when members of a pacifist preacher's family in Atlanta, Georgia, were arranging to have him tucked away in a state insane asylum because of his pacifist activities. It also coincided with the action of the district court of Massachusetts in sending to a state training school children of Jehovah's Witnesses as habitual school offenders for refusing to salute the flag on religious grounds.

The growth of industrial unionism, to meet the new industrial centralization, has caused reactionaries in fright to seize new weapons for the destruction of basic rights and to erect new barricades between the public and its Constitution. American employers of great masses of men have largely conceived of labor liberty as the inalienable right of a man to work ten to twelve hours a day at twenty-five cents an hour, and overtime at the same rate or merely for the joy of working. With industry organized for years, parallel unionism—requiring each craft union to make its separate agreement with employers—became as outmoded as threshing with a flail. Centralization of industry, vast interlocking directorates, and holding companies which brought many industries under one management required co-ordination on a grand scale. But industry—as well as craft unionism—has consistently opposed a like move on the part of labor. Labor had not merely one small employer who could be faced to fight. Industrial monopolies had grown up with the sound of battle in their ears, and they had no intention of allowing labor, without a fight, to encroach on their profits.

Extreme disparity between the bargaining power of the individual and that of his employer has been generally recognized by the public, by legislatures, and by the courts. In a decision of the Supreme Court, we find this statement: ". . . the proprietors of these establishments and their operatives do not stand upon an equality, and their interests to a certain extent are conflicting. The former naturally desire to obtain as much labor as possible from their employees while the latter are often induced by fear of discharge to conform to regulations which their judgment, fairly exercised, would pronounce to be detrimental to their health and strength. In other words, the proprietors lay down the rules and the laborers are practically constrained to obey them" (from a report of the National Labor Relations Board).

Louis D. Brandeis, in a report of the United States Commission on Industrial Relations (1916), says: ". . . the main objection, as I see it, to the large corporation is that it makes possible—and in many cases makes inevitable—the exercise of industrial absolutism. It is not merely the case of the individual worker against employer, which, even if he is a reasonably sized employer, presents a serious situation calling for the interposition of a union to protect the individual. It is the fact that we have the situation of an employer so potent, so well organized, with such concentrated forces and with such extraordinary powers of reserve and the ability to endure against strikes and other efforts of a union, that the relatively closely organized masses of even strong unions are unable to cope with the situation. . . . There must be a division not only of the profits, but a division of the responsibilities; and the men must have the opportunity of deciding, in part, what shall be their condition and how the business shall be run."

However, such statements, as fair and democratic as they are—and this is by no means an isolated instance of such judicial opinion—do not go with present-day American employers. On the contrary, we see Ford shutting down his plant some ten years later without any concern as to the hundreds of lives affected by such a decision. Food and clothing and housing went on the same for Henry as before; while, for many thousands of idle workers, radical changes in living were imposed by one man.

Even before this, in 1904, we saw the same determined working of the doctrine of individual liberty in the campaign of California fruit growers to induce cheap labor to come to the state. Ten thousand people were moved across the continent for $3,500, according to Carey McWilliams, the author of *Factories in the Fields*. The workers were worked a few months, and then turned loose to find their way back East, or starve.

The technique of coercion of employees by employers, in this new battle between democracy and wealth, has been worked out so thoroughly that it goes generally now under the name of the Mohawk Valley Formula. This was the name given it by its inventor, Mr. James H. Rand, Jr., of Remington Rand. First published in the *Labor Relations Bulletin* of the National Association of Manufacturers, it was summarized in a N.L.R.B. Report. Here it is briefly:

1. Label the union leaders as "agitators"; conduct a forced balloting in the plant to ascertain strength of the union, then misrepresent the strikers as a small minority imposing their will upon the majority; disseminate propaganda to the press, falsely stating the issues involved; threaten to move the plant; organize a Citizens' Committee.

2. Cause the community in which the agitation occurs to mass press, legal, and political weapons against imagined violence.

3. Call mass meeting of citizens to co-ordinate "public" sentiment against the strike.

4. Bring into the community—its strike area—a body of armed guards furnished by private military establishments organized to furnish such hired mercenaries to corporations in order to intimidate the

strikers—and order these to use their newly acquired authority to the limit.

5. Heighten the demoralizing effect of this by a back-to-work movement publicized by a pro-corporation press, an intimidated ministry, the anti-labor opposition of the police, the local sheriff, and what not else, and you have an anti-strike atmosphere calculated to convince strikers that their cause is hopeless. The general public, which knows nothing of all this, is then strengthened in the belief that the majority of the workers wish to resume work.

6. When a sufficient number of employees have fallen for back-to-work hokum, a large area around the plant is roped off—protected by the local police.

7. The opening is then theatrically staged with speeches and an American flag-raising.

8. When a moderate number of strikers have been induced to return, capitalize on the seeming demoralization of the strikers still out by continuing the show of police force.

9. Close this total barrage on the theme that plant is at full operation, however false this may be. Poverty and starvation will eventually do the rest.

The current concern among industrialists as to whether unions are democratic is an extension of the old Mohawk Valley Formula. In this struggle between unions and corporations—truly a battle to decide the strength of democracy—we find a thousand men and women and children forcibly deported from a lumber town in California. Why? Several hundred members of a C.I.O. union were on strike. With their families they sought refuge in a near-by town. The attorney-general of California refused to restore them to their homes, or to prosecute their assailants.

In southeastern Missouri, over a thousand sharecroppers took to the road when they were evicted from their homes, and threatened violence was narrowly averted.

In New Mexico, two men are serving forty-five- to sixty-year sentences for merely being present at a riot in Gallup wherein the sheriff was shot.

In New Jersey, Vice-Chancellor Berry, when granting an injunction, made the astounding announcement that free speech is a "qualified Constitutional Right" inferior to the "absolute right of acquiring and possessing property." This opinion was expressed in restraining the Furniture Workers' Union from distributing circulars and picketing stores purchasing from an anti-union company.

Still, and despite all the holes that have been shot in them, we have our "democratic institutions." We have, or rather are supposed to have, freedom of speech, of the press, of religion, of assembly. And whether we have had them or not to the degree that we might have had them (and we have not), most of us agree that they have worked out fairly well in practice in the past, under less advanced conditions of knowledge. Do they work now?

Also we have a system of "checks and balances." Whom do they check and whom do they balance?

The customary way to find out is the hard way—by examining each carefully and analyzing its mechanism. All this ever succeeds in doing is to produce a mountain of theoretical abstractions which add up to nothing.

There is a much easier way. Look at the results.

Who is going to rise up in meeting and tell us that it is the will of the majority of Americans that we should destroy our forests and fields and crops, and hoard food by the billions of pounds and bushels, while every other American child is born into a family on relief?

How can such a condition be democracy? Is it not obvious that, if every adult has a vote (and of course millions don't have), and such conditions exist, the vote is for one reason or another ineffective?

In the past two years four major mine disasters, "entirely preventable by proper mine inspection and proper management," according to John L. Lewis, have taken a toll of 1,538 lives. Is that democracy? Is it not clearly the result of the miners', who know about mines and have to face the dangers, being denied any voice in the operation of mines?

In a letter to the Hearst newspapers, H. L. van Tynne writes:

"I see the spiritual body of America in back of politics, good and bad. I see the great idea of individual rights and liberties as opposed to the divinity of the state idea. That is the soul of America."

Fine, Mr. van Tynne. But who is in effect the state? Have you asked yourself that? And isn't it, as far as the distribution of material things which really matter are concerned, just as divine here as elsewhere?

Replying to a correspondent who wants to know "Can a man eat his personal liberty?"—a good, intelligent, American question—a Hearst columnist writes:

"Millions of men have foregone food in order that not only they, but people still unborn, should enjoy personal liberty (the soldiers of Valley Forge, for instance)."

Have they? Wasn't it liberty to eat that they fought for primarily? Didn't they want the liberties of speech and assembly and press in order to insure themselves and their children this most fundamental of liberties? And have the "people still unborn" got what the men of Valley Forge fought to give them?

If certain people feel that this is un-American, I am sorry. It is realistic, and it is American enough for me. It belongs to the America I know.

The conditions of our national economy which I mentioned under "Scarcity and Plenty" have been pointed out again and again by the Technocrats and other "subversive" groups. But how often do you see and hear them in the newspaper and on the radio, under our "freedom of speech" and "freedom of the press"?

Once in a blue moon, perhaps, and then in a remarkably half-hearted manner. Why? Because the implications of them are revolutionary and those who own our newspapers and radio chains are the Sons and Daughters of No More American Revolutions. At first Howard Scott of Technocracy was taken up by our respectable universities. He was dropped like a hot potato when the political implications of his words—which he himself tries in vain to wish into thin air—were realized.

And now we are told that to speak the truth about America is to espouse "alien isms," from which at all costs our impressionable youth must be shielded. The president of Harvard tells us that "our present generation will go on being educated for social conditions in the future, which will not be unlike social conditions in the past."

Could Jefferson in his wildest nightmares have imagined that a leader of American higher education would ever make such a statement? The president of Harvard appears to have omitted from his acquisition of wisdom the study of history, which shows how the world changes. It changes by steady continuity and also, at periodic intervals, by jumps to something new: the water gradually heats, then changes to steam.

Such a complete change in kind, such a jump forward, is implied by what the Technocrats tell us about the present state of America. But if this makes the Technocrats alien—if giving the Americans the food they grew instead of throwing it away is alien—then evidently I must be Chinese.

What is throughly alien to the American spirit is, on the contrary, the present orgy of prejudice against this opinion and that opinion, the attempt on every hand to suppress those who do not think as the big business minority thinks. Why should we concern ourselves, anyhow, about whether an opinion is "alien" in its origin or not? We are all aliens in this country except the Indians, and they originally hopped over from Russia, which perhaps explains why they are Red. The founding fathers were not too proud to base our Constitution on the ideas of the "alien" Rousseau, or to work with the "alien" Tom Paine to mold it. If we are not big enough to consider all ideas, wherever they come from, and take what is good from them and reject the bad, then we are not worth two cents. If we stuck to our Constitution and the rights of man therein expressed, we would do so.

All our business leaders are attempting is to build a second feudal China, a mandarin society, instead of building our Constitution. We pander to the mere vanity of the great millionaires who do not need their billions but say: "You think you're as good as we are—we'll show you." In a short while, at this rate, we shall just have a few Sons of Heaven in their palaces, with all the rest of the mere coolies without the walls. But there is so much wealth that we cannot let a small group have it. To deprive anyone, for any reason, of basic needs for living in this age is fantastic.

I do not cast lustful eyes on the billions controlled by Mr. Morgan when I say that technology has brought us to the necessity of social change. I don't want his billions or anyone else's. It isn't a question of my desire or Howard Scott's desire or Earl Browder's desire, but of nature's command.

Democracy is at stake here because you cannot by any known means make the masses of the people indefinitely submit to want in the midst of plenty, and if you don't let them have their share of the wealth by democratic means they will eventually take it by violent means. All history proves that. Nature's way of making these changes has generally been violent revolution. Whether or not we can make the change like intelligent human beings, by rich and poor sitting around a table and blueprinting a society of plenty, is the test of our democracy.

Surely it must be obvious that if the majority of our people had effective democracy the change would come peacefully and quickly. The ordinary American wants neither to be hungry nor to fight against his brother. Give him just once the power to vote on what shall be done with our "surpluses" of food—and that will be one time when it won't be necessary to sit up late listening to election returns. It is true that at the present stage of development only 3 per cent of men do any original thinking, while 22 per cent can be taught by the 3 per cent, and 75 per cent are largely controlled by instinct and can only be led. But it does not take original thinking for a man to know he is hungry, and that his babies are crying out for milk which is being thrown into the sea.

Why is our democracy inefficient? First and foremost because the mass of our people are deliberately kept in ignorance about the realities of their country's present condition, about the new potentialities discovered by science, and about the changes that have to be made in order to distribute the potential wealth.

If they do get wind of the extent of our present system's inefficiency, they are told: "Yes, indeed. These little maladjustments are unfortunate. But our knowledge of how to distribute has not quite kept abreast of our knowledge of how to produce."

Utter, unmitigated nonsense. People need food and clothes and houses: they produce them out of the materials at hand in order that they should have them. Could anything be simpler? The truth is that we know perfectly well how to distribute wealth. What we don't know —what nobody will ever know—is how to distribute it with anything approaching equity and still add to the ducks'-eggs of the millionaires. For the ducks'-eggs only grow out of scarcity. But that is what the mass of the people must not be allowed to find out.

Let us, very briefly, blueprint a democracy that would be effective today. Not a perfect, utopian democracy, for there can be no such thing. But a democracy which, admitting that it must always suffer from natural limitations, would not suffer also from glaring man-made limitations. A democracy, then, which is not merely political, and which gives the people power to change the social structure when it is worn out as well as to make changes within the existing structure. That is nothing more than the Declaration of Independence and Bill of Rights call for.

In order to do these things intelligently and only when they are necessary—for nobody wants constant upheavals—it must be an *informed* democracy. Notice that the first thing the avowed enemies of democracy, the Hitlers and Mussolinis and Francos, do is to cut off all possible sources of accurate information.

How can the people be informed, fully and accurately? Only by the organs of information—mainly newspapers and radio—being placed in the hands of the people; which means being taken out of the hands of small moneyed groups and of advertisers. Every newspaperman knows that at present news is presented, exaggerated, or suppressed according to the interests of advertisers and owners. But don't ask your newspaperman acquaintance for confirmation of that, unless you know him well. He has his job to hold, and jobs have a strange amount to do with freedom of speech.

In the case of Senator LaFollette, there was a national conspiracy of silence inaugurated against him. No matter what he said the papers reported *nothing*. The same now applies to Howard Scott and to Earl Browder. Browder spoke in Los Angeles to over 10,000 people, and the papers did not even mention it. The last time Scott spoke in Los Angeles he addressed 10,000 people. After his lecture hundreds of people climbed up on the stage to greet him—and yet the next day no one paper carried a word about his talk. The same thing has happened to me on many occasions in some of the larger Eastern cities. And I notice how very little is said any more about Steinbeck—now that the social import of his book *The Grapes of Wrath* is really understood and known.

Just the same, full and accurate information about everything comes first. Hence this democracy of ours must start at home. The citizen must have power not only to put one of two men in the White House, but power in those things that are of immediate concern to him.

That means power, first, to demand his right to a job, to a self-respecting place in the social mechanism. (Also he must have the freedom to do no work, and the freedom to starve that by the basic law of nature goes with it.) Democracy that in our day doesn't offer every man a job, however humble, plus the limitless opportunity to fit himself by education for something better, is not democracy, for a man with no place in the social structure is not a man. This is not asking the state to "baby" weaker citizens. On the contrary, it is asking the state to make men of millions who today, because they are social outcasts from birth, tend toward futility, irresponsibility, and crime.

Second, it means democratic power at the point of labor, so that each citizen can assure himself of a house and clothes and necessary food and medical care and holidays and education for his children in return for his labor; and so that each may have a voice in management of the farm or factory or mine or office where he works. You cannot have democracy politically if you have a Fuehrer-principle in business and industry such as exists in America today. Theoretically a man is free to quit a job where conditions are bad and go elsewhere, but in fact all our major industries are now monopolies run by chambers of the leading millionaires, and there is almost nowhere else to go. Every working man and woman knows that. As for "democratic control" through shareholders, this is a long-exploded illusion. The ordinary small shareholder is just as helpless in the hands of the Sons of Heaven as the worker is. There remains the privilege of voting for a representative at Washington, but the Sons of Heaven are interested also in that matter and

> "Whatever happens, they have got
> The million bucks, and he has not."

In place of his political vote offer the average American a vote at his place of work, the problems of which he has a chance to understand and is vitally interested in. There is no doubt which he would take. But of course he should have both. Democracy in our time implies nothing else. And the cardinal point of the American credo is that without democracy life ceases to have any interest. Without it we might as well stop bothering.

Now we are being told by our Sons of Heaven that the people of our democracy "want" to take sides in another European dogfight.

What a magnificent contradiction in terms! The people of a "democracy" going into a war which can profit them nothing! What kind of democracy is that? Do our Princes of Heaven now tell us that the human race is a race of suicides?

Haven't we enough trouble of our own to put right without going to start more trouble somewhere else?

The Sixty Families of America had better sit down and do some realistic thinking about that, and do it quick.

Laugh or weep or look the other way as you will, Sixty Families. You still have the choice of accepting facts and adjusting yourselves to them reasonably and peacefully.

You may not have it much longer. The kettle is very near the boil.

CHAPTER THIRTEEN

What Are the Objectives of American Finance?

TO MAKE clear and interesting what is involved by this certainly ponderous title I shall have to begin by asking what is the object of any human being who desires to live and grow? Is it not to obtain the things that will permit him to satisfy his desire—that is, food, clothing, shelter, protection, warmth, advancement among his kind, or anything you care to name in connection with the desires or the necessities of any social being? The problem broadens not a little when you think of the so-called individual as not exactly a real individual but one-half of a sex mechanism that involves not only its other half, male or female, but the results of such a mechanism, which as everybody knows are children or, to use that much nobler word, progeny. And, in addition to that, the state or society or social organism in which they must all move if they multiply and endure. And once you make that fact clear you have the wants of the individual not single or double any more but treble and even more (when you think of relatives and society) as he or she proceeds from infancy to death.

The objects of a child, male or female, are food, clothing, toys, entertainment, and the desire, unless it is trained differently, to possess something which it has not but which another individual or nature may happen to have. The same is true of the young man and the young woman until marriage, when they begin to repeat what their forebears repeated before them: to wish to possess all the things that will make their new arrangement—the family—a "go." In other words, the male and female half of the mechanism thus joined want some things for themselves, but as much and sometimes more for their children. And then, as the complicated organism proceeds, you find the children wanting things, not only for themselves, but for their parents and even for some of their relatives. And collectively considered, those can certainly be called the objects of the finances of that social organism.

However, in our modern state, when the male of one of these mechanisms finds himself gifted in the matter of acquiring money, which is the medium by which some things (not *all* by any means) can be procured, he usually finds that his path is smoothed by that medium which can be exchanged for so many other things. And unless he has been instructed in the history of the race and the development of the modern thing called a State or Society (which is not often) he acquires, and quite naturally from what he sees going on about him, the thought, and pretty soon the conviction, that money is the answer to nearly everything that is worth while in this world.

For, as a rule, he sees that the possession of it opens the way to preferment in many forms. With it, if he is so gifted as to acquire a considerable quantity of it, he can hire labor and even brains in many forms, to work for him and help him for what he pays them, to make more money. Lawyers will provide him the law that he does not know. Physicians will use their years of study to rescue him from illness. Men with schemes to make money, but without the necessary money in hand, will approach him with the purpose of interesting him in return for what they can get—sharing their discoveries or schemes with him. Politicians will open the doors of legislatures to him, and for a return in money to themselves, will translate some of his plans or schemes into legal enactments. He can, with their aid, and those of the paid representatives of the people, obtain rights or franchises to do or control this, that, or the other—build railways, acquire oil lands, dig wells, establish telephone and telegraph lines, buy up sailing vessels or steamships, or get hold of a large variety of patents for things which the public desires and must have, such as machines and implements of all kinds from a coffee grinder or a plow to a typewriter or a moving-picture mechanism or a broadloom.

And with these patents or franchises or rights in his name (or that of the corporation which he chooses to organize and hide behind) he becomes, at last, what we know today to be a financier—a man of vast financial equipment and even genius; someone who like Mr. Morgan or Mr. Rockefeller, Mr. Mellon or any other you choose to list, controls not only patents and banks and railroads and lawyers and politicians, but newspapers and educators and religious representatives in pulpits.

For he is an example of that strange arrangement which according to our modern psychologists holds in nature, but which man did not invent and which he does not appear to be able to change. . . . And that is that 3 per cent of the people born in the world, and *only* 3 per cent, have the amazing ability to do what we call "Think." It may not be, and as I see it, positively *is* not, anything which an individual consciously does. He is, as science can easily show today, a reacting mechanism which chemically and physically reacts to certain changing phases of his environment. When it gets too hot he moves to a cooler spot if there is one. But that, as you can see, is not a thought but a reaction. If a man starts for him with a knife, and he is physically hale and swift and a chair is handy, the chair, not he, will suggest to him that he seize it and prevent the man with the knife from doing real harm. But that is not *thinking*—that is reacting. For if there were no chair he would not think of any chair. And if he had never seen the man with a knife, or never heard of one descending on another in this fashion, it would not occur to him that the man intended him any harm. In other words, there would be no thought on that subject.

But the point of all this is merely to make clear that, thinking or not, there are just 3 per cent who are gifted with the reactions toward life and circumstances which permit them to guide themselves and others, not always to their own ultimate advantage or that of these others, through this labyrinth called living. I am thinking of the Rockefellers and the Morgans, the Caesars and Napoleons, as well as of the Galileos, Newtons, Faradays, Edisons, Wrights—and also of the Buddhas, Platos, of Jesus, Mohammed, and others. At the same time, as the psychologists seem fairly well prepared to show, there are 22 per cent more of all the population that are capable of understanding, carrying out, executing (if they are progressive, for they are not always so) the discoveries, instincts, and understandings of the 3 per cent—making them work, as it were. This 22 per cent includes, of course, the educators, artists, musi-

cians, poets, playwrights, actors, dancers, soldiers, doctors, lawyers, legislators, and indeed the studious and skilled workers in all fields; but, at
that, leaving the 75 per cent to fill the world—the young, the aged, the
feeble or ill, and the stupid, but not necessarily totally incompetent by
any means—perhaps those who are not financially, and more important
still, acquisitively, constituted.

And it is this arrangement which man himself did not make, but
which none the less appears operative in nature, that eventually—perhaps always, perhaps not (human society is not really old enough to let
us know—ants and bees suggest something else again)—creates an unbalance all too frequently resulting in internal crises: uprisings, rebellions, changes of government, etc. You have only to think of the endless
rebellions of the subject peoples of Rome, of our American Revolution,
of the French Revolution, the Russian Revolution, the Mexican Revolution against Diaz to know what I mean. The 3 per cent plus the 22 per
cent have usually acquired too much of a given country's goods—its
powers, privileges, wealth, etc.—to permit the remaining 75 per cent to
endure. And, hence, revolt. This is always proclaimed unlawful by
those in power: for they never appear to grasp the fact that nature's
laws, which make for balance and proportion between all things in
nature—even classes and degrees of intelligence in society—are not
subject to their wishes or orders, but operate in spite of anything they
may feel, think, or do. For, as you can see for yourself, if you meditate
upon the matter a moment, the 3 per cent and the 22 per cent are in-
escapably beholden to the 75 per cent not only for their wealth and
power and fame but for their very achievements, because without this
group these other two classes would be meaningless. For it is obvious
that if the 75 per cent were removed, the remaining 25 per cent would
lack that vast body called the public, for whom, by whom, through
whom all of these so profitable things with which the 25 per cent busies
itself and by which it rises would not be. For in this world there is not
only the creator and builder, but the *consumer,* the *ultimate consumer,*
for whom as well as through whom all of these things that make for
the distinction of the 3 per cent and the 22 per cent are to be done. If
you doubt that, just ask yourself: "Where would the railway magnate
be without his passengers and his freight, to say nothing of his laborers? And again where would be the corporate owner of the mines

of coal, gold, lead, silver, iron and copper, tin or whatever, without the laborers as well as the ultimate users of these things in whatsoever form they are ultimately molded?" Take our giant telephone monopoly and ask yourself where it would be without the millions and even billions with their desire to talk with each other—to tell each other that they are either sick, or well, or happy, or the reverse? Indeed, speaking of the monopolist in any field, his first requisite, if he is to be great and glorious, is the mass that needs, or at least can consume, what he has to offer—what he monopolizes. No mass, no monopoly—no financial titans.

And so, at long last, we get to the place where we are prepared to ask—if not answer fully—what should be the objective not alone of our American 3 per cent but of the 3 per cent in any country. If they must have each their mass, and their mass must have them and neither can do without the other, what are their obligations, if any? And if they do not acknowledge any—as for the sake of argument we may assume at least—then we can ask, What apart from any obligations to the mass are their objectives? Power, for power's sake? Or fame, for fame's sake? A rather silly question this, for without a mass to acknowledge the power of an individual or his fame, where is he? How is he to have any sense of either? For they must want this vast control for some reason or other.

The best way to answer that, seeing that it is not easy to interview them on the subject, the living or the dead, is to study their actions and observe how, having obtained great power and wealth, or what can be looked upon as major social control, they have done or are doing with these things. In this connection the citizens of America, at one stage or another of their history, have seen some amazing goings-on. Cornelius Vanderbilt I, for instance, truly the earliest of our great financiers and the founder of the immense railway system that dominated America and the East in his day, was content to live with his wife and his children for a period in a quite simple house in or near Washington Square, New York, and have her do the family cooking. He had no education in the modern school or university sense, although ever since his death any number of schools and universities have studied his instinctive actions and financial greed with the greatest care. When once he was asked whether he could flout the state law of New York by uniting two railways east and west of Albany without a franchise, and building a bridge to connect the same without a franchise, his answer was: "Haint I got the power?" And most certainly he had. For he could, as he himself said, "buy and sell the State Legislature any day." And he not only so said, but did.

But he was not the only one so to act by any means. The entire period in which he appeared, lived, and died was alive with what are now referred to in research books and histories as brigands of finance—also, more respectfully, robber barons. This group indulged themselves in the most untutored and fantastic forms of display. One need only study the "mansions," the estates, the receptions, entertainments and social goings-on generally of the so-called Four Hundred from 1840 to 1910 to know. These same years and the actions of the so-called giants have given rise to volume after volume of the most astonishing social nonsense, which you can read for yourself if you choose. Multi-millionaire after multi-millionaire, as fast as he arrived at that stage of wealth permitting of the application of that description, proceeded to indulge himself in mansions, servants of course, yachts, private railway cars, membership in the most exclusive clubs, a fifteen- or twenty-five-thousand-a-year box at the Opera in New York, a hunting lodge in the Adirondacks, etc., etc. In connection with these there followed of course, since there were wives and children, visits to England and the European continent in the hope as well as the determination on the part of these great magnates to contact royalty—the possessors of titles and of similarly accumulated masses of money outdating their own in the matter of years—in order to show them who was who in America; and incidentally that they were worthy rivals of these foreign social advantages and equipment, whatever the same might be. One peacock strutting in the presence of another.

And in consequence, and not before so very long either, international yacht cruises, with the hope of achieving thereby social intimacy with the equally ridiculous and fantastic nobility of England: having the honor, for instance, of racing the Prince of Wales somewhere on the high seas! There was the Diamond Horseshoe at the Metropolitan Opera House, so that the originals and their heirs would have some place to go where they could show themselves in all their luxury (the diamond tiaras, the diamond stomachers, the diamond cuff buttons) and of course be seen by the mass. The Hollywood première of today is all that is left of the high mental concept, by which you can know what I mean. (Incidentally, multi-millionaire carriages with two horses, a driver, two footmen, and harness glimmering with gold and silver.) There were of course—as there are today, but in a sadly modified form —the endless receptions in New York in the winter season, and at Newport, Bar Harbor, and other established resorts in summer. And always the great question of who was to marry whom—and naturally, in the country that boasted no titles of any kind, an eye toward the young nobles of such European lands as did. The most prized gems were English dukes and French princes, the daughter of a father worth one hundred or two hundred million being always of course the most eligible.

Whether by reason of ironic laughter or boredom or the growth of too many newer and rawer fortunes in America, plus the social unrest that was beginning to seize on the masses who were working in the mines and the fields with scarcely more than their daily bread, around 1907 this contest ceased and a new change of procedure came about. The showy mansion, the "Tandem," the Diamond Horseshoe, the international races, became decidedly *de trop*. Silence was now the word. Lack of ostentation. A quieter form of publicity which came with the fear of parading the enormous holdings of given individuals and groups. This was the period of the elder Rockefeller, who followed the first Vanderbilt and who could give $35,000,000 to a university or $250,000,000 to an educational foundation, but who would not pay more than a bare living wage to anyone if he could avoid it. Fame was confined to statistics, rumors to the financial pages of the papers, including the *Wall Street Journal*. And, of course, gifts for the completion of cathedrals in France or the erection of museums in Egypt or South Africa, or the providing of hospitals and universities for the Chinese, and occasionally for the Hindus. In fact, the first suggestion of a social obligation to the masses was that provided by Rockefeller, who confined his gifts to educational funds, research laboratories, and the like. It had not occurred to him then, as it did a few years later to his successors in the work of accumulating millions, that laboratories could prove the sources of even greater fortunes than he had ever dreamed of. Hence they followed not a little later. Need I mention the duPonts and controllers of General Electric, General Motors, and Mr. Mellon's University of Pittsburgh?

However, a thing that was coming into the picture at this time had more to do with the new trend than any other reason. It was the fact that American industrialists and their associate financiers, having prospered so, and organized their interlocking directorates or holding companies, now not only were in a position to control the resources of America, but were beginning to see that the as yet undeveloped resources of other lands were also suitable objects for their development and control. Oil for the lamps of China! It was Mr. Rockefeller who first found an enormous field for his Standard kerosene in that country. However, at the same time it rapidly became apparent to many that with the proper political and financial intrigue, it was also possible to enter Europe, Asia, Africa, and South America. Oil, as the Standard Oil Company discovered, was to be found in many places. Motor cars, tobacco, electrical equipment, improved American machines were to be manufactured and sold abroad; or if not that, these industries, these companies, could establish overseas branches in Germany, France, Turkey, Italy, the Argentine, Mexico, and where not else. And with the success of various of these ventures preceding the first great World War, as well as after it, there was brought into the mind of the American financier, his banker and diplomatic agent, the thought or conclusion that finance, money, once you have enough of it, is not a thing that need necessarily be confined to the country of its birth. It could travel and enter nations or small states hitherto unaware of its power or methods—and it could bribe or buy their statesmen or officials, acquire franchises for this or that, just as these had been acquired in America. And with money in such quantity as was now in their possession—never, never, never in any way to be divided with the American people or the land of their origin and opportunity—these franchises could be developed. And, if they became too powerful for the governments of these new lands in which they were seeking to entrench themselves, these same governments or their officials could be taken over, suborned, or made to do their biddings in so far as it was possible for them to do it.

I am discussing the objective of American finance, remember.

If you doubt what I say, consider Chile, its copper and nitrates, and the Guggenheim family; Bolivia and the Standard Oil Company; Paraguay and the Royal Dutch Shell; and the great three-year war in the Chaco (the green hell) that these two countries conducted in the years 1931–1933, which cost these two companies jointly about $600,000,000 and the lives of 100,000 men—soldiers employed by their respective armies. General Motors and Mr. Ford opened their plants in Germany. The Standard Oil Company, in association with England, took over the oil fields of Rumania. The American Tobacco Company, after a number of sessions with a minor English tobacco company, decided to join hands with it to supply America and the British Empire with tobacco.

What developed finally with this, of course, was understandings and conferences between American, British, French, German, and other groups or phases of finance in the important countries of the world. With this went the problem of their protection, by either their native land or the land which each or both had invaded. And for that, of course, in case of international financial quarrels, both armies and navies were necessary. Hence armies and navies to threaten Mexico, China, England, Japan, Germany, anybody and everybody who chose to interfere with any English or American corporation. So, even before the first great World War, you had the picture of American and British and German and other agencies of finance invading various alien countries with the money of their native lands; and once there, employing the cheapest labor, charging the highest prices, competing sometimes even with their own native land by underselling themselves in their native lands.

Yet, at the same time, in case of any quarrel concerning or danger to their property anywhere, expecting and calling upon their native country to help. them. English warships arriving in Venezuela in 1895 to demand payment of loans that were made to Venezuela in order to secure an interest in the asphalt lakes. The Guggenheims exacting international intervention on the part of America in connection with the passing determination of Chile to seize their copper mines or make them pay better wages. The Standard Oil Company calling upon the United States to protect its interests in Manchuria at the time that Japan seized that country, in Mexico, in Central America, etc.

The only eventual object—if one looks acquisitive international finance squarely in the eye—being the eventual domination of the world by some one international financial group, with so-called nations as mere local forms or puppets, under their control, but with the avowed purpose to do what?

Pay better wages to all the laborers in the world wherever? Advance the education or technical training of the millions here in America or England or elsewhere? Build them better houses? Provide state medicine for the millions of the underpaid and sick? State hospitalization? Assured labor for those able to work? Old-age pensions for those who have worked and are no longer able to do so? Food, clothing, shelter, education for the children of widows or the orphans of the dead? Establish peace and plenty for all? What do you think?

Do you truly think their hearts or minds are touched or appealed to by any such objectives? If so, study the newspapers and radio speakers of our day. Or are they blazing with that same old individualistic vanity which causes them to look on private and personal possessions and supreme power as the be-all and end-all of human existence? Imagine!

If you look at the first great World War in which 40,000,000 people died from starvation or other causes, and after which America as well as Europe sank into twenty years of poverty and fear—and realize that it was nothing more than a quarrel between the financial leaders of England, Germany, and such other powers as England could influence, as to which was to have the financial domination of Europe and Africa and Asia, and nothing more and nothing less—you can judge for yourself. There was no Jewish question in 1914 and there is none now in so far as these warriors are concerned. Neither is democracy, human liberty, nor any other truly and socially respectable thing being fought for. Power, wealth, dominance for one or the other is all that is sought. And England cares no more for America than she does for Germany or India. She is out for herself and so are our American financiers. But not the American people.

This latest war that is raging in Europe is about just that: the determination of Germany, after twenty years of sufferings due to its defeat in the first war, to recapture at least some of the power that it once dreamed of obtaining. Determination of England, which has one quarter of the world—and when I say England, of course I mean its financiers, not its undernourished masses—to see that not one acre of its quarter of the world is yielded or lost to its rival financial mechanism that will control Germany if Germany wins. And although, as you know, it prates of saving civilization and democracy, it has no such purpose in mind, for it is a financial oligarchy of the worst type and, as I have shown in another chapter of this book, it has never been anything but that. Victorious, it does not intend to free the 380,000,000 Hindus whom it causes to live on a cent or two a day; nor does it intend to do anything for the blacks of its various colonies in Africa and elsewhere, who at this time slave for a mere pittance to grow its sheep and wool, its tobacco, its coffee, its cattle and rubber, any more than it intends to improve the condition of the working man in Canada or Australia or British South Africa, or British Guiana or England, or Honduras, or anywhere in its quarter of the world.

It has not done so and it will not do so because, as I have shown, the British Empire is built on the theory of the dominant 3 per cent whose obligation is to no one but themselves. And as for our American financiers, if you can judge by what they do and not what they say, you can see that their objective is precisely the same. We have, as we all know, "our" Mr. Morgan who at this hour dominates American finance, and yet is co-operating as closely as one human being can co-operate with another with the English House of Morgan (part and parcel of the American house)—and whose ideals, as shown by the history of the House of Morgan, here and in England, are those of the English royalists. And, mind you, out of these close ties comes pressure on us to enter the war. The mass is not worth bothering about. It cannot do what the 3 per cent or the 22 per cent working together can do. So why bother with it? Let it die. Or if not that, give it just enough, the lowest possible wage always, to permit it to create for the 3 and the 22 per cent —never the 75 per cent—the things that you wish to manufacture and sell, and to buy at the highest possible prices (all the traffic will bear) what it has ready for sale. It wants no American flag except for the protection of its particular interests throughout the world. And it does not give a tinker's damn about the welfare of the people of any of the lands that it invades, and at the expense of whose labor, time, and necessity it wishes to prosper.

Does the world progress? The English ruling clique does not give a damn for that unless the said progress spells more money and power, and so grandeur, for it and its particular group. Such questions as progress and the welfare or happiness of the people as a whole it leaves to crack-brained theorists, such as Plato and Aristotle, Lao Tze, Confucius, Buddha, Jesus, St. Francis, Bacon and Samuel Johnson and Thomas More and Henry George and Edward Bellamy and Karl Marx and Lenin, and such tripe. After all, we live but once. Why should I not have everything for me? Why bother about you? Is not the greatest social aphorism in use in the world today "Let the devil take the hindmost"? And so it will remain unless and until the present and past-day objective of finance can be modified to include that great 75 per cent which through all time and up to this particular hour it has consistently and autocratically ignored.

CHAPTER FOURTEEN

Have English and American Finance Co-operated with Hitler to Destroy Democracy?

I DON'T KNOW how many people there are left in America who accept the noble idealism of public statements by political and business leaders and newspaper editors. If such there are, they will regard the question above propounded as preposterous on the face of it.

Still, the strange transatlantic romance between England and America remains to be explained. If England in its relations with us has given us so little cause to love it, what is this thing all about?

If we go back to essentials and put the terms of our proposition under the microscope, we can see who loves whom, and why.

We have already observed how little the term "England," as broadly used to describe the effective functioning of the Anglo-Saxon islanders in world affairs, involves the great majority of Englishmen. The great majority of Englishmen live in little gray houses and tenements on family incomes well below $1,000 a year—almost ignorant of the national, let alone the imperial, economic structure of which they are part; voting every few years for a party-nominated Member of Parliament who as like as not lives far outside the constituency and whom they may never see; concentrating almost everything they have on the pressing daily problem—the problem of getting enough to eat.

As far as effective realities go, "England" in world affairs means the propertied families who, because of the rent and interest and profit they derive from it, have a stake in England and the Empire: the one-half of one per cent of the population who get over 10 per cent of the total national income. These have something to defend on their own and their descendants' behalf; they defend it in what seems the most practical manner. Their method of defending it and increasing it is the policy of England.

Now if you say, What about the savings of the masses, what about their jobs, what about the wide distribution of stocks and shares: don't the mass of the people have these to defend?—I answer that, by Economist G. D. H. Cole's statistics, at least three out of four Englishmen die leaving no taxable property at all, and of the fortunate fourth nearly two-thirds leave less than $5,000. Also that not more than 1 or 2 per cent of the people have enough stocks and shares in any enterprise to give them the very smallest voice in its management and policy. Also that the notion that capital "creates" jobs (as if people would sit down and twiddle their thumbs if it were not for some magical marks on pieces of paper) has been exploded by Abraham Lincoln and every other man of plain horse-sense who ever examined it.

No, it is the one-half of one per cent of the English population who speak and act for England, because they have a tangible stake and because their money gives them the power. It is they who are the eastern partner—the partner carrying the club—in our strange transatlantic love affair.

Possession of wealth under the scarcity system places them automatically under the jurisdiction of certain laws by which they must act. The concept of human "liberty of action" and free will is, as we have seen, an illusion. Everything in nature functions according to the laws of its being. The poor man functions according to the elementary law of life, the law of hunger. The man of property—property that depends on maintaining scarcity for the mass without which there is no "value" —functions according to the law of money, which is that money must not lie "idle" but must "earn" more money.

Because of that law, the scarcity-dividend system at first sped the wheels of progress: profit was made out of one thing and was immediately invested in something else to make more profit. But after a time, since the mass never received enough wages to buy them more than a bare livelihood (I am still speaking of England, although the same is true of other lands), there necessarily came about a shrinkage in the profitable outlets at home for the accumulating hoard of capital.

The English masses wanted the products of new industries but had no cash to buy them. Hence the seizure of colonies to provide new outlets —and hence also the search beginning for capital outlets in every part of the world, colonial or not.

Hence, finally, the clash between all the different groups, each seeking outlets in the same finite world. The group that got the most money had the most power and was able to eliminate the smaller fry from the increasingly grueling race. So that there came about the last and greatest contradiction of the system—the formation of monopolies for the purpose of eliminating that very competition on which the system was based: a state of affairs obviously containing within it the seeds of disaster, as we plain and bewildered little animals discovered in 1929 and the years following. Trying to run a competitive world without competition is like trying to run a bathroom without any soap. It means dirty weather ahead.

But we have noticed how these reachings-out of capital into foreign countries, in order to find some way of turning dividends into still more dividends, formed combines and monopolies not only on a national but on an international scale, thereby producing such an extraordinary mass of contradictions that words and concepts such as "England" seemed to lose all meaning.

What is "England" today? Let us take a look at some of the men of wealth who for all practical purposes are "England," and see what the interests are that they call upon Englishmen to defend with their blood.

A good place to start is the Council of six business magnates appointed by the government in 1938 to co-ordinate the national armament effort for "England's" defense. Here are four of them:

Sir Geoffrey Clarke: Managing director of Telegraph and Maintenance, Ltd., which owns half the stock of Submarine Cable Company, Ltd., an affiliate of Siemens, the great German electrical trust. Former member of the Anglo-German Fellowship.

F. D'Arcy Cooper: Chairman of Unilever, Ltd., the giant soap and margarine trust, with a number of subsidiary companies in Germany and in what was Czechoslovakia. The Czech subsidiary, confronted with evidence that it had given $250,000 to the Sudeten German Party—Hitler's John the Baptist before the Advent—never denied it. Unilevers was a corporate member of the Anglo-German Fellowship, and the Fellowship's meetings were held in a room lent by Unilever House in London. Cooper was on the Fellowship's Council.

P. F. B. Bennett: Director of Imperial Chemical Industries, the Empirewide chemical monopoly, which has a working arrangement with Germany's I. G. Farbenindustrie chemical trust, shares ownership with it of several enterprises, and has $55,000,000 invested in it.

J. S. Addison: Managing Director of Courtaulds, Ltd., the artificial-silk trust, which has very close business connections with Germany's Vereinigte Glanzstoff Fabriken and Italy's "Snia Viscosa" with interchange of shares— and has its own factories in Japan.

So the Alice in Wonderland situation, which gets curiouser and curiouser as we look further into it, begins to take shape for us. "England" is at war with "Germany." The people of neither country have the smallest desire to fight each other. Of six Englishmen appointed to supervise the armament effort, four have business interests in Germany. They have in consequence, and quite naturally, been directly or indirectly connected with the Anglo-German Fellowship, a post-Hitler organization set up specifically to cultivate friendship with the Nazi regime. Now you begin to see why this was called the Cock-Eyed War.

A further glance at the pre-war membership of this Anglo-German Fellowship—it has presumably now been given an interment "for duration" in the interests of public decency—completes the bewilderment of the plain man on the sidelines. The members included twenty-eight Lords and twenty-seven Members of Parliament, among them Sir Thomas Moore, who said in 1933, "If I may judge from my personal knowledge of Herr Hitler, peace and justice are the key-words of his policy"; Sir Arnold Wilson, who reported in 1934 that "there is no militarism in Germany . . . we should study, adapt and adopt much of the German method"; Lord Redesdale, Guinness Stout magnate, father of Unity Mitford and father-in-law of British Fuehrer Oswald Mosley; Lord Londonderry, one of England's most powerful political and business figures, frequent host to Von Ribbentrop—and to Neville Chamberlain—and fellow-guest with Mussolini at Goering's "summer residence"; Lord Nuffield, England's Henry Ford; the Marquess of Lothian, late Ambassador to Washington; the Marquess of Carisbrooke, grandson of Queen Victoria. Lord Halifax, former Foreign Secretary, did not join but was the society's guest of honor.

Now hold your hats and we're off again. Among the London concerns—all with German interests—which were corporate members
of the Fellowship were the Lazard Frères', the Schroeders', and Guinness Mahon's banks; Firth-Vickers Stainless Steels, Unilevers, Thomas
Cook and Son, Combined Egyptian Mills, Dunlop Rubber Company.
And here are some other concerns which had one or more directors belonging to the Fellowship: Bank of England, Midland Bank, Lloyds
Bank, Barclays Bank, National Bank of Scotland, National Bank of
Australia, British Linen Bank, Ralli Brothers Bank, Coutts Bank, National Bank of Egypt; Commercial Union, London, London and Lancashire, Eagle Star, Phoenix, and Guardian Insurance Companies; Imperial Chemical, L.M.S. Railway, L.N.E.R. Railway, Shell Transport
and Trading, Anglo-Iranian Oil, Tate and Lyle (sugar trust), Hudson's
Bay Company, Distillers Company, Gas, Light and Coke Company;
P. and O. Steam Navigation, Birmingham Small Arms (Neville Chamberlain's family business), Imperial Airways, Thomas Firth and John
Brown (shipbuilding), William Beardmore, Consett Spanish Ore Company.

Whew! What a list! We have got there most of the great corporations
and trusts and big-money interests of the British Empire. But don't
get heated up and start calling these charming English gentlemen
names. They were pro-Nazi for good and sufficient reason. If they
didn't have private interests in Germany to be protected, they were
sympathetic with anyone who was willing to go the lengths of a Hitler
to hold in check what threatened their collective interests—the onsurge
of world democracy. If you had been in their shoes there is little doubt
that you, too, would have turned up at the Fellowship meetings at Unilever House, to heil the Fuehrer and plan how to create "better understanding" with Nazism.

Many of the same people, and for the same reasons, also belonged to
the Friends of Italy and the Friends of National Spain. When Mussolini was mustard-gassing the wretched Ethiopians, Lord Mottistone of
the Friends of Italy thus addressed the House of Lords:

On the one hand are millions of bloodthirsty tyrants [the Ethiopians] to
whom it is proposed to send arms, on the other the honorable and humane
army with 100,000 or 150,000 mouths to feed. . . . It is a wicked thing to

connive at sending arms to these cruel, brutal men while denying them to others who are playing an honorable part.

Observe the human animal cutting the coat of morality according to the cloth of material interest? Observe it again when Franco and Mussolini and Hitler's dive-bombers were butchering the almost defenseless Spaniards and gaily sinking British ships. Captain Cazalet, M.P., called Franco "the leader of our Cause today," while Sir Henry Page Croft, M.P., said: "I recognize General Franco to be a gallant Christian gentleman." Sir Patrick Hannon, M.P., a director of Chamberlain's Birmingham Small Arms, said:

Whatever critical attitude the people of the British Empire may feel impelled to take up in relation to Germany and Italy in the complexities of international affairs, it must in its soul feel convinced that both these great countries are now acting with strict correctitude in relation to Spain.

Possibly Sir Patrick's reading of the soul of the British people was a little off, but his reading of the soul of England's coupon-clipping circle was most accurate. These gentry had $200,000,000 invested in Franco Spain (according to Chamberlain, when refusing to embargo Franco's shipping to England because the investment might be endangered). The principal company concerned, Rio Tinto—a limb of the world-wide copper monopoly which in holy profit's name has restricted production to as little as 20 per cent of capacity—has among its directors a noble relative of Viscount Wimborne, who has two brothers and a son in the House of Commons. (Now watch the rabbit closely.) Rio Tinto owns European Pyrites Corporation jointly with the German Firm of Metallgesellschaft A. G., and Metallgesellschaft has an English director who is related by marriage to Viscount Wimborne. And chairman of Rio Tinto's board is Sir Auckland Geddes—former Ambassador to Washington (they send us all their very best people), until recently Air Raid Precautions adviser to the British government, and father-in-law of an attaché (the Prince of Hessen—remember Hessen?) at the German embassy in London.

Clearly neither Hitler with his intervention in Spain, nor Chamberlain with his "non-intervention," could have acted with greater correctitude—on behalf of the real rulers of both countries, the Wealth International. It's all in the family—but what a far-flung family!

What does become increasingly difficult is to disentangle "England" and "Germany" out of this skein of financial interests. The group in control of power in England has interests everywhere, including Germany. And the group in control of power in Germany has interests everywhere, including England. We find, for instance, the huge Siemens trust—as big as Ford's, duPont's and General Electric put together—with affiliates throughout the world, including a big one in Canada and a $25,000,000 company in England. Obviously when a war starts the same firm goes to work making equipment for both sides.

"Curiousest" of all are the international ramifications of the arms industry, the sole interest of which is to start wars. Krupps of Germany have branches or subsidiaries in Holland, in South America, and in the East. Vickers of England have direct interests in arms factories in Holland, Spain, Italy, Japan, Rumania, France, and Switzerland. France's Schneider Creusot controlled 56 per cent of the stock of Skoda in Czechoslovakia. And while they are in one sense rivals, they all work together from time to time—as various commissions of inquiry have shown—in the business of stirring up war scares and bribing selected army and navy officers and editors of all lands. Their business is unlike any other because each business coup by one firm operates to the advantage of the "rival" firm: in other words, if Krupp can sell some tanks to Brazil, Vickers can make a sale to the Paraguayans by calling upon them to view the Brazilian frontier with alarm.

So there were found sitting on the board of Skoda, side by side with the honorable Frenchmen whose government was pledged to defend Czechoslovakia, two pro-German Czechs who were heavy contributors to Hitler's Sudeten German party. And according to *Fortune* there is a strong inference—"close to inescapable"—that Skoda, that is, Schneider Creusot, contributed as a corporation to Nazi Sudeten party funds. Anyway, the arms business was doing poorly before Hitler came along, what with all the "sentimental" demand by ordinary people for disarmament or nationalization of the industry; and immediately afterward it began to pick up very satisfactorily. The Paris newspapers controlled by the De Wendels, French armament kings, led the piercing cries of denunciation of Hitler and the shrieks of "We must arm—*Pour la Patrie!*" But their first interest was still to sell where they could get the highest price, and between 1933 and 1936 the export of French iron ore to Germany rose from 95,000 to 547,000 tons.

No aspect of the international arms hook-up is more fascinating than the De Wendel family—which actually has a Von Wendel branch across the Rhine. If the De's don't get it, the Von's must. The first world war did the family proud. The iron mines and smelters belonging to the "De's" in the Briey Basin were captured by the "Huns"—but the French never fired on Briey because the De Wendels' property was sacred and they were able to give the government orders. It was explained later, when this came out, that if the French had fired on Briey the Germans would have fired on Dombasle, where equally large-scale mining operations were supplying France with its raw materials of murder. "Of course," as *Fortune* pointed out, "if the French and Germans had each leveled the other's smelters the war would have ended sooner—and so would war-time profits. . . . Here the proof of the international operations of the armament makers is open to no question at all. . . . The De Wendels need have felt no great concern. Regardless of the national tag attached to these mines and smelters they remained in the placid control of one or the other branches of the family." After France's victory some of the Von Wendels changed their names to De Wendel. One supposes that now, after France's defeat, the De's will become Von's. What's in a name?

And meanwhile, so it was revealed after 1918 by a British rear admiral who was naval attaché in Denmark, "England" was all through the war exporting nickel to Sweden—nearly all of it to go finally into German armaments to kill Englishmen.

Who was this "England"? Obviously not the ordinary Englishmen who had to get killed by their "own" metal. Obviously a very small wealthy group who, even in wartime, had to act according to the laws of their wealth and make profit wherever they could find it.

Even while they were still picking up the pieces of the dead in the first world war, the grim and crazy process went on as before. The mood of the common people in England was pretty ugly and the rulers could not ignore it—so "England" abjured war forever and embraced the idea of collective resistance to anyone trying to start it. But the big-money men still existed, with bank accounts more inflated than ever before; and to have all that money was necessarily to act according to its laws. "Civilization"—as they knew it—still depended upon making profits *ad infinitum*. They still had their ancient foe, democracy, to fight and to help their foreign brothers of the Wealth International to fight. And inside the International the foreign brothers had to be competed against for places nearest the gravy. But just as competition at home had more and more been eliminated by monopoly, so on the world scene there was an increasing tendency to international monopoly trusts. The old national boundary lines became dimmer—in one sense. Nevertheless, overlap though the different imperialist groups did at certain points, the overlapping represented not a real fusion but a political expedient in a fiercer death struggle than ever. The law under which they functioned was a law of fundamental contradiction—a law of expansion in a world that refused to be made of elastic. The irresistible force and the immovable object.

Were they, then, headed for unavoidable collision and disaster, involving a yet more ghastly orgy of death and torture and suffering for the poor bewildered people of Europe? Yes, undoubtedly, there could be no other end unless the people saw it coming and took action to control the juggernaut of high finance. And the people could not see it coming because the juggernaut itself controlled their newspapers.

But while the clash between imperialisms could not be avoided, it could be, so the more internationally minded finance groups thought, postponed. It could be postponed by opening up that one-sixth of the world where the dividend-scarcity system had been abolished—Soviet Russia: at one blow to smash the new system working toward the ideal of plenty for all and to replace it with scarcity for most—by opening up a huge field for hungry capital. The hope of doing this was many times expressed in the House of Lords and Commons and the Paris Chamber. Not to understand the strength of this hope in the minds of all branches of the Wealth International is to understand nothing that has happened in the last two decades.

We have seen that England, Grand High Master of Europe's lodge of Haves, has always sought to get others to fight its wars for it. And in this case, who was to be elected to strike the blow at Russia? Obviously Germany—with Japan to do some harrying and keep half the Russian army occupied in the east. Germany was geographically in the right spot. And ever since Bismarck it had been the rising imperialism, threatening the possessions of the older powers. Conditions in Germany after the war showed that either its capital would have to be allowed to expand in some direction, or else if the country was held down by force the whole dividend system would be overthrown and the plague of plenty would spread further west. (This plague was what Prime Minister Baldwin was referring to when, addressing a Wesleyan Methodist meeting in 1926, he complained that "since the war the manifest forces of Satan have been more conspicuously at large.")

Germany could be allowed—and even helped—to become strong again provided there was reasonable assurance that it would turn its new strength eastward, smash the new phase of democratic experiment, and leave a vast war-weakened area all the way from the Rhine to the Pacific as a playground for London and Paris capital in addition to German capital.

Well, Japan began to do its bit—the green light having been flashed from England—by seizing Manchuria. And then the God of Bankers gave London's stock exchange and the Paris Bourse their Western answer with the rise of Hitler's Nazi party. Hitler's whole philosophy was violently and laudably anti-democratic; his remarkable vocabulary of invective was equal to the task of finding appropriate names for Russia. A perfect man for the job! He did not have the majority of the German people with him, but money could push him over the top.

Who, then, really created the Nazi regime? Big German capitalists, yes. We know that the supreme economic council set up by Hitler in 1934 consisted of Krupp, arms king (private fortune, $30,000,000; capital represented, $75,000,000); Thyssen, steel king (private fortune, $30,000,000; capital represented, $2,700,000,000); Siemens, electrical king (private fortune, $32,500,000; capital represented, $62,500,000); Bosch, dyestuff and chemical king (private fortune, $10,000,000; capital represented, $275,000,000); and Voegler, steel king (private fortune, $30,000,000; capital represented, $200,000,000). And we know how handsomely Hitler paid them for their support, at once dispelling the fear of social revolution and eliminating the big magnates' remaining competition, establishing and legalizing their monopoly stranglehold. Krupps and Vereinigte Stahl, which had paid no dividends in 1933, paid 6 per cent in 1938, and other profits of the monopolies rose likewise. Working hours rose, wages fell, trade unions were killed. (Our lying press seriously expects us to believe that Hitler is anti-capitalistic, hoping to prove it by the downfall of small business and, recently, of Thyssen. In fact, of course, the small capitalists were sacrificed merely so that the great monopolists of heavy industry could survive in a war economy run hogwild—so hog-wild that it was bound to lead to still further eliminations, placing the monopolies in still fewer hands.)

Those were the men behind Hitler. But who was behind them? Beyond a doubt, their brother-monopolists in the "democracies." These people have not gone around bragging about it, but we know enough to put two facts with two indications of facts and make four. We know that Vickers of England has business connections with the German arms trust through subsidiaries in Holland and elsewhere; that England's Imperial Chemical has business connections with Bosch's I. G. Farben; and that English electrical interests are closely knit with Siemens. We also know that directors of these and other English monopoly groups promptly joined the Anglo-German Fellowship to establish "friendly relations" with the Nazi government. And that a leading spirit of the Fellowship was Frank Tiarks of Schroeder's Bank in London, which has a branch in Cologne. Tiarks is a friend of Montagu Norman of the Bank of England and an open admirer of Hitler's financial juggler Dr. Schacht—and he was also president of the International Commission of Standstill Creditors. The enormous increase in the profits of Hitler's monopolist-backers in Germany since 1933 was really given to them by the City of London under the standstill agreement on Germany's foreign debt. Schroeder's Bank was known in London as the "bridge" between Hitler and Lombard Street.

A great deal more evidence has come out. It has been stated and not denied that Schneider-Creusot contributed funds to Hitler. Sir Henri Deterding of Royal Dutch Shell never, so far as I know, disproved the charge quoted by Edgar Ansel Mowrer in *Germany Puts the Clock Back* that he "put up a considerable sum for the 1932 presidential election in the hope (or on the promise?) of being granted an oil monopoly in the Third Empire."

Lord Rothermere, England's biggest newspaper owner, openly backed the Nazis with such statements as:

The sturdy young Nazis of Germany are Europe's guardians against the Communist danger. . . . Germany must have elbow-room. . . . The diversion of Germany's reserves of energies and organising ability into Bolshevik Russia would help to restore the Russian people to a civilized existence, and perhaps turn the tide of world trade once more toward prosperity.*

So the little game went merrily forward. In December 1934, wrote John Gunther in *Inside Europe*, "the Bank of England granted a $3,750,000 credit to Germany in order to 'facilitate the mobilization of German commercial credits'; i.e., so that Germany might have means (and credit) to meet old debts—and build airplanes that can cross the English Channel in seven minutes." Vickers began advertising their tanks in German arms trade periodicals, and a treaty was made allowing Hitler to build up his fleet of submarines, although according to Versailles Germany was absolutely forbidden to rearm. And "everyone who was anyone" in England's wealthy circles was now charmed with Nazism.

Lord Lothian chatted with the Fuehrer in 1935 and returned to praise him in the *Times* for having rejuvenated Germany. Hitler gave a tea at Nuremberg for Lord Stamp of the L.M.S. Railway, who had said in 1935 that "democracy produces unbalanced lives." Von Ribbentrop, later to be cursed with all the oaths in the Mayfair vernacular as a "traitor," was wined and dined in all the best English homes.

The London Stock Exchange *Gazette* breezily gave the show away in 1935 by remarking:

Who finances Germany? Without this country as a clearing house for payments and the opportunity to draw on credits under the standstill, Germany could not have pursued her plans. We have been so ready to sell to Germany that the question of payment has never been allowed to interfere with the commercial side.

By 1938 Hitler was said to be buying on credit from the English and French empires (whose leaders paused now and again to deplore the pogroms and make speeches about "the sanctity of treaties") 26 per

* *Daily Mail,* November 28, 1933.

cent of his iron ore, 33 per cent of his lead, 50 per cent of his chromium, 52 per cent of his rubber, 60 per cent of his zinc, 61 per cent of his manganese, 62 per cent of his copper, and 94 per cent of his nickel. That these figures are probably accurate is indicated by what the foreign editor of London's respectable *Financial News* wrote in 1939:

There can be no doubt that practically the whole of the free exchange made available to Germany for the purchase of raw materials was supplied directly or indirectly by Great Britain. If the day of reckoning ever comes, the liberal attitude of the British Government in this matter may well be responsible for the lives of British soldiers and civilians. War materials, which will eventually be used against this country, could never have been produced but for the generosity with which Great Britain is giving her enemy free exchange for the purchase of raw materials.

You see, some of the big-money men were beginning to get worried by that time. Their protégé, Hitler, just would not turn his face the right way—toward the east. Such ingratitude! But who could blame Hitler for it? He is, after all, a plain and honest buccaneer—which is more than can be said for England's imperialists. He doesn't care whether he gets white meat or dark off the turkey as long as he gets a heaped plate. And the more England and France "appeased" him, the more clearly he could see their fatal weakness.

Finally England and France gave him Czechoslovakia to chew on, plus the $50,000,000 of Czech gold that was in the Bank of England as a free gift. But after Munich Hitler could no longer have any doubt which way he was going to move. He had met Chamberlain and Daladier and learned to despise them—a Hitlerian sentiment which we can all, for once, share. At the same time he knew (what was suppressed at the time but was later admitted by Benes and published in a remote corner of *The New York Times*) that Russia, alone of all the powers pledged to help Czechoslovakia, had been ready to the last to fulfill its obligations—and that Russia's morale and military preparedness (this is Benes' word against Lindbergh's) were of the highest. To the east the Fuehrer saw a frontier bristling with modern armaments in the hands of a determined people. To the west he saw frontiers bristling with umbrellas, and behind them two hopelessly bewildered peoples who did not begin to know what the real score was—who placed their hopes in a democracy that did not exist.

Yet even then the City of London did not give up hope of turning the Nazi wrath in the other direction. If politically they abandoned outright appeasement, financially they redoubled their appeasing efforts. A few days after Munich a delegation from the Fellowship of British Industries went to Berlin for "unofficial" trade talks with the Nazis. One of the four delegates was an iron-and-steel-trust representative, one was a Unilever man, and one was our old friend Mr. P. F. B. Bennett of Imperial Chemical Industries: all three men with considerable business interests in Germany. The idea was that, since Hitler obviously couldn't be cheated of his "rightful" share of imperial gravy, he could be appealed to on the ground of England's and Germany's common business interests, and a deal could be made for "economic co-operation and a common export drive."

While the talks were going on, Hitler did what everyone knew he would do, and grabbed off the whole of Czechoslovakia—thereby publicly breaking Chamberlain's heart with a bang that could be heard half across the floor of the House of Commons. The delegates took no notice of this little rape scene—they, of course, also knew all along that it would happen, since they and their friends had planned it—and continued chatting. At the same time the *Quarterly Business Review,* organ of the Fellowship of British Industries, began setting out the arguments for giving Hitler a free run of southeastern Europe. The *Financial News* talked of "uniting the policy of collective resistance to aggression . . . and the policy of appeasement previously followed by Mr. Chamberlain." Delightful!

But not so fast there in Berlin! It began to ooze out that what was really being discussed was Anglo-German co-operation (English capital and the unorthodox but highly successful methods of Dr. Schacht) to exploit South America in return for this "free hand in the east" for Hitler. And now the United States stepped into the picture and gummed up the works. Secretary Hull announced that "if two larger nations enter into a discriminatory arrangement between themselves . . . other nations inevitably will take defensive economic measures, and instead of establishing peace, economic rehabilitation and progress, the result

is bound to be a general collapse." In other words, that's our turkey
and you boys better keep your elbows to yourselves. So once again the
best-laid schemes of the Wealth International were thwarted by the
contradictions inherent in its own system.

At the same period the "democracies"—the Haves—were trying to
buy their way into a deal with Franco. A group headed by the Lazard
Frères Bank (whose chairman is a director of the Bank of England) and
former Belgian Premier Van Zeeland were offering the Spanish gener-
alissimo a bagatelle of $100,000,000 in credits. In this little deal the inter-
national ramifications of world finance were particularly striking. Van
Zeeland had just become a director of the Spanish-American Electric
Company, part of a huge international combine on the various boards
of which sit French, German, Italian, and English interests, including
Lord Swinton, Chamberlain's Minister for Air until 1938, and the Duke
of Alba, Franco's London ambassador who throughout the war in Spain
kept his finger on the non-interveners to make sure they wouldn't stop
intervening.

And in Japan, the same kind of finagling. The more pairs of British
trousers the Japs removed at Tientsin, the more England strove for a
deal—for were not the Chinese, whom Japan was trying to smash, dan-
gerously infected with the disease of democracy? Here again, the hope
was that Japan would crush democracy on England's behalf but would
suffer so much economically in so doing that the City of London's gold
would eventually win the day, saving English investments in both Japan
and China. That is still the kernel of England's Far Eastern policy. Last
March British Ambassador Craigie told a distinguished Tokyo gathering that England and Japan were "ultimately striving for the same objective—namely, lasting peace and the preservation of our institutions
from extraneous and subversive influences." Three days later the world
heard that Anglo-Iranian Oil, in which the British Government has a
controlling interest, had sold Japan a million barrels of crude oil. Just
by way of helping them "strive for the objective of lasting peace."

Of course, as anyone with a grain of perception could see from the
start, Hitler and Franco and the Japanese monopolists have merely been
trying to take the Have boys for all they could get while hardly able to
refrain from laughing in their faces. Every new loving approach that
England could make rendered it more certain that England, with its

huge and sprawling and undefendable empire, was the one that was going to get it in the neck. Why should the upstart financiers of Germany and Spain and Italy and Japan co-operate with England to divvy up the swag, when they could bump England off and take all?

So much for "England's" role in building up the Frankenstein that is now devouring it.

But "Mamma goes where Poppa goes." We started off to examine a certain strange transatlantic romance between "England" and "America." Just who is this "America," and to what extent has "America" kept by its true love's side?

Well, we have seen the answer. This "America" is the group known as our Sixty Families, who have the big stake in American business and who must travel far and wide across the world, following wherever their homeless millions may lead in search of a place to settle and grow.

This "America" is not Mr. and Mrs. Smith who for a wage—when they can get it—screw on bolts and type invoices for Ford. Not Mr. and Mrs. Jones who run the corner drugstore in Omaha. For what are the Joneses and Smiths interested in? Simply and solely and exclusively in America—in producing and distributing more food and clothing and houses and commodities for themselves and their fellow Americans. They know these things are here for the producing and are not being produced in sufficient quantity to satisfy half the need. They want only to produce them and have them.

And what are the Sixty Families who run the great corporations of America interested in? More and more every day in foreign lands—because the stimulus to which they answer is that of their wealth, and the purchasing power of the American people continues to shrink while millions go short of necessities and millions of acres lie idle, so that here under the scarcity system there is no more work for their money to do.

To say this—to point to the divergence of interest between the wealthy fraction and the vast mass of the people—is to be accused of "fomenting class antagonisms." (The next verse of that number being "We must have unity. What destroyed France?") But it isn't fomenting. It's pointing out something that exists and that must exist in America as it is now organized. "America" as a single entity is as illusory a concept as "England." "Americanism" should mean concentrating on the welfare of America—but those who use the expression most are those whose interests lie more and more outside America.

What do the Joneses and the Smiths know about the finaglings for profit and profit on profit that go on in the smoke-filled rooms? What glimmering are they afforded of the discussions between their "representative" Sumner Welles and the Hitlers, Mussolinis, and Chamberlains? Most of what they see in their wealth-controlled press or hear on their wealth-controlled radio is the sort of high-flown Halifaxian flapdoodle, bearing not the smallest relation to realities, that Roosevelt addresses to the Pope—about "seekers of light and seekers of peace" forming a "friendly association to overcome the forces of evil." What an insult to a supposedly educated people to expect them to swallow that kind of thing and look no further! Honeyed words, addressed to the man who blessed the ruthless massacre of Ethiopians and Spanish Catholics, from a man who knows perfectly well what part wealthy Americans have played in creating these very "forces of evil."

Yes, "America"—the fraction of one per cent of our people who speak for their private wealth under the guise of speaking for us—has likewise been concerned from the start to suppress democracy in Russia, in Germany, in Austria, in Spain, in China, in Czechoslovakia. It has likewise lent a helping hand to whichever "force of evil" would at any cost hold back the age of plenty. That, and no less, is what the seeking of new outlets for accumulated capital, in a non-elastic world with a scarcity economy, involves.

Now we are "threatened" by an enemy so diabolically evil that we are told we must abandon our democracy in order to defend ourselves. Which means, to any person of normal common sense, that rather than wait for this "force of evil" to cross the ocean and establish dictatorship here, we will do the job ourselves. We may not like that but won't that old "force of evil" just look silly when he lands!

The evidence we have certainly suggests that we have done as much as anyone else to create the "forces of evil" and make them strong.

Once upon a time, as you may recall, a mountebank "socialist" named Mussolini saved the day by force for the scarcity system in Italy. The same Mussolini whose "stab in the back"—meaning his carrying out of a long-standing treaty agreement with Germany—our President recently denounced with such indignation.

This man did a fine job for old man Scarcity. He increased working hours, decreased wage scales, abolished trade unions and all the country's liberal parties. With the greatest efficiency and thoroughness he took the fillings out of the Italian people's teeth. They didn't need them. There was only spaghetti to eat and hardly any of that.

He did this, like Hitler a few years later, on behalf of the big bankers and the equivalent of our National Association of Manufacturers. Naturally the American N.A.M.'s applauded. Thomas Lamont of the House of Morgan told America that Mussolini had saved Italy from Communism and that the Italians "wanted" Fascism. He did not stop to mention that out of the 452 members of Italy's democratic congress, eighteen were Communists and thirty-two Fascists.

Mr. Morgan felt that such a man was worthy of support—in gold. By 1926 Italy had been brought to the verge of ruin. Mr. Morgan, of course, knew this quite well. It was even reported in the Chicago *Daily News,* whose correspondent Hiram Motherwell cabled that Fascist finance was a flop, the country was bankrupt, the living standard was sinking lower and lower. But Mr. Morgan had enough control of our press to sell America the exactly opposite story, emphasizing the remarkable precision with which Italian trains were now supposed to be running. Americans subscribed a $100,000,000 bond issue which was used to save Fascism. Without that loan Mussolini would have collapsed. That was the first nail America drove into the coffin of democracy.

Today, according to George Seldes, the former American correspondent in Italy who is our greatest authority on the subject, "America's" financial stake in Italian Fascism is more than $600,000,000.

To put it in the simplest way, "America" and "England" really forged the dagger for the 1940 "stab in the back." The Nye Commission—most of whose findings, thanks to our corporation-controlled press and radio, the American people have never learned about—found that American business had equipped Italy's air force with the most up-to-date American instruments: horizon and directional gyroscope devices, searchlight and sound locators, operating control gear. And in addition, enormous quantities of "our" scrap iron have been sent to Italy—and the greater part of Italy's steel, more than half of which goes into munitions, is made from scrap iron.

The Department of Commerce shows that in 1938, when President

Roosevelt was so passionately devoted to "neutrality" during the mass assault on democracy in Spain, "we" exported over 400,000 tons of scrap iron to Italy to kill Spaniards with. We exported the same amount again in 1939, and in the first third of 1940 we exported to Italy 200,000 tons of scrap iron. To only one of all Europe's belligerent governments have "we" ever effectively barred sales of war materials; that is, to the democratic government of Spain, which threatened nobody except wealth and privilege and was shamelessly set upon by international brigands. To China, set upon in a similar way, we have sold a little, but not a fraction of what we have sold to the aggressor Japan. China is moving toward greater democracy, and "we" cannot sympathize with that kind of Bolshevik business. That is why, while you hear so much of the horrors of Nazi bombings in Europe which result in a few score of hundreds of casualties, there is hardly a mention of such raids as those on Chungking from August 17 to 20 last, where 25,000 people were killed in just one day—25,000 democratically minded Orientals! What right have such vermin to American sympathy?

That is "Americanism"—export model.

Now what about Hitler, Lord High Beelzebub of the "forces of evil"? What stiles have we helped the lame but rabid dog of Berchtesgaden over?

Well, what do you make of this: Henry Ford, Charles A. Lindbergh, Thomas J. Watson, the International Chamber of Commerce's former head, Vice-President James D. Mooney of General Motors, and "a number of influential educators" are named by the newspaper *PM* as having received Hitler's "Order of the German Eagle," which is given to foreigners deserving well of the Nazi government. Watson has returned the medal. *PM* says that it "has not heard that any of the others have returned their Nazi honors."

Mooney is known as a friend of Gerhard Westrick, the Nazi trade agent who has got some undesired notoriety owing to one of those unfortunate off-guard moments we all have. Recently, according to *PM,* Mooney published a pamphlet written by himself which parallels current Nazi propaganda. He has a key job in America's defense. They do it that way in England; why not here? He is executive assistant to the president of General Motors, in full charge of all negotiations involving defense equipment. General Motors' president, Knudsen—a character carefully home-spunned by his press agents in *Saturday Evening Post* articles—was appointed organizational Director of Roosevelt's national defense against "the forces of evil."

Why not? What better man for this job than one who so frankly and warmly expressed his admiration for Nazism on his return from visiting Hitler's Germany?

America's men of wealth fit into the picture in much the same way as England's. General Motors is known to have a large interest in Opel, the biggest auto-manufacturing concern in Germany. Out of this Knudsen garners some of his company's millions. Somebody asked him the other day what this plant was now producing, and he said: "I don't know."

There is also in Germany a Ford plant, 40 per cent of which belongs to Ford's Nazi business partner I. G. Farbenindustrie. And Ford's Mr. Cameron, the one-time editor of the Dearborn anti-Semitic newspaper, who every Sunday between selections from *Scheherezade* expatiates over the radio about his lord's generosity, says with an air of brisk finality: "We don't know what has happened to it." Without doubt the German Ford plant has for duration of the war been lifted up miraculously upon a cloud of Mr. Cameron's inspirational phrases.

And so on down the line. Rockefeller's Standard Oil, like Imperial Chemical in England, has "entered into relations with the various German companies and groups including the I. G. Farbenindustrie" (quoting Dr. Plummer, the Oxford University economist)—all in a giant international tea-party involving Shell Oil (English and Dutch) and Anglo-Iranian.

Last February, Standard Oil announced that it had acquired from I. G. Farben the rights to the Buna process of making synthetic rubber. It did not announce what was the other half of the deal—but it is obvious that Hitler would not in time of war release such an important war process to a potential enemy without some form of payment which would immediately benefit Germany as a "force of evil" against "civilization." The news sheet *Uncensored* comments: "The most probable explanation is that Standard will make direct payment in the oil that Hitler's war machine so desperately needs—through Rumania." Yes, Standard Oil controls 12 per cent of all Rumania's oil production, and sells oil to Germany through a Standard-owned company called Deutsch-Amerikanische Petroleum Gesellschaft.

These are but straws in the wind which happen to have come into view. Nobody knows just how far the thing goes. But do you catch the echoes of the Briey Basin, of the delightful "De" and "Von" Wendels?

Come war, come deluge, come anything and everything except popular uprising against the scarcity-dividend system, the international machine of profit-making must pound on. Consider the case of Texaco's Mr. Rieber which recently leaked out in connection with the revelations about Nazi agent Westrick. We learned that "our" Mr. Rieber had turned over to Franco $6,000,000 worth of oil during the Fascist rebellion—American oil produced by democratic American workers. (That was non-intervention in practice: oil for Franco, scrap iron for Mussolini, nothing for the legal government of Spain.) This oil must have helped Franco as much as anything else to smash democracy in Spain. Now, I do not charge any connection between the two events, but Rieber subsequently got the monopoly of Fascist Spain's oil market— which came in particularly handy for supplying oil to Germany indirectly through Spain when Hitler began to need vast supplies for his tanks and dive-bombers in the present war. As *The New York Times* said: "Many American oil concerns own tankers flying foreign flags. These are not banned from visiting Spain under the Neutrality Act." For months after the start of the present war our newspapers were hurling all their terms of obloquy at Russia for supplying the Nazis with oil. But eventually, when the Westrick case opened up, *The New York Times* admitted that "far more oil has been reaching Germany from America since the war started than Herr Hitler has obtained, or can hope to obtain, from Russia."

When our government hypocrites are confronted with such facts, they lift their hands helplessly and infer that this is the shortcoming of democracy, businessmen being "free agents" who may do what they like provided they stay within the law (that is, get around the law and make a joke of it). That is the great lie of all lies, for is it not obvious to anyone that the majority of our people, if they knew about these things, would insist on their being stopped? But the people are not informed until after the acts are committed, if then; and democracy that is not informed isn't democracy at all.

Not that the Riebers are any worse than the larger bloc of our men of wealth, whose money is mainly invested in the English cause. If the majority of our people had a word to say about it, they would not allow one penny of American money to be gambled on either side in a European war, for they know that where American money goes, there sooner or later goes American flesh and blood to "protect the investment." But the Riebers dramatize more effectively the hypocrisy of our American Fuehrers who keep up a never-ending geyser of moral preachments against Germany and for England. Rieber turns out to be just what you would expect—a union-hater who "curses the New Deal as freely as any big businessman"—something which is held up for our admiration by *Life* magazine, in a panegyric printed in cozy proximity to a page advertisement for Texaco in three colors. He returned from his last trip to Germany, after the start of the war, bearing a message from Goering to Roosevelt. And how many more Riebers are there?

He resigned from Texaco when these things leaked out, and because at the present time Nazi Germany is officially hated by "America." But note how sudden and how recent this hatred is. It barely peeped out—that is, in effective action, for words mean nothing—as long as the Nazis were doing the job of smashing democracy in their own and other countries. It came screaming forth when Hitler went against our true love, England—when it became finally clear that he would not do the job for which he was built up, the job of attacking Russia. That was Rieber's bad luck. He, too, as his whole record shows, would have given almost anything to have the Nazis go for Russia. He thought they were going to do so, and "our" leaders in Washington thought so too, and for that reason never discouraged Rieber or anyone else.

Discouraged, did I say? In 1936 the Nye Commission revealed that Pratt and Whitney, Curtiss-Wright, and other aircraft concerns sold hundreds of planes and plane engines to Hitler ("whole trainloads of them," according to none other than our new Secretary of the Navy, Knox); and that this was done with the knowledge and consent of "our" War and Navy Departments. United States exports of aircraft to Germany came to nearly $2,000,000 in 1934. Yet our blood is asked to curdle now on account of Hitler's "terrible dive-bombers," as if this were a special and devilish invention of the "forces of evil."

The Nye Commission also revealed that the common stock of Dynamit Aktiengesellschaft, the German explosives trust, is held by Imperial Chemical Industries and I. G. Farben and duPonts of America. DuPonts had a deal with both English and German firms whereby "each party . . . upon making or obtaining any patented invention or discovering or acquiring any secret invention" must "disclose in writing to the other party immediately or in any event within six months thereafter, full particulars in respect thereof." Does it still have such an agreement? It was further revealed that "the Sperry Gyroscope Company has been delivering automatic pilots and gyro-compasses and other instruments, sufficient to equip at least 50 planes in Germany a month."

Yes, in those days it was most respectable to assist the Nazis. "Our" investment in Hitler's regime is placed at $1,400,000,000. "We"— meaning the financial house of Dillon, Read—lent seventy millions to Voegler's Vereinigte Stahlwerke and forty-six millions to Siemens; and Voegler and Siemens financed Hitler and made him dictator of Germany.

Here, as in England, it was all in the family and the family extended right into the seats of government. "Mysterious" financial figures flit about the Congressional lobbies and the White House, keeping all the boys in touch.

"We" have a stake in the Nazi side, trifling though it is compared with "our" stake in the English side. But it is not really either side that "we" have a stake in, but the defense of the Wealth International by whomsoever it can best be defended, and in war itself.

Just as for the Von and the De Wendels, the war is a source of profit for our Sixty Families no matter who wins. From the last quarter of 1938 to the last quarter of 1939 the lowest rise in a steel company's profit was 100 per cent, the highest over 2,000 per cent. That is only the beginning of the expected war boom.

The law of concentrated wealth is expansion and travel, and if the American people do not insist on controlling it they must inevitably travel after it and again become fertilizer for some foreign field.

CHAPTER FIFTEEN

Can the British Empire Endure?

IN THIS the most critical situation the human family ever faced, the smallest decision we make carries in it tremendous implications for the world of the future.

The world is going to go on anyhow, come hell or high water—make no mistake about that. It is going to move forward as it has always done. Not all the stupidities and obstacles that the tortured brains of our generation can devise will be more than a twig which it brushes from its path.

But that is the cosmic view, and we do not happen to be gods. We are mortal men and women, and the immediate future is of tremendous importance to us. We cannot afford to let our wishes and emotions run away with us. We have to be ruthlessly practical.

England as I see it is the issue concerning which we must be most ruthless and most practical. Forgive me if I bore you by harping on this subject, but unless we make up our minds finally about where we stand on it, none of our other deliberations and decisions mean anything at all. Therefore I say, put aside all sentimental feelings you may have about England and present this question to yourself: If we tie ourselves to England, are we tying ourselves to a live and growing concern or a dead horse?

Forget what you *wish* for the British Empire, whether you'd like to see its glory burn still brighter or whether you nominate it for oblivion. Ask yourself what *is going* to happen to the British Empire.

That isn't just a question for crystal-gazers. It is a question to which the facts of history and of geography and of nature will provide an answer.

Take your map of the world and consider the matter from the practical businessman's point of view.

The English collected their Empire by Hitler's methods precisely—and for one reason: because there was profit in it. We have already had a glimpse of the magnitude of those profits. They did not mind how far afield they went for imperial loot, and the Union Jack was planted in every part of our globe. They could do that because they were the leading naval power and their navy ruled the seas. As more and more colonies were added, the maintenance of the Empire became an ever bigger and more complicated business. In order to hold India they had to have control of Egypt and Suez and Aden and Gibraltar. Also naval bases at Malta and Cyprus to keep the Mediterranean safe for their ships. Also control of Iraq and working "deals" with the various slave-running sheiks of the Persian Gulf. In order to hold Malaya and Australasia and their Chinese interests, they had to have bases at Singapore and Hong Kong. Hence the Dutch, who had the East Indies, had to be made weak and subservient. Also, Spain and Portugal had to be weak in order that the English might not get shoved off the rock of Gibraltar, and to keep the route to British West and South Africa unobstructed. Likewise, if the Japanese could not be held back from becoming a power, it was important for England to have a working arrangement with them.

These things could be done, and were done most effectively, up to the first decade of this century. Everything the Empire needed to keep its communications open, it took. The protection of the swag called for a more and more gigantic navy—but this offered no difficulty, for the increasing size of the swag more than paid the bill. England began to clothe itself in white raiment and pose as the generous protector of the poor defenseless peoples of the Empire. Actually, of course, the protection those peoples got was the same sort of protection the poor defenseless Chicago storekeepers got from Al Capone. They paid a dollar to Capone for fifty cents' worth of protection—from Capone. It wasn't on a very high moral plane, but what big business is? The only thing that mattered was that it worked.

The first world war seemed to have still further entrenched the

English as self-appointed protectors of lesser breeds. For, with our
asinine aid, she had disposed of her one growing European rival—Germany. Hence, as supplementary protection of their Suez route east, they
were able to take and make a new naval base at Haifa in Palestine,
with an American-British oil pipe-line running to it from the Iraq
wells. Also Germany had its possessions adjacent to the British in Africa
and the Pacific taken away. Japan was stronger but was still officially
England's ally. Italy and Spain were delightfully weak, and France
was broke and subservient.

But the historical process of development in man's whole way of
life and relation to nature was moving to an accelerated speed. New
forces came into play and began to eat like termites into the foundation
of what England fondly believed to be a majestically permanent edifice.
Do not forget that the thought of individual liberty had been growing
all over the world. The poorest, dumbest native anywhere was beginning to hear of electric lights, automobiles, airplanes, telephones, the
phonograph, moving pictures, ice boxes, washing machines, to say nothing of advertising billboards, newspapers, books, machine guns, Mergenthaler linotypes, etc. Also, rival powers were growing in the East and
the West, and the protection of the Empire was becoming a grimmer
and more difficult business every day. In sum, England's position was
not unlike that of Capone, who had not only to deal with rival gangs
but also with the Federal Government, which was rising in wrath
against the whole institution of high-powered gangsterdom. England
saw rivals such as Russia and Japan and Italy and Germany rapidly
building up their war-making power, and at the same time had to face
the rising wrath of the colonial peoples against the institution of imperialism.

Three things changed the relationship that had once existed between
England and its rival imperialist gangsters. In the first place, with the
success of the revolution in Russia, the rivals were able to play much
more effectively than before on England's fears of the whole institution
tottering, so that when they wanted to expand and threaten British
world dominance they were able to say: "If you try to stop us, there
will be a revolution in our country—and you know how highly infec-
tious the revolution disease is: our country today, your empire tomorrow." That has been Hitler's trump card all along, and most effectively

he has played it—and Italy and Japan and Franco in Spain have followed suit. Over and over again in the last twenty years England has been faced with the unpleasant alternative of letting one of the new gangsters grow in power by conquest, or of possible revolution and the spread of anti-imperialist ideas such as those of the Soviet Union. Also there have always been two groups in England's leadership, one of them favoring the first alternative (the Chamberlain appeasers) and the other willing to take a chance on revolution rather than weaken the British Empire in any way (the Churchills).

The second point that complicated the imperialism racket was that, except for Ethiopia and a few polar icebergs, the whole potential colonial world had already been appropriated—so that any gain by one power must necessarily mean a loss by another power.

The third point was that discoveries of new slaughtering methods—notably, of course, the bombing airplane—had changed the whole technique of attack and defense. England was having great difficulty keeping control of the seas: the rival gangsters were increasing in number, and the navy, large as it was, could not be everywhere. But even so that was no longer enough. An empire so spread out over the face of the earth was tremendously vulnerable from the air. Had it been closer knit—a widespread but solid territory such as the United States, Russia or China—England might have been able to produce enough planes to reach any point that was attacked and so defend itself effectively. But an air corps capable of defending the whole Empire would have to operate out of a dozen bases, each one of which would need as many planes as any potential attacker. There was some talk of disarmament, as you recall—of abolition of bombing planes by international agreement. Very nice for the great Have country, England—in theory. But factually English imperialism was at last and hopelessly caught up in its own contradictions once again. It had to have not only a navy attempting to rule the waves of all the world of 1940 but also bombing planes to keep the colonial people in order locally—so that it was England itself that came out flatly in opposition to the idea of no bombing planes, and so killed it.

However, from a purely geographical standpoint the British Empire cannot be defended today and is therefore an anomaly in the age of airplanes. Enormous though the tribute is that the little wealthy group

in the south of England takes from the Empire, it is still not enough
to provide an adequate defense for so far-flung a world. The con-
founded thing costs too much. Its upkeep has become greater than its
income; the Empire is in the red. If you doubt that think how much
England owes us. And the imperial profiteers in England have for some
time realized that this is so from a military point of view. They know,
for instance, that Australia, a country sixty times as large as England,
with a total population considerably less than that of greater London,
could not possibly be defended against Japan. The nearest great British
naval and air base, at Singapore, could perhaps not even defend Malaya
itself. England has therefore had to make all sorts of compromises and
deals with its bristling rivals and to try and keep them in check by the
power of its gold. It has sought more desperately than ever to get its
rivals to fighting with one another, hoping that they would thus weaken
themselves and England would be able to control the final outcome
when they came to London for reconstruction loans. But Hitler has
made sausage-meat out of gold as a weapon of power, demonstrating
that with sufficiently ruthless control of internal economy a country can
grow powerful and get what it wants by means of barter.

But quite apart from this fatal geographical weakness, and regardless
of whether England sits in the driver's seat or Germany or Japan pushes
England into the gutter, such an empire as this cannot endure. History,
bearing out what seems to be nature's law, tells us that no empire based
on the forcible exploitation and holding-back of subject peoples has
ever endured. It also tells us that no people taking away the freedom
of other peoples can itself be free. The story of every great empire has
been the same: the grandeur that was Greece, the glory that was Rome,
Persia, the Byzantine and Mongol empires, Spain, Portugal, France.
Too much wealth produces decay at the top; too much poverty produces unrest at the bottom. That is just as inevitable as Tuesday, and
there are only two ways it can end. Either the oppressed mass in the
empire itself, or the youthful strength of some rival imperialism which
in turn will later decay and die, upsets the apple cart.

Of course the rulers of the British Empire claim that theirs is a new
kind of Empire. The gentlemen of England, we are told, carry a white
man's burden, and though they get remarkably well paid for the work
it hurts them more than it hurts the burden to be trussed up on their

shoulders. Their Empire is not a means of robbing the weak, but a "Commonwealth of Nations" in which each nation is kindly and patiently developed toward the time when, as an equal partner, it can walk by England's side.

The burdens say they want to walk now. England says that is impossible; their legs would give under them and they'd just die in the gutter. The burdens say that's a lie, and if England would put them down just for a minute they'd prove it. Be patient, says England: all in good time.

Certainly we have to give the British Empire credit for being new in one sense: it is the first empire that ever made such a claim for itself. All other empires have been quite frank about their predatory motives, and so England was in the early days. But because England makes this novel claim, millions of people with no access to the facts—we poor corporation-propagandized and so uninformed Americans among others—are willing to believe that its Empire is new in fact as well as in self-attributed theory. It sounds so good and beautiful to us world-rescuing and -saving and -healing Americans (outside the United States, that is)—the "British Commonwealth of Nations."

And the English "liberal aristocrat" who puts forward the claim is an exceptionally convincing fellow. He is convincing because the English have made a national fine art out of convincing themselves that black is white before they try to convince others. Indeed, many of these English "liberals" do not merely *pretend* that the "Commonwealth of Nations" dream is a reality: they *desire* it to be real with all their noble hearts. The editorials in London newspapers, and the speeches in the House of Commons, after some new Royal Commission has made public the unfortunate results of British imperialism in this or that colony, are often passionately sincere. But unfortunately the English cannot make it work in practice, desire and hope as some of them may. The laws of their own economics are against them. So that, considered objectively, these editorials and speeches become the very pinnacle of hypocrisy.

If I have been at pains to point out how wretched England makes the existence of hundreds of millions of its subjects—if I have challenged anyone to explain just how those subject peoples could be any worse off under, say, the Nazis—it has not been done to satisfy any personal animosity against the English, nor to demonstrate that the individual Englishman is "evil" by comparison with individuals of other races. If America had an empire like the British Empire, you can depend upon it that the inhabitants would be in precisely the same condition. Indeed, you have but to look at Puerto Rico—where the people are starving and without democracy and where only the other day (according to the Associated Press) two native political leaders were arrested and charged with the crime of "making speeches and publishing letters"—to see that in such colonies as we now possess we do exactly what England does in India, Africa, and the West Indies. We do it on a smaller scale of course, because our possessions (you will, by the way, find nothing in our Constitution about our ever having any possessions) are few. But the net results of imperialism by whomsoever practiced are and must be the same, without the slightest relation to the benevolence that may or may not glow in the hearts of the rulers. The imperialist economy makes it necessary for the subject peoples to be held back from normal industrialization—and at that point man clashes with nature, and we know who is bound to win in the end. You cannot get the peoples of colonial Britain—nine-tenths of all the people ruled from London—excited about the "threat of falling under the Nazi heel." They have nowhere to fall, since they are under a heel now, and no matter who owns the heel it feels just as uncomfortable under there.

How can we possibly maintain that the English claim to be "developing the backward peoples of the empire for equal partnership" is true in any real sense? Or that we owe it to civilization and democracy to help them maintain this international lie? The best their own statistics can claim is, as we have seen, that in India and the Gold Coast everyone will read and write by the years 2851 and 2631, respectively, if populations remain static, which they won't. As for effective democratic rights, the movement is if anything a backward one. It is bound to be, since the subject peoples inevitably crave industrialization and since, equally inevitably under imperialist economy, they are getting year by year less rather than more industrialization. As the world stands today, the getting of mechanized industries is the foundation on which all material and cultural progress can alone be based. But in India we find that, in the twenty-year period for which official figures are available (1911–1931), the number of people employed in industry fell by over two millions, while the number dependent on agriculture kept on rising. The whole picture is there, in those figures. Even now, with its "back to the wall" at home, England's promises to India are and cannot help being just as nebulous as ever.

At the very best, then, the British Empire's claim to a future and to our sympathy is founded on wishes. And that gives the Empire no future at all. For history and technology are streaking forward like a stratosphere plane and simply will not slow down or concern themselves in any way with the pious wishes of a few gentlemen in London. The Empire could endure only if it were what it claims to be—if the "development" of backward peoples were going forward as fast as history and technology, which, as the mathematicians say, is absurd. If it were what it claims to be it could put arms in the hands of the colonial peoples, give them factories in which to produce their own airplanes, and let them defend their countries. It can never do that because it knows against whom those arms would be turned. What interest have Indians and Egyptians and Malays in defending England's right to oppress them?

And this is seen by men of detachment in England, who have dug to the roots of our present-day world, just as plainly as I, a mere vulgar and interfering American, see it. In his recent book *The Common Sense of War and Peace,* H. G. Wells says that society has evolved to a point where life will be intolerable unless there is a world-wide change involving centralized control of production and distribution. He then writes:

Let me ask you now what the setting-up of one sovereign peace in the world and one general economic control, means. It means World Revolution. I ask you not to be afraid of the word Revolution. Speak English. Don't think of Revolution as an affair of street barricades, the heads of beautiful ladies on pikes, and tumbrils going to the guillotine. Our Glorious Revolution in 1688 had none of these ingredients, and the Revolution that established the Hanoverian Succession was practically bloodless. You can have a Revolution without massacre or violence. But anyhow, I submit that organized world peace and welfare mean such a Revolution in human life as will dwarf all previous revolutions to comparative insignificance. It means such a universal scrapping of time-honored institutions as mankind has never faced hitherto. . . .

I put it to you with the utmost deference that anyone who runs about now demanding permanent world peace and who is not prepared to scrap the sovereignty of his own government and amalgamate the general control of political and economic life into a world-wide system, is either muddle-headed or insincere or both. This means the end of the British Empire quite as much as the end of German Imperialism. You have to face it.

"You have to face it," says one of England's most fearless and original thinkers. But the rulers of England in their most despairing hour are not facing it, and they are not because they cannot. Their privileges—which in their minds go through a chemical process and become identi-fied with "civilization"—depend on not facing it. They are compelled by forces far stronger than themselves to keep on fighting for the con-tents of their stable after the horse, for all practical purposes, has already been stolen.

Ever since the present war began, vulgar and interfering people at home and abroad have been calling on them to say what their war aims are—and we still don't know. What answer do we get from the London *Times,* accepted spokesman for the ruling class of England?

In the European order of the past 20 years Hitler finds one of his easiest targets. He finds another in the contradictions of our social and economic system. . . . The chronic unemployment, the inequalities of social privi-lege and vested interests, the burning of wheat and coffee while men go hungry, the senseless accumulation of gold in Fort Knox, Kentucky—all these reproaches have been flung once more at the old order in the attempt to convince Europe that the time is out of joint, and that Hitler was born to set it right. . . . Preoccupied though it is by the needs of defence and offence, the British Government should not allow Hitler's challenge to go by default. Much harm may be done to our cause, both in Europe and over-seas, by the insinuation that we stand for the old order and that our only aim is to restore the status quo in Europe and to maintain it at home. This charge should be emphatically and authoritatively refuted.

Bravo! It is going a long way for the London *Times* to admit, as it does, that the Nazis' "appeal for a planned economic unification of Europe is not without its force." But what on earth is the good of "em-phatically and authoritatively refuting" unless you have some practical suggestion to offer? What kind of "new order" has England to put forward? From the vague details vouchsafed one can only gather that this "new order" is just as futile as the "new order" of 1919. It would still be based on that system of privilege and artificial scarcity which is the core of the British Empire and which is rapidly becoming the core of this our American democracy and which was responsible for both the world wars. Germany would presumably be split up, with Englishmen to police it, and we should be back more or less where we were a century ago. If this is England's "new order," who is to blame people "overseas" for concluding that, for all his barbarism and cynicism and lust for power, Hitler has at least one grain of reason on his side, England none at all?

What do we get from Lord Halifax, who speaks for God and (as Secretary for Foreign Affairs) His Majesty? This gentleman, who as Viceroy of India kept Gandhi amiably chatting about things of the spirit while his police beat up the starving Indians, drifts away into the empyrean with talk of "putting our hand in the hand of God."

"Where," he inquires of his Oxford-accented heavenly voices, "will God lead us? Not, we may be sure, through easy or pleasant paths. That is not His way. He will not help us to avoid our difficulties. What he will do is to give those, who humbly ask, the spirit that no dangers can disturb. The Christian message to the world brings peace in war, peace where we most need it—peace of soul. If we can really do our work, whatever it is, as well as we can in God's sight, it will become His work, and we can safely leave the issues in his hands."

Believe it or not, American newspapers reported that speech, made almost a year after the start of the second world war, under the headline:

"EMPHATIC 'NO' TO HITLER'S ULTIMATUM."

But perhaps Mr. Dooley reflects more truly the average American's reaction when he says: "Th' English dress up f'r a Methodist preacher, stick a piece iv lead pipe in th' tails iv their coat in case iv emargency, an' get all the money there is in th' line."

Halifax speaks of "That lasting and righteous peace which the British Prime Minister and the President of the United States have both declared to be the only peace which is possible." So far as the reference to our President is concerned, it is only too well justified: Roosevelt seems every bit as unconcerned about the details of the "righteous peace" as Halifax and Churchill are—provided it puts the English back on top of its Empire and of the European manure pile. But Halifax's whole cathedral approach to the subject of British war aims, while it might be eminently suitable if he were a bishop in a pulpit, is infantile, coming from a man in his political position. It reveals the complete and astounding bankruptcy of England as a force for progress or for anything at all in our day. Of the Halifax pamphlet, *The British Case,* H. G. Wells justly remarked:

This publication is calculated to damn us utterly in the eyes of America [from America he evidently excludes President Roosevelt and his circle] and all neutrals—even our ally France. I challenge you to read it and say whether Halifax is the fit and proper person to continue in charge of our foreign affairs. I believe you will say with me that if this is the stuff for which we are fighting, it is foolish to fight. . . . Why all this hysterical trust in our Government? Is it psychologically different by only a degree from what is happening in Germany? The Germans adhered to Hitler because they feared complete chaos if his gang broke down.

The very nearest we can get to anything positive in the future policy of England's rulers is that they have shown themselves "friendly disposed"—nothing official, of course—toward the proposals of Clarence Streit in the book *Union Now.* "There is little doubt that something along this line will have to be given very serious consideration when the time comes to lay the foundations of a new order"—that kind of thing! But even had they come out flat-footed for *Union Now,* every intelligent economist knows this to be a mere compromise with something which just will not be compromised with. Instead of such a world union as Wells calls for, *Union Now* suggests a union of the fifteen "democracies" that are "satisfied." It sounds very beautiful until you try and find fifteen democracies and fifteen countries that are satisfied —"there ain't no sich person." But it is a nice harmless toy for England to give its people and Franklin Roosevelt to play with, since under it there would be a deputy in the "Union" parliament for every million citizens, and that would give England and its satellites more deputies than any other bloc. Nothing more, in fact, than the dear old Pax Britannica in a new, if slightly used, hat! The dear old Pax which is not Pax at all, since there would still be the Have-Nots growling and muttering at the gates, and we lesser breeds outside the law would still be taking orders from England and some of us would kick.

If the speeches and statements of England's leaders appear to come from a mummified corpse already ticketed and displayed in history's museum, let us see whether we can find any spark of life-force in their actions.

First, look at the government of "national unity" which now, after many months of public protest against the Munich "old gang," is conducting England's holy war. Most of the leading members of the "old gang" are still there—slightly reshuffled but with no less power than they had before. Chamberlain, who certainly deserves to go down in history as the most horrible and pitiful figure of the ages, until recently remained on the right hand of Churchill, the new Prime Minister. From his new chair about half a yard from the old one, Chamberlain told the world: "Certainly I know that no section of the Conservative party wants peace. We are absolutely united. . . . There are no differences between the Prime Minister and myself. . . . Our minds run in the same channel. . . . If I disagreed with the Prime Minister I should resign and go in opposition. But intrigue—*never*. . . . We feel ourselves trustees for civilization as we have known it."

Churchill, who in 1936 wrote in the London *Times* that "another great war would extinguish what is left of the civilization of the world, and the glory of Europe would sink for uncounted generations into the abyss," stoutly defends Chamberlain and has added exactly nothing to his predecessor's zero score in the department of precise war aims. He is more bellicose than Chamberlain, more vitriolic in personal abuse of Hitler, but affords us no glimmer of what he has to offer humanity which is superior to what Hitler offers.

Halifax, the ineffable man of God, who is responsible before the bar of history for the intrigues preceding the betrayal of Austria and Czechoslovakia to Hitler, has run foreign affairs with the same ineffable and inimitable futility. Hoare, whose name is a stench in the nostrils of every decent man for his plot with Laval to sell out Ethiopia, has become His Majesty's special plenipotentiary at the usurper Franco's court, where obviously any new Munichs and betrayals that the situation calls for at any time must be plotted—until such time as Hitler orders Franco to come out openly on his side.

There are some "Labor" men, some "socialists," in the new war government: Greenwood and Attlee, the mild little Major, in the Inner Cabinet, recently joined by Minister of Labor Bevin and Dalton, the Old Etonian "socialist," as Minister of Economic Warfare. Bevin is the "socialist" who, when Spain turned to British labor for help in 1936, told her "in the name of the entire British-socialist movement" that he "refused to accede to [her] demands." The only member of the troupe with a half-way decent record is Herbert Morrison.

These are the very men who for years, while Europe crumbled about their ears, refused co-operation against Chamberlain with the Liberal Party because they "could make no compromise with any group not pledged to socialism." Now they co-operate with the Chamberlain group in opposition to all liberalism, doing little about that "socialism" which they are "pledged" to introduce. How much real power they have, how much they are really opposed to what Chamberlain and Halifax and Hoare stand for, is shown by the fact that they have not only made no effort to get the Munich men removed but have actually expelled from the Labor Party others who advocated their removal! And this is the group of men which is holding God's hand and asking us to do the same and fight the good fight alongside them. (You will have noticed that, in time of war, God has an unlimited supply of hands. Hitler, of course, is holding one, and Mussolini is using the one he and Franco held jointly between 1936 and 1938 while butchering two million Spaniards.)

And now look who is Minister of Information, officially in charge of all British war propaganda: none other than Alfred Duff Cooper, pride of Mayfair and Park Avenue drawing rooms, who in April of this year declared that the crimes of the German militarists are "The crimes of a whole people"—and called for war to extermination on the whole suffering Nazi-dominated German race, ending with a "peace" in which their common "crimes" must not be forgotten. Exactly one year before, in a speech quoted in the London *Times,* Duff Cooper had said: "Hatred of any race is a sign of mental deficiency and of lack of a broad conception of the facts of the world." But in May of this year this self-confessed contradictory soul was appointed Minister of Information. A wise choice, under the circumstances—but what now, my Lord Halifax? Are you still holding God's hand or have you let it slip?

Now where else can we look for enlightenment about the sort of world we would have if the British Empire should by some miracle endure?

Perhaps the recent "recognition" of Haile Selassie, so that this Lion of Judah might become an ally against Italy, is as revealing as anything. When England itself and its right to hold colonial peoples in subjection is attacked, England will always fight to the last Frenchman, or American, or Ethiopian. If those same people are so foolish as to want to fight for the integrity of their own country, England is not interested. Cast your mind back two years to the cozy little séance of the League of Nations in May 1938, when the wretched Haile Selassie was graciously permitted by England to make this statement:

Ethiopia placed her confidence in the signature of members of the League and has been betrayed. Now, at the request of the most powerful State in the world, it is proposed that the problem should be written off. A deliberate infraction is proposed of an undertaking, accepted by League members, not to recognize ill-gotten territories. . . . Is it not absolutely incompatible with the spirit of the Covenant to sacrifice a State member of the League to insure the tranquillity of other powers?

The answer, vouchsafed by my Lord Halifax after due consultation with his Voices, was no:

I do not overlook the fact that there are many in my own country, as perhaps in others, who feel that any action designed to facilitate recognition of the Italian conquest does infringe on principle, and who would, therefore, deplore the adoption of such a course [wiping Ethiopia off the slate as a State and League member]. I respect, but I cannot share their view. . . . No cause is served by vain lamentations over the past. Great as is the League of Nations, the ends it exists to serve are greater than itself, and the greatest of those ends is peace.

Perhaps—I proceed with Halifaxian caution—you still retain illusions about England's noble purposes and England's vitality? "After all, even if they have made mistakes, they are fighting Nazism."

Are they? Do you know that, as I write this, practically all the most powerful Englishmen—and there are many—who before this war were avowed sympathizers with Hitler are circulating in England just as freely as ever—many of them in the Houses of Lords and Commons? And do you also know that hundreds of determined and implacable foes of Nazism in England are now in concentration camps—held incommunicado, husbands separated from wives? George Strauss, progressive Labor M.P., has listed many of the most flagrant cases of this in a challenge to Home Secretary Sir John Anderson: a boy of sixteen —a deaf sculptor of sixty and his wife—a man of German birth who has lived in England for forty-three years and was not even interned in the last war—Rudolf Olden, author of *Hitler the Pawn,* who has spent the last fifteen years fighting the Nazis—Heinrich Fraenkel, author of *The German People Versus Hitler,* who is personally known to me as a man who has martyred himself for many years to draw public attention to the Hitler menace. These and hundreds like them have been imprisoned, it is said, in response to "an 'Intern them all!' demand from the public." There has been no such demand from the public. The truth begins to appear when you look up the record of Sir John Anderson and find that he was Fuehrer of the Black and Tans in Ireland and, as Governor of Bengal in 1931, established himself as the most ruthless and tyrannical administrator in the whole of British imperialist rule in India.

In other words, Sir John Anderson—Home Secretary in the government defending "civilization"—has by his own actions shown himself to be as much like Hitler as two peas in a pod. In the name of all reason, is this "a war against Nazism"? No, it is a scrap between Hitlerdum and Hitlerdee.

If an empire built on such hypocrisy and blood can endure, then you and I might just as well abandon all our efforts to establish a decent world, all our faith that such a world is possible and not far distant. It is consistent in nothing except the defense of profit and privilege. It fights for "Democracy" in Europe, and continues appeasing aggressive dictatorships as merrily as ever in Asia by stopping the sale and transport of arms to China. That is done by that same Winston Churchill who on August 11, 1939, said: "It is of the utmost importance that neither Great Britain nor the United States should allow their local material interests in China to be used as a lever of blackmail to induce them to take sides against the heroic resistance of the Chinese people. . . . It would be far better, if the worst happened, to abandon temporarily our concessions and interests in China, and suffer all the losses entailed thereby, rather than to fail to aid and comfort the Chinese in their agonizing, but ever more hopeful, struggle for Right and Freedom." Typical words of a British statesman not in office—words which are always and inevitably forgotten when the man who spoke them has the defense of English imperialism on his shoulders.

The contradictions within this Empire have become so fantastic that it is a matter of moments, from the historical aspect, before it commits suicide. When the end comes, it may look like murder, but suicide it will really be. All pretense of being an economy of peace has now been discarded. The Empire has abandoned itself to a complete war economy from which—just as from Hitler's Nazi economy—there is no retreat: a trail at whose end lies inevitable disaster.

The wealthy class of England is splashing around in a stagnant, reeking pond of blood-profits. Last March, for the fourth year in succession, Vickers, the great armament firm, cut a 10-per-cent dividend melon—a ceremony in no way reflecting the huge profits the company has made by selling arms to more or less anyone who would buy. Only a few years ago Vickers was advertising its superior line of instruments of murder in German publications—at a time when Germany was officially "forbidden" by England to buy any arms at all. Asked to explain this, Chairman Sir Herbert Lawrence uttered that armament kings' classic: "The question of the manufacture of arms by the State or by private firms has been obscured by a certain amount of prejudice. . . . The prejudice is the expression of an honorable but mistaken ideal respecting the sanctity of life and the iniquity of war." Actually, while this year Vickers distributed some £400,000 to shareholders, its total profit for 1939 was £1,295,541—the rest being salted away as "reserves," etc.—"for the look of the thing." Reserves—millions of pounds of reserves ready for those future mass massacres to which the directors of Vickers look forward with calm certainty; for they do not or will not realize how few grains of sand are left in the British Empire's hourglass.

Even Vickers' blood-bath is a puddle compared with that of Imperial Chemical Industries, which holds a monopoly of all the Empire's chemical industry so vital in time of war. For 1939 its gross profit after taxation was no less than £9,313,485—an all-time high. Again, many millions of pounds of reserve, ready to be used for mass asphyxiations of the human surplus in years to come. And notice—of course it may be just a coincidence—all the scores of directors, ex-directors, and share-holders of Vickers and I.C.I. sitting at Westminster in solemn deliberation about the future of civilization as they know it; conducting the policy which is leading England straight to destruction and into Winston Churchill's "abyss."

There you have the picture of a great empire committing suicide, which from the first it was fated by the law of its being to do, before the eyes of what should be—and as far as the vast majority are concerned, is—a grateful world. The profit madness gets into these people and because of it they cut their own throats.

If only they would do it quietly in a corner, nobody would object at all except Roosevelt and Morgan. The tragedy is that the innocent millions of plain people in England and the Empire and throughout the world, who know nothing of the gruesome finagling going on behind the scenes, have to be dragged into the ocean of blood.

This whole thing goes far beyond the question of war or of peace between Britain and Germany. If Britain seeks peace now, then the British Empire is gone. And this will be so regardless of what Germany will or will not demand. Britain will lose India through revolt. Boer South Africa will withdraw from the Empire. Britain will no longer have a voice in Egypt or Palestine. Gibraltar will be lost and so will Hong Kong and all the English holdings in China. Australia will be easy prey for the Japanese, however loyal the Australians may be.

And peace or not between Britain and Germany, Japan will continue on its way and so will Russia. My guess is that no matter how this present segment of the conflict comes out, there will then be an even greater war between the winners of this one.

It is not a lovely thought, but that is the kind of world man in his surpassing wisdom has made. We could make it better if we could learn to be wiser.

CHAPTER SIXTEEN

Will American Democracy Endure?

HISTORY IS rushing forward so fast now that no man can fore-tell what is in store for us next year, or even next month.

That democracy will eventually grow far beyond its present limita-tions—indeed, that men will one day look back on this era and wonder how we could even think we had democracy—is, I think, certain. The widening of democracy and liberty is the natural order of things, the natural result of the advance in our knowledge of nature and com-mand over its forces.

But the developing process, as ever, is uneven in different parts of the world—and it can take a step back while gathering force for three steps ahead. Whether America, which has led the world in the first great stage of democracy's development, will be the leader in the next stage—or whether history is tossing the ball to those whom we now scorn, the Russians and Chinese—is something we do not yet know.

Democracy is something we don't talk about much except when we are in trouble. The word came into popular use here for the first time when Wilson proclaimed our war with Germany, to make the world safe for democracy. Judging by the attack on democracy *after* the war, in the handbook issued by the War Department, and recently quoted in Congress, we hadn't in fact accustomed our own shores to it. Democracy, that particular handbook argued, is a form of mob rule leading to attacks on property.

In different words—for no American dares any longer say such things openly, and that in itself is something gained—the same is being

225

said of it now. And in a way the statement is true. If mob rule is the rule of the majority, and if property rights are defined as a minority's right to pile up limitless wealth far beyond what they can spend, then certainly it is mob rule leading to attacks on property.

The first thing we have to realize is that without attacks of the most uncompromising kind on property as thus defined, democracy in America is doomed as far as the visible future is concerned. We must make no mistake about that. If 742 corporations (about one-sixth of one per cent of all corporations reporting in 1939) continue to have over half the cash, nearly half of all notes and accounts receivable, nearly half of all capital assets and approximately two-fifths of other assets, and nearly two-thirds of non-tax-exempt investments, then democracy has an eclipse ahead.

For what is the inevitable result of such maldistribution of wealth? The great corporations have far more money than they can use for honest purposes, and for the residue there is only a dishonest use to smash democracy. They have taken charge of the press and the radio and the state legislatures, through their lobby system. They elect the Congressmen and Senators they want and are enormously influential with local judges. They own the police and the Chambers of Commerce. Whatever they want they can put over by a veritable blitzkrieg upon the people from all directions at once. We get it by roaring earfuls from the "Veteran" organizations, the lunatic women's clubs, and it is plastered all over the newspapers while real news is completely suppressed. They neglect nothing in the way of noise. Then a man like Dies—whose "election" to Congress by only 5.3 per cent of what should be the electorate in his district makes him eminently suitable for the work—marks for smearing and breaking down real men of the people —a John L. Lewis or a Harry Bridges—who raise their heads and look "dangerous." If the smear is ineffective they can do the job equally well by a conspiracy of silence such as that visited upon LaFollette and all those who try to tell the people the truth. They can reach the schools and distort history so that the corporations are shown in a lovely light and the really great American figures are neglected or lied about.

Huey Long said that $5,000,000 should be the greatest wealth any one man could possess—that this would be "sufficient incentive." That is already ten times too much in my view. But at present the only "incentive" seems to be five billions, and still repletion is not attained. Propose the smallest curb upon it and you are told that you "kill business incentive." Yet hunger is incentive enough to make a poor man work for eight dollars a week.

Nowhere does "Americanism" go more crazy than over this question of "incentive." The financial editor of the New York *Sun* wrote last May that "it is difficult for many Americans to understand how Britain can expect anyone to make the tremendous extra productive effort required by war without some stimulus other than the vague one that it is necessary to save the country." What kind of incentive is this—just saving the country? How hopelessly "vague"! And when the workers in Kearney's shipyards struck for an extra ten cents an hour—less than the increase in the cost of living—Congressman Barden of North Carolina lectured them: "This is no time for labor to try and grab off ten cents an hour more!" A dime for a workman is "grabbing off" and nothing less than treason. A billion for a corporation is hardly incentive enough to set the wheels of defense-production turning.

Or recall the holding-company case in the Supreme Court of Massachusetts, where no ruling could be handed down because it was "not humanly possible" to understand all the interlockings of profiteering corporations in the case. I would have ruled, and any man of ordinary common sense would have ruled, that if it was as mysterious as that then it was outside the law and the companies should be dissolved until someone *could* explain it.

It is to these "mysterious" corporations—mysterious in everything but their ruthless drive for more and more profit—that the mass of our people are in effect becoming enslaved. Our jobs depend on them. The inevitable end is that the corporations want to take complete control of the government, as they did in Germany and Italy and Spain, so that the shackles on the people may be legally fastened.

All efforts to curb this corporate wealth, in the interests of the people as a whole, have so far been ineffective. We have the income tax law, and death taxes. But the very people against whom they are mainly directed have been able to evade them. The man who gets $3,500 a year on the whole calculates his income tax scrupulously, but the man with $3,500,000 sets his legal staff at work to find every possible loophole by which he can avoid paying his tribute to the very government under whose protection that fortune was made. His wealth buys him immunity.

The same is happening with the new excess-profits taxes which are supposed to curb profiteering out of defense production. There are so many loopholes in them—placed there by the corporation lobbies—that practically no concerns will be hit by the higher taxes of 40 and 50 per cent. Exactly the same loopholes are in England's wartime excess-profits taxes, and almost nobody is actually paying them to any extent. They are just there to look good on paper. But the taxes payable—and paid—by the poor have bounded up enormously. Meanwhile the National City Bank of New York tabulates the returns of four hundred corporations and finds that, after deducting taxes and deficits, they made $649,000,000 in the first half of 1940 as compared with $409,000,000 in the first half of 1939.

Who are these men who suck all the wealth from the body of America? Mere nobodies, in fact. They don't really do anything. Nothing comes out of them except the collection of money and more money for their families and groups. They do not invent anything—in fact, they spend a great deal of their efforts seeing to it that the inventions of others shall not see the light of day, while the inventors are never heard of. A young research physicist says of the attempt to break the atom and create a new source of cheap energy: "If such energy were harnessed it would not be used until after all the coal and oil in the world is gone, for it would disrupt the economic setup. The secret would probably be buried in Fort Knox with the world's gold." In other words, the discoveries that big business cannot turn to its immediate profit are sabotaged. So you see this economic setup *depends* and *must depend* on scarcity for the many—plenty for the few. Make the masses work hard for what they get and they will respect us—those who have gathered in this wealth they create plus the national wealth they should socially share.

Albert Einstein, summarizing the condition of our land and the world in A.D. 1939, says: "The production and distribution of commodities is entirely unorganized so that everyone must live in fear of being eliminated from the economic cycle, in this way suffering from want of everything." But take no notice of him—the man is an alien.

The tremendous power our men of wealth have in our legislatures they use, because of the demands of their wealth, only to prevent progressive legislation from being introduced. And so chain five-and-tens, chain hotels, chain drugstores, chain oil stations, chain radio stations, chain restaurants, chain bakeries, chain barber shops, chain auto agencies, chain movie theaters, chain newspapers, chain telegraph offices, chain railroad and bus stations: a chain slave-service in the new all-clerk nation. Verily it is said: "Man is born free and is everywhere in chains." And all the chains howling in chorus that the "American way" is for the government to stop interfering with them, so that—there can be no other motive—they can still further enslave the slaves. Everyone knows that without government "interference"—without immense subsidies paid out of the people's toil—half the corporations would not even exist today. The government saved the banks in 1933 —saved them from themselves. It saved the railroads and is still saving them with our money, while the railroads bite the hand that feeds them in the national magazine advertisements. Even benefit checks to farmers land for the most part in the laps of the privileged. That poor old patched-jeans dirt farmer, Metropolitan Life Insurance, got $257,000 from the government in 1937. Just 272 persons or corporations got checks of $10,000 or over in that year, and yet the average check—the check the real farmers with the real need received—was just $75.

Do not be deceived by the specious arguments offered by newspapers and magazines which are themselves a branch of the corporative interests. In the same year as the Declaration of Independence Adam Smith wrote: "Civil government is maintained for the defense of the rich against the poor." At that time, he said, "For one very rich man there must be at least five hundred poor." That is just as essentially true for America as for any other country under this system, all the cant about "the American way" to the contrary notwithstanding: except that now the owners of our corporations are not content with a mere five hundred slaves. They require and have thousands each, even though they know not who or where they are. Indeed, since the first world war our great fortunes have doubled and redoubled until those with an income of one million or more a year make a large directory;

and since they cannot spend a quarter of it, most of it lies in bank vaults, and its presence there is used to prove that because of high taxes it cannot be profitably invested.

Is it any wonder that these people admire—secretly now for the most part, perhaps openly pretty soon—the Fuehrer of Germany who succeeded in legally enslaving his entire people? A recent publicity release of California's "Associated Farmers" (a group of bankers and multimillionaire corporations) put it better than I can: "Ruthless totalitarian dictators in Europe, using fifth column traitors to destroy peaceful nations unsuspecting of their danger, have done in a few short weeks the job we have been striving to do for years."

Well, certainly our democracy cannot endure if things go on this way.

"It is no use"—I am quoting J. A. Hobson, the leading English Liberal (not left) economist—"for free traders to preach the pulling down of trade barriers, for economists to lament the waste of money upon competing armaments, for democrats to bewail the collapse of popular institutions before the rise of despots, for rationalists to appeal to the material and real advantages of a world pooling of raw materials, science and social co-operation, so long as the real source of trouble lurks unrecognized in the background, *viz.,* the insistence of the owning classes in each nation to cling to their 'rights of property' and to utilize those rights in such ways as to breed class and international discord."

Un-American, is it? Written by another mere alien?

But which is the more un-American—to speak plainly about the troubles of our own land and the causes of them, or to cast out wildly over the waters and far lands of the earth in search of profit upon profit upon profit?

Is that the "American way"—to mortgage the lives of American boys for the sake of extra billions from Europe and South America and the Far East when we are not making use of half what the good Lord gave us right here at home? Is following England on the path of world imperialism "the American way"? What is American about the insane scramble of the old imperialisms to become a World Power? Who wants to be a World Power? What ordinary, normal American?

Being a World Power has done nothing for the people of England.

See how they live now. See how little they have of material things, how little democracy. Not all of the vast tribute from India and the colonies has been able to put butter in the ordinary daily diet of the English masses.

This world-power business is an obsession. You see the next fellow doing it and a natural instinct makes you run him a race, all apropos of nothing at all as far as the people are concerned. For world power means millions bowing down to you. It means dictatorship in your subject countries and leads by quick stages to dictatorship at home. It means competition in armament-building—and that means war. Armaments have never yet been built to rust in storerooms, and never will be. Every wise man drew that conclusion from the first world war. Lord Grey of Fallodon, British Foreign Secretary from 1905 to 1915, wrote: "Great armaments lead inevitably to war. If there are armaments on one side, there must be armaments on other sides. . . . The increase of armaments that is intended in each nation to produce consciousness of strength, and a sense of security, does not produce these effects. On the contrary, it produces a consciousness of the strength of other nations and a sense of fear. Fear begets suspicion and distrust and evil imaginings of all sorts."

A commonplace in the years following 1918. Forgotten now in the hysteria and panic of a new armaments race resulting from nothing but the inter-imperialist dogfight to redivide the world.

Here in America, however, we have at least found, in the course of our very hasty search, a few ways *not* to make our democracy endure.

We will not make it endure, for instance, by intensifying our efforts in the imperialist racket, which is the very essence of undemocracy. There is no democracy for us, any more than there is for the inhabitants whom nobody ever consults, in America taking over British and French colonies in the West Indies. Does it ever occur to you, gentle reader, that there are people who are born and die in these colonies, people who yearn just as much as you or I for freedom? Do you perhaps think those people would get any advantage out of being "transferred" to our loving care? Read what a Jamaican had to say last June:

I love Jamaica with as great intensity as Englishmen doubtless love England and I resent any suggestion, no matter how well intentioned, that in order to save England our island home should be a sort of sacrificial lamb.

. . . There is no proof that "materially a transfer of sovereignty to the United States would be an advantage." . . . Puerto Rico, although American for forty years, is still desperately poverty-stricken. The masses of the people are landless and their standard of living unbelievably low. The former Danish West Indies, now American, was not long ago described by former President Hoover as an "effective poor-house." . . . No one suggests selling Newfoundland or any of the Dominions. That kind of talk is reserved for countries inhabited by "natives."

Or again, if you have illusions about "American" imperialism being different from other brands, read Theodore Roosevelt, Jr., on his return from Puerto Rico in the boom year 1929:

In the last six weeks I have traveled all over the island. I have been through school after school. I have seen hundreds of thousands of children, and I write now not what I have heard or read, but what I have seen with my own eyes. . . . I have seen mothers carrying babies who were living skeletons. I have watched in a classroom thin, pallid boys and girls trying to spur their brains to action when their little bodies were underfed. I have seen them trying to study on only one scanty meal a day, a meal of a few beans and rice. . . . The death rate from tuberculosis was higher than that of any other place in the Western Hemisphere, and four and a half times the death rate of continental United States.

And of the formerly Danish Virgin Islands already mentioned by our Jamaican, the wife of an American Confederate army general who visited them recently said: "The island natives, both black and white, are living under economic slavery more cruel and oppressive than the chains which shackled the slaves of the Old South."

So our Mr. Hull trips down to Havana to make the domination of the United States more secure than ever over the "way of life of the Americas," as our President puts it. It is not enough for the Wall Street finance groups that already most of "the Americas" are groaning under dictatorships just as cruel and much more long-standing than those of Europe. No, these wretches of "the Americas" must also be brought under the wing of the United States eagle.

How shall that be expeditiously achieved? First by telling the Central and South American "democracies," which for the most part never were democracies, that in democracy's name they must be less democratic than ever because Wall Street capital wants to come in. Second, by conscripting a huge army in the United States to show we mean business. Third—well, how about appointing a Rockefeller as the National Defense Council's "co-ordinator" of relations with "the Americas"? The Rockefellers are the very people who have been charged by the Mexican government and many others with arming rebels in Mexico to compel subservience of that country to Standard Oil. Who better to act impartially on behalf of the great democratic American people? And so Nelson Rockefeller, son of John D., Jr., and third in line in his great dynasty, gets the job. As a San Francisco columnist says, in thumbing his nose at the Dutch government for suggesting it has anything to say about the Dutch West Indies, "this is an age for utter and brutal realism."

All this, of course, under the somewhat threadbare cloak of the Monroe Doctrine, which had to do with entirely different conditions and is today nothing more than a snare to lead the American people to disaster. We talk of "protecting" these countries for a certain "way of life" which we claim to exist in them. In the first place this "way of life," which only partially exists in our own land, is a complete myth in 90 per cent of the rest of this hemisphere. In the second place, what interest have the American people in "protecting" an entire hemisphere? Since our "sphere of interest" is now said to extend to Greenland and the Azores and West Africa on one side and the Dutch East Indies on the other, where does the thing end—if it does end? The fact is, of course, as anyone knows, that the people of "the Americas" have far more in common with the European way of life than with ours.

Let us speak frankly. Every word of this talk about "the way of life of the Americas" and about "protection" and "hemisphere co-operation" is pure and unadulterated hypocrisy. What is happening, quite simply, is a gigantic world struggle between monopoly groups for the exclusive right to use South and Central America as a source of more profit. The only difference between the German and Italian monopolists on the one hand, and the English and American on the other, is that the former frankly call it conquest and the latter call it "protection." England's "protection" is exactly the same as England's domination. After the last war it was called a "League Mandate" but it was still the same kind of domination. If you think our "protection" is any different, you are living in a dream. It's the grab that counts, not the name.

If you think the people of Central America really want to be "protected" by us, you ought to see a doctor. And if you think there is one particle of democracy in all of this for anyone at all, you need the prompt attention of an alienist. There is nothing in it but swag for the Wall Street boys, and inevitable wars for us suckers.

Nor will we make our democracy endure by screaming like hysterical schoolgirls about the terrible Nazis and the terrible Fifth Columnists and the terrible Communists, without ever taking the trouble to find out just what Hitler could really do against us and what sort of defense we need—or to find out who the real Fifth Columnists are—or to find out what the Communists are. These are not at all difficult things to discover—indeed the real cognoscenti of Wall Street know the answers now, whatever they may pretend.

As to what Hitler could do to us: all we get from our President is shrill cries for an army of two million and dark hints that "from the fjords of Greenland it is only six hours by air to New England," while "the Azores are only two thousand miles from parts of our eastern seaboard." Now mark that word—"only"! Not a word about the fact that Hitler hardly began to bomb England until he had got within twenty miles of its coast. No mention of Winston Churchill's speech last June, when he said: "In the Skaggerak, because of the distance [four hundred-odd miles from England] we could give no air support to our surface ships and consequently, lying as we did close to the enemy's main air power in Norwegian waters, we were compelled to use only our submarines." And only the day before President Roosevelt uttered his ridiculous forebodings, the Senate Naval Committee had reported that "airplanes on the continents of Europe and Asia do not menace us." And they had added: "We cannot be attacked directly by the armed forces of any powerful foreign nation. We cannot be blockaded by any surface vessels or submarines. We cannot be starved. We cannot be invaded. Nor can our cities or homes be bombed from the air by foreign airplanes, if we make sure that we command the sea and air approaches."

Well, what is this? A monstrous practical joke? Are our President and the committee of experts down the road at the Senate no longer on speaking terms? Of course we need to see that we "command the sea and air approaches" against any possible enemy. But why all the hysteria —and why, in the most breath-taking defiance yet of all legality and neutrality and democracy, make England a present of fifty of our destroyers when we are told our own defenses are so sadly deficient?

The reason is only too obvious. We have no clearly announced defense policy because our real policy is imperialist aggression on Wall Street's behalf, not defense on the people's behalf. We are being rushed into war hysteria and prepared for war itself because our economic problems have become insoluble under this system and the only course left to our Fuehrers is to establish dictatorship, which can only be done under the guise of "national defense."

No democracy there. Not a shadow of it.

And we are really up a gum tree to find a way out. We have let this thing go so far that the ballot box can do little for us. We know how Wilson and Hughes both prattled about peace in 1916. Elections are not won on frank espousal of war—the people are against it. Democracy means winning an election by promising peace and then immediately declaring war.

I am an oldish man and I have seen and heard some hypocrisy in my time—but if there has ever been anything to beat the New Deal's contradictions I would be interested to hear about it. "Freedom of information and the press, freedom of religion, freedom of expression, freedom from fear of attack, freedom from want"—those are the "ideals of government and peace" according to the New Deal policy. Yet President Roosevelt becomes positively angry when anyone seeks information on how his private love-affair with England is progressing, and leads all the other Wall Street voices in whooping up hysterical fear of a geographically impossible attack—and strikes millions off relief rolls because they happen to be of foreign birth. According to Senator Clark of Missouri, the man's hysteria is such that the war plank he tried to insert in the Democratic platform would have committed us to aid the Allies *until all democracies everywhere were restored to their former estate.* Senator Clark sarcastically added: "If the higher ethics require that no government established by force is to be recognized, I trust that no one will embarrass us by asking by what authority our flag flies in the Philippines."

And how well does it bode for America—the America you and I

thought we inherited—that our land, once a haven for the "tired, the poor, the huddled masses yearning to be free"—has now become the asylum of all the foulest scum of Europe's decayed aristocracy? How do you like to see the refugee ships from Europe bringing tattered Grand Dukes and Princes, runaway bankers, old cast-off Bourbons, and the children of English aristocrats—even, on one ship which turned away human beings for lack of space, the two dogs of one Lady Mendl —while our government not only refuses entry to hundreds of thousands of homeless people who have really tried to fight Fascism and Nazism, but actually brings pressure on Bolivia and Chile to cancel visas they proffered to anti-Nazi writers? That is but one of many signs of our present rulers' real sympathies with Fascist dictatorship. Signs of American Fascism appear everywhere, either unchecked or encouraged or promoted by our government. New vigilante groups springing up in Connecticut and elsewhere to take "private action" against "those endeavoring subversive activities." Pennsylvania state employees ordered not to wear buttons with the words "The Yanks Are *Not* Coming," on pain of dismissal. Aliens thrown out of work by the thousand and denied relief as an immediate result of the monstrous fingerprinting law—as if a man's place of birth, instead of his bankroll, were the measure of his probable loyalty to democracy. Millions still denied their constitutional right to vote in the South of "Democrat" Dies. Plans under way for industrialists to be allowed to maintain private storm-troopers against possible "unrest" in the factories. The hunt for "Fifth Columnists" openly led by the Ku Klux Klan—itself America's Fifth Column Number 1—in Florida. The K.K.K. boasting in its official publication that "It must be a source of great satisfaction to Klans-people everywhere that the President of the United States has come out boldly in defense of the Klan program." "Wartime" ordinances passed in McKeesport obliterating all civil rights, on the insistence of an American Legionnaire that they must pass "regardless of the Constitution." Students threatened with expulsion in Berkeley, California, for daring to oppose the Burke-Wadsworth Conscription Bill. Labor leaders sentenced to long jail terms under an Anti-Trust law which was introduced to control the monopoly corporations—and under which no corporation man has ever been imprisoned. Legislation before Congress for sedition laws which would end free speech, press, and

assembly for citizens and non-citizens alike; for destruction of what remains of the Wagner Act; for a domestic passport system similar to that of Czarist Russia; for denial of constitutional rights to all minority parties; for silencing trade unions, churches, and fraternal organizations on all political issues. Plans completed for complete dictatorship on "M-Day," when wages would be fixed, the right to leave a job would be withdrawn, strikes and picketing would be forbidden, habeas corpus would disappear—all this to be administered by Fuehrer Stettinius of United States Steel. Exactly and precisely that Hitlerism which we are asked to get so excited about! What a picture of "democracy in action"! Who would not lay down his life for so glorious an ideal? The same fatal idea that destroyed France—the idea of abolishing that which the people are asked to defend in order to defend it.

If Americans knew how far we have already gone toward abolishing our democracy, they would rise in anger now in defense of their most precious possession. But millions don't know, because the only sources of information they have deliberately keep them from knowing. The National Federation for Constitutional Liberties has issued a statement listing the grossest recent newspaper suppressions, showing that:

Only one large newspaper in the country printed anything about the petition to discontinue the Dies Committee which was signed by one hundred outstanding Americans including six college presidents;

Only two or three papers printed the "Defense of the Bill of Rights" issued by sixty-two prominent Americans;.

Scores of protests against the Dies Committee and against conscription by C.I.O. and A.F.L. unions were unmentioned in the press;

About 2 percent of the press mentioned the state and city conferences against anti-alien bills, in which delegates representing millions of Americans participated;

Most papers suppressed altogether the American Bar Association Bill of Rights Committee's warning to the nation against certain Congressional actions;

More than three hundred leading American writers issued a declaration against American entry into the war—it was ignored. And to that let me add that when some six thousand delegates from forty states, representing many millions of Americans, made the trek to Chicago in September for an American Peace Mobilization—possibly the most remarkable spontaneous demonstration of its kind in our history—hardly any newspaper even mentioned it, and those that did dismissed it in a few lines as "Communist," merely because some of those taking part had been given a red label by the preposterous Dies.

So we have gone a long way from democracy already. We go further every day that passes. The movement is so rapid that, as I come toward the end of this book, I cannot tell whether it can be printed in time to appear before all free speech legally disappears.

Yet—maybe I am the victim of delusions, but I still believe our democracy has a good chance to endure.

I believe it because all these demonstrations and protests, despite the sabotaging of the press, have occurred and are occurring. The people are still alive to the issues, however much Wall Street tries to hide the immediate truth from them.

Lincoln said you couldn't fool all the people all the time. I think he was right. We are not only a fundamentally democratic people; we have a tradition of fighting for our democracy. And we *are* fighting. If the avenues left open to us by our governmental and financial Fuehrers are small, we simply have to broaden them by mass pressure or find new avenues.

American democracy is not quite such a frail flower as Wall Street imagines. It may not be the most beautiful that the world can ever develop—though in good weather Americans are inclined to think so—but most certainly it has proved to be a slow-growing, tough-fibered thing that has withstood Civil War, widespread plunder and graft, unprecedented centralization of wealth, slow starvation, and undernourishment and other assorted evils.

For as you know, it did not burst into full flower at the Constitutional Convention of 1787, nor did it thereafter receive careful cultivation. It was a seed sown by our forefathers; and the gardeners grossly underestimated the hardiness of the seed and the productivity of the soil. For long periods subsequently it has been neglected, even forgotten. But in time of its greatest peril the people always seem ready to rise in its defense—and they find their own ways of defending it.

The greatest democratic tradition of America is the tradition of Labor. Our people are given to "spontaneous mass movements and sudden manifestations of tremendous violence, especially when peaceful or lawful channels seemed blocked." They do not resort to such violence until they are convinced that it is the only alternative to far greater and more ruthless violence by the enemies of labor. The tradition comes down through John Brown, through the Know-Nothings of the '50's, the Anti-Renters and Barn-Burners, the Molly Maguires, the Green Corn Rebellion, through "Coxey's Army" of '94 and the Bonus Army of more recent years. The flame has only been fed by the savage anti-labor violence of the Haymarket Affair, of Ludlow, Wheatland, Gastonia, Centralia, Harlan County, Homestead, Lawrence, Everett, and the Memorial Day massacre of Chicago in 1936. The cry back of all these movements has been: "We'll make democracy work!" And if it were not for the American spirit in the common man through all these events, then indeed there would be no hope for America.

Where do we find this spirit today? Not in the majority of labor leaders, who have been just as corrupted by the system, and have become just as strong a vested interest against progress, as have their counterparts in England. But it is not difficult to recognize the labor leader who does have this genuine love of democracy in him. The more savagely he is smeared and assaulted by the billionaire press and the other tools of monopoly capital, the more certain we can be of his genuineness.

I know Harry Bridges, who is now being depicted for Americans as Satan in person complete with horns and tail. I would not have to know him to know that he is honest and genuine, but to meet and talk to him is to be convinced beyond doubt. His "crime" is very simple. He has successfully organized the waterfront workers of San Francisco, whom the employers had done everything in their power—with permanent success, they thought—to prevent from being organized. He has put vitality into the whole labor movement of San Francisco and of the West. In figures, here is his crime: hourly wages in San Francisco average $1.19 for newspaper employees, 83¢ for stone, clay and glass workers, $1.00 for book and job printers, 85¢ for furniture workers, 79¢ for food and tobacco workers, 81¢ for metal workers, and 55¢ for canning and preserving workers. The equivalents in Los Angeles, still a citadel of the "open shop," are 97¢, 64¢, 82¢, 67¢, 67¢, 72¢, and 48¢.

Terribly un-American, isn't it? Just chockful of Alien Isms? Shockingly bolshevistic and subversive? How can America survive this attempt to put purchasing-power into the pockets of the mass? How, tell me how, can industry survive when people actually have money to buy its products?

Believe me, for I speak of what I know: Harry Bridges is a better American than most Americans ever dreamed of being—and that goes too for John L. Lewis, his chief, whom Bridges calls "the greatest force in the world today between complete reaction and the maintenance of civil liberties." They may possibly not always be thus; Lewis, certainly, was not worthy of that praise in the past; but you will know when they have changed, if they do—by the cessation of press and Dies attacks on them.

It is with the leadership of men of that stamp that American democracy can only be saved, by the mass of working Americans. Not by just passing laws and sitting around, expecting them to be enforced. Only by a continual pressure from the bottom, where the need for more democracy and more consuming power is. For as Bridges says:

The Wagner Act was a great gain for the workers. But, as it is now, it protects us only as long as the unions are on the job to have it enforced—not by leaving it up to the government. Likewise the Security Exchange Commission, and the maritime laws: they aren't beneficial just by being there— but they can be made beneficial. We complimented Roosevelt on his intentions when he was doing something for the common people. Now we're scared of his intentions. It seems to me he has sold out the common people, and we are fighting him as far as we can.

And speaking of the union leaders who have "sold out," he says understandingly and without bitterness:

It is partly money, partly weariness—and age has a lot to do with it. As these people get old, they haven't the strength or ability to bounce back from the constant blows and pounding. It has an effect on them and weakens them. You have to have quite a little youth to take this pounding, otherwise you haven't the ability to bounce back.

The men, like Bridges, who bounce back, are the hope of the masses in America—the hope of democracy in America.

What blows and pounding he has taken and is still taking! "You have to have quite a little youth" . . . yes, and America will have to have quite a little youth, and use every ounce of it, to save democracy in this land.

CHAPTER SEVENTEEN

"The Lesson of France"

FROM LEFT and right and center, from upstairs and downstairs, we are being urged to look at France—and learn to be wise.

Excellent advice: I am all for it.

A few of us crackpots were urging Americans, a long time ago, to look at Austria, and Czechoslovakia, and Spain—and learn what happened to them. The lesson was the same but nobody bothered much with it then.

The crumpling up of France was such a shattering spectacle, a thing so humiliating and shameful, that none could ignore it. To those who hadn't previously acquainted themselves with the rough outlines of what is happening in the world, it must have been quite bewildering. Still more bewildering, perhaps, is the variety of explanations offered. It reminds me of the dam that collapsed outside Los Angeles some years back, killing several hundred people. Explanations ranged all the way from the simple one that the dam was faultily constructed, to the inspired theory of a Los Angeles *Times* reporter (or perhaps of his employer, who had reason to lift his eyes skyward) that "the finger of God toppled the dam over."

On one point all the theories about France agree—that "the real enemy is within the gates." The Fifth Column, you know. It is a point everyone likes because it enables one to lay the finger on whomsoever one does not like and say he should be locked up or guillotined lest he do the same here.

For all that, the point happens to be true. And consideration of the evidence with the utmost detachment we can muster, so that we may

241

identify the villains correctly, is urgent and vital. It is just as important for us not to lock up the wrong people as it is to lock up, or at least place where they can do no harm, the right people.

What is it about democracy that produces these traitors? Is this an incurable disease of democracy, and does it mean that democracy isn't all we have cracked it up to be?

Before proceeding to the evidence and bringing in a verdict, we would do well to examine France and find out how much democracy there was to destroy.

France was an empire, similar to but smaller than the British Empire. With a home population of forty-one millions it controlled a colonial population of sixty-five millions. Those colonial people performed the same function for France's bankers and industrialists that the people of India and British Africa perform for England's bankers and industrialists. They were a supply house of tribute and raw materials for the "motherland," and consequently had to be forcibly held back from natural progress. The sixty-five millions had no effective political democracy at all. Of the forty-one millions at home, nine and a half millions cast a vote in 1936. The unusually small figure is largely due to the fact that women's suffrage, long accepted in every other self-styled democracy, had been nine times voted in by the elected Chamber and nine times thrown out by the "indirectly" elected Senate.

So much for political democracy in France.

Taking the yardstick of material possessions—What do the people want, and what do they get?—here is the picture given me by a decidedly reactionary acquaintance who lived many years in France:

France is the only great "advanced" State where millions of people never possess a pair of leather shoes, and where a suit of clothes or a dress is something to be passed down from generation to generation and worn till it falls apart. For a great number of the ordinary families, 60 cents a day is the highest income they ever hope to see. The laboring man has a long revolutionary tradition but in the end, such is the concentration of power and wealth in a very few hands, he never gets what he revolts for. He strikes often but usually ends by going back to work under the same or worse conditions. Paris, with a huge working-class population, is run exclusively for wealthy foreigners. Nothing of any consequence has ever been done for the mass.

That describes very briefly how much democracy, in general, the French had to lose.

And now, in particular, how much did they have at the time their government declared war on Germany for the third time in seventy years?

On this we may refer to the account given by the sober but intelligent American writer Elliot Paul, on his return from France a month after the war began:

In a few short weeks the last vestige of democratic parliamentary government has been swept away. Every gain made in a constitutional manner by the workers under the Popular Front has been nullified by decree. A censorship the like of which has scarcely been seen in any totalitarian state has been set up and is in operation, so that not a word of truth regarding the events of the day reaches the eyes or ears of the helpless public. . . . France was bankrupt before the war started and is nearer collapse than at any time in modern history. There is no enthusiasm, no confidence in Chamberlain (who manipulates Daladier in foreign affairs), less confidence in Reynaud. . . . Bonnet, roué and simpleton who was instrumental in alienating Russia, has been given free rein in history's most thorough and unbridled red hunt and has landed in prison practically every member of the Chamber who voted against the Munich sellout. . . . The Paris police force, consisting of strong young men, has been augmented until there are three or four officers on every corner. . . . Industrial workers work twelve hours a day, seven days a week. . . . No payment is made for overtime. Unemployed women, such as servant girls who have been thrown on the country by the tens of thousands, collect about 25 cents a day, if they can get it, from the government. . . . Travel restrictions have been imposed that would have seemed harsh in Tsarist Russia. . . . No parliament, no press, no freedom of speech or assembly, labor unions almost helpless and growing more helpless daily, controlled currency, troops and petty officials everywhere, no national income, no money. That is only a partial list of Daladier's accomplishments.

Such was the state of affairs for which the masses of France—and unfortunately, nobody has yet found a way to fight a war without the masses—were asked to go forth and die.

"Yes, yes," you say. "Very sad and distressing. But it was only temporary—*c'est la guerre*, and all that. The French people would have understood that and fought as they fought in 1914, had the Fifth Column not deprived them of weapons."

All right. Now we have to find that Fifth Column. Who were they, what did they do, and why did they do it?

Here is one selection of theories, garnered from the most respectable sources:

"Paid agents of Moscow and Berlin," says Scripps-Howard Foreign Editor Simms (note which he honors by putting first). "Communist agents of Hitler," says Ambassador Bullitt. "Communists," says the intellectual pugilist Tunney—and calls for "a suspension of civil liberties so far as Communists (in U.S.A.) are concerned, in order to avoid the fate that befell France." A very popular theory points to "the crimes of the Popular Front government," the greatest of which, according to the Chicago *Tribune's* Colonel McCormick, was "sending all its airplanes to defend Communist Spain." The Los Angeles *Times* specifies the "crimes" as: "Collective bargaining through a strong union organization—a boost of wage rates—a political drive on the 200 families supposed to control the Bank of France and on French capitalists in general—the nationalization of the arms industry."

Whoa, now! Let's take it easy and try to make some sense out of these theories, if that is possible. Already we are up to our thighs in the kind of pure mysticism—the solving of problems by name-calling and insisting black is white or possibly pink—which today passes for intelligent analysis of events. We must proceed to extricate ourselves from the morass of distortions and outright lies involved in the above-quoted theories.

The Bullitt and Simms theories are based on the proposition that Communism and Nazism are identical and were in an alliance against French democracy. To this we must oppose that (*a*) France was not democratic; (*b*) Dies and all other great philosophers to the contrary notwithstanding, every line of official Communist and Nazi theory plus the material results obtained in Russia and Germany show the two concepts to be exactly as much alike as plenty and scarcity; (*c*) Russia and Germany are not allies against France or anyone else—they merely agreed not to attack each other, while on the contrary France itself *was* a full ally of Russia until recently, bound by treaty to come to Russia's aid, and vice versa.

As for Ambassador Bullitt, we can estimate how much he even knows the meaning of words by his statement that he "does not think it right to call the Pétain government Fascist." With this remarkable assertion not even President Roosevelt or the Los Angeles *Times* can agree— and for my part I think it eminently right and exceedingly generous, since we are name-calling, to call Bullitt a half-wit.

And now in the matter of Colonel McCormick. The Popular Front government did not send any airplanes at all to the Spanish government, and the Spanish government was not Communist. Assertions to the contrary are barefaced lies without a shadow of evidence, which people like the Colonel apparently expect Americans to believe merely because of constant repetition. The Popular Front government's crime —a crime in which we were accomplices—was on the contrary that it would not sell airplanes to Spain's legal government, which by international law it was bound to do.

We must get a few historical facts straight about the Popular Front government.

This government came to power in 1936 and lasted a little over a year. Except for Blum's short-lived cabinet in the spring of 1938— eighteen months before the war—the French government has at no time since then even given lip-service to the original Popular Front program or anything resembling it.

And as for its "crimes": if the Los Angeles *Times* sets them forth correctly, what democratic American with his roots in the Declaration of Independence and the Bill of Rights would not applaud such "criminality"? The Popular Front's program was to restore wage and salary cuts made during the depression, to create a national unemployment fund, to shorten the working week so that some of the millions rendered idle by technological progress could get work, to inaugurate a public-works program and old-age pensions. Isn't that terrible? Isn't that the most un-American thing you ever heard? This Popular Front dared nothing less than to suggest that the masses of the people should get a tiny fraction more of the wealth they produced! It was the very same program of bloodthirsty revolution that got the Spanish government the name "Communist."

They did nationalize, only partially (for many aircraft, frame, and accessory concerns and the two major aëro-engine companies were left in private hands), the arms industry. For this half-hearted attempt to remedy what all civilized people have long recognized as one of our society's greatest evils—making war a source of profits—there was an overwhelming demand from all sections of the French people. The Chamber passed the bill by a majority of 484 to 85, and even many ultra-conservative deputies voted for it. Even the editor of *L'Aëro-nautique,* the leading aviation journal, wrote that "the private system has drained almost the entire aëronautical industry of its substance; it has forced it to be dependent on banks to whom has thereby been conferred the authority, in respect to matters of defense, which ought to remain in the hands of the Government." But Gene Tunney and Bullitt and the Los Angeles *Times* and the other great minds will tell you that the editor erred. The partial nationalization of armaments was Communistic.

Under the new set-up the government struggled to step up arms production. But as everyone knows, it takes a long time and a lot of capital to equip such an industry to function efficiently; and the capital still had to be borrowed from private sources, since the timid Mr. Blum had not dared to nationalize the banks, and it was still not possible in France—not even for Blum's successor, Daladier—to adopt the Hitler technique of simply seizing money from the Jews.

And here is an account by a "respectable" American newspaperman in Paris—Frederic Sondern of the San Francisco *Chronicle*—of what the Two Hundred families of France did in face of the poor little "threat" of social progress:

The villains of the piece are a small group of bankers and industrialists. These oligarchs have exploited their country during the past years on an almost incredible scale. They have controlled the press, the huge manufacturing and financial trusts, and many Deputies and members of the General Staff . . . they have been liquidating their assets and reinvesting their capital in the United States and other havens of refuge. The exact amount of these transfers is not available. But indicative is the figure given by one French banking house specializing in large industrial accounts—75 per cent of their capital has been sent abroad, chiefly to the United States—in the last two years. Crippled by this outflow, the whole French armament industry was left unmodernized and totally unfit to deal with the present emergency.

In other words, it was not the working people but the owners of wealth who went on strike and stripped France of its power of defense.

They went on strike in just the same way that American big business went on strike against the timid reforms of the New Deal; in just the same way that our armament kings have been on strike against the outrageous suggestion that blood profits be restricted in any way.

There were no workers' strikes at all in the French arms industries after June 1936. In 1938 the working week was raised to forty-five hours, strikes were forbidden by law, and "absence from work" was declared punishable by beheading. But so woefully lacking were the factories in equipment that there simply were not forty-five weekly hours of work available for the existing labor force—which was less than a quarter of the German aircraft industry's labor force in size. In factory after factory the workers pointed out this condition, in answer to Daladier's sneer at the unions for "unwillingness to sacrifice."

"There is," says the American millionaire press in solemn judgment on the French debacle, "no magic substitute for the toil and sacrifice which alone can guarantee that no such price as France is now paying will be demanded of America." And even while they write, the Sixty Families of America are doing just what the Two Hundred of France did. They offer the working people of America toil and sacrifice—but you cannot stop invasion of a country with toil and sacrifice. It takes guns and tanks and planes (not to mention a forthright, consistent foreign policy which would probably stop the invasion from ever happening), and these the Sixty Families will not produce unless all restrictions on wages and hours, just as on profits, are removed.

That this is the real lesson to be learned from France is so glaringly obvious from all the facts at hand that our lying press can only fool the people by keeping them ignorant. Turn to our own country, and you find that, when the excess-profits tax bill was being prepared by the House Ways and Means Committee, lobbyists on behalf of big business invaded the hearings: representatives of steel mills, chemical plants, aviation interests and the like all paraded complicated reasons why they should be exempted from any such tax. What they said, in effect, was that they would lie down on the defense program unless they were allowed limitless profits out of it. Note, by the way, that the aviation concerns which led this treasonable movement were the very same firms that the Nye Committee had shown in 1936 to be helping Hitler build up his air fleet. And look what they got! New factories literally

donated by the government—that is, by you and me—for still further
skinning the public in the holy name of defense! And now the excuse
of "defense" is put forward for refusing the workers any pay increases,
any share of the huge new profits, not only in defense industries but
even—believe it or not—in the ladies' garment industry. The employees
in these sweatshops tried to strike this summer against their dreadful
working conditions and were told by their own "leader" that this was
practically treason—as if the United States Government were going to
put its conscripts in ladies' cloaks!

Perhaps the simplest refutation of the charge that the democratic
elements in France were the betrayers is the fact that England, where
highly reactionary governments have been in power since 1931, was
even less prepared for this war of its own making than was France.
In England likewise big business was and is sabotaging the defense
program in order to make astronomical profits. Even in the summer of
1940 Herbert Morrison, then English Minister of Supply, revealed that
the only up-to-date steel mill then existing in England was still only
running at two-thirds of capacity. Why? Because the old-fashioned
mills are in a cartel, controlled by Montagu Norman of the Bank of
England, which was a power at Westminster and must be first in the
profit-taking jamboree even though it means less steel production for
defense.

And just recently a columnist in the London *Daily Mirror* wrote:

The mortal bankruptcy of this country has been unmasked in the last
few months—a degrading, terrible spectacle. It ranges from selfish money
scavengers to disreputable remnants of the worst gang of political pests who
ever sabotaged the future of a great, honorable nation.

Is he referring to some Popular Front? No—to Chamberlain and Sir
John Simon and Sir Samuel Hoare and Lord Halifax. And of course
during the period leading up to the war, the period during which
France and England were making war inevitable but not preparing to
fight a war, the French politicians in power were men of exactly the
same stripe, whose one burning ambition in life was to destroy democracy.

Do we now begin to learn the lesson of France as it applies to our
own situation? We have arrived at the period of boundless potential

plenty for which humanity has struggled up through all the ages—
and our leaders tell us, in the name of "democracy," to vote for hardship, sacrifice, and suffering. It is for these noble aims that our sons
must be conscripted and sent abroad—yes, no such army as we plan to
raise could possibly be needed for defense of our own land—to die. What
a wonderful consummation to the process of human liberation set
going by Washington and Jefferson and Paine! How gratifying for the
spirit of Abe Lincoln!

Doesn't the picture begin to get clearer? Elliot Paul reported in October 1939 that "the French people are as desperately in need of help
against Daladier as the German people are in need of help against
Hitler." The same exactly is true today of the English people and the
Chamberlains and Churchills—and of the American people and its
hysterical leaders.

Do you tell me that all this is sad but unimportant, because France
and England were threatened by armed force and therefore, however
bad their governments, the people were compelled to fight and accept
discipline for sheer self-preservation?

I tell you to look at what happened in Spain. Spain and France—
what a startling contrast! Spain, too, was violently attacked: the people
had to fight and have discipline. But they had a government whose
program was to create and distribute plenty, not to preserve scarcity—
and so discipline did not have to be imposed from above. The people
imposed it on themselves—and that, as the results showed, was a very
different thing.

The Spanish people were so bereft of arms that at the start of the
Fascist rising they had to defend Madrid almost with their bare hands.
To the very end they suffered from an infinitely greater inferiority of
equipment than the French did in 1940. But they held Madrid for two
years, and even then the Fascists could not take the city: it was handed
over by traitors inside—the original Fifth Column.

They too had Hitler's tanks and dive-bombers to contend with—
but they had no horde of panicky refugees gumming up the works
for the simple reason that the people knew it was their fight and all
took part in it. A boy who fought in Spain has described how the
Loyalists were in position behind Madrid with "no Maginot Line, no
trench, no river, nothing except a little ravine and the dry earth parched

by summer sun. Each man dug himself a fox hole. That was all the protection we had. . . . The Fascists were throwing artillery shells over at the rate of twenty-eight per minute all day. At 10 A.M. the Nazi bombers began, and they didn't stop till sundown. They had from five hundred to seven hundred planes, attacking in waves or shuttle formation from their airfield about an hour away. . . . Not for one minute was there a let-up of that hell. . . . Anti-aircraft guns? We didn't have any. Roosevelt wasn't interested, then, in saving democracy. We just had to rub our noses in the dirt and take it. . . . When the dive-bombing stopped, the Fascist tanks and infantry attacked. But we beat them back and counter-attacked—singing! . . . Dive bombers? Do they 'paralyze front-line resistance'? Not if your soldiers have something to fight for."

Perhaps you give a superior smile—such a thing isn't possible. But facts are facts. Madrid held out for two years—and as for the amount of war material and men Hitler and Mussolini sent to Spain, just check with the figures they themselves have boastfully published. The same story is being repeated now in China, where despite terrific odds the people, who feel they have a real stake in what they are defending, seem to be unbeatable. Yet Paris falls without a struggle—the whole of France is overrun in a month.

The boy who fought for Spain has the answer: "Not if you have something to fight for."

What had the French to fight for? Let Lloyd George, First World War Prime Minister of England, take up the tale:

From the start of the campaign, whilst blazoning liberty on their banners, the rulers of France constantly pursued a policy of repression in their decrees. They ruthlessly and stupidly censored the press; some journals which supported the action of the government in challenging Nazi aggression were suspended. They were suspended because of criticisms which were ultimately proved to be completely justified by disastrous events.

Freely elected members of Parliament were thrown into prison for no breach of law, for no act or word of treason to the state, but purely because they held the same views about the social and economic reconstitution of France as the country with which France herself was in alliance up till two years ago—by the way, an alliance which, if it had been honored, would have saved Europe from its present catastrophic condition. . . . Of those who elected these persecuted members to the Chamber of Deputies and municipal councils there were at least 500,000 men who were actually enrolled in the armies defending the frontiers of their country. What a mockery it must have appeared to them in these circumstances to be called upon to face death for liberty, equality and fraternity, which were trampled underfoot by their own government! Liberty is not merely an ideal to be achieved; it constitutes the most formidable weapon by which that ideal can be won or defended.

Some days later—but, interestingly enough, Hearst despite his contract for Lloyd George's writings did not print this—the veteran Welsh statesman referred to the Communist Party of France as "by its sympathies more hostile against Nazism and Fascism than almost any other section of French opinion—a powerful political party held in special abhorrence by the plutocracy." That opinion—with which you may or may not agree—is heresy number one to the Hearsts and at all costs the American people must be kept from knowing that it is held by such a man as Lloyd George. If Americans stopped thinking that Communism and Fascism are the same, one of the main foundation stones of our Sixty-Family lying propaganda would vanish.

Let us look further to see what a mockery it was for Frenchmen to be called on to defend liberty, equality, and fraternity.

They had seen their government laugh in the faces of the German republic's leaders, who came imploring for help to stop Hitler from seizing power. They had seen their government stand by while Hitler marched into the Rhineland in bold defiance of the treaty France had imposed.

They had seen their government turn a deaf ear to the cry of the people of Austria when Dollfuss and Schuschnigg smashed democracy there, preparing the way (as Daladier and Reynaud were to do in France itself) for their own gory end at the hands of a mightier tyranny.

They had seen their government, blandly ignoring the wishes of the electorate, stand by to watch, with pleasure they did not try to conceal, the smashing of democracy in neighboring Spain.

They had seen their government make Hitler a free present, at Munich, not only of Czechoslovakia and its democracy but also of Czechoslovakia's 1,482 airplanes, 501 anti-aircraft guns, 2,175 artillery pieces, 785 trench mortars, 462 tanks, 43,876 machine guns, 114,000 revolvers, 1,000,000 rifles, more than 3,000,000 shells, more than 1,000,-000,000 cartridges, and bridge-building materials, sound detectors, searchlights, and trucks. All these and more would have been at France's disposal to use against Hitler if Czechoslovakia had not been betrayed. Yet Frenchmen were asked to believe, and Americans are now asked to believe, that the only people who voted against that betrayal are the ones who betrayed France!

They had seen the small new liberties and reforms of the Popular Front period swept away, and most of the liberties they had before that swept away with them. France had become a complete, open dictatorship in order to fight the dictators. Is it any wonder then that—to quote Frank C. Hanighen, ace American correspondent in Paris—the French people "went to war with no enthusiasm"? For "The great hope characteristic of the early days of the Popular Front had long since evaporated. The prevailing mood of the people was one of disillusioned apathy. ... The sabotaging of the Popular Front meant the sabotaging of the morale of a people who had to fight a war."

And when the war came, what then? The government's first concern after suppressing and jailing those who disagreed with them was to reassure the world that they had always been nice to Hitler and the man was really most ungrateful. In an official book they disclosed how the Nazi ambassador had called on Bonnet in July 1939 to berate him for not being undemocratic enough, and Bonnet had "finally told the German ambassador elections would be suspended, public meetings stopped, Communists brought to their senses." And Hitler's orders had been most conscientiously carried out. The Communist Party had been outlawed a week before war began—the Communist press, a month before. But meanwhile, as the Paris correspondent of Lord Beaverbrook's London *Daily Express* wrote:

Men who, slavish in their advocacy of Hitlerism, are down in police records as having taken Nazi money in peace time, still went free in Paris. The Cagoulards, who plotted against the Republic in the times of the Popular Front, were all released from jail the day after the war started and returned to their regiments. The truth was the French military and police were too busy on another track—hunting down the Communists.

Well, do you see anything like that happening here, or don't you? Who are officially the great enemy, the "forces of evil"? The Nazis. And whom do our political leaders spend most of their time hounding and hating? The "Reds." And who, pray, are the "Reds"? Well, to judge by the actions and speeches of a man like Dies the term takes in everyone who ever stands up for the Bill of Rights and the Declaration of Independence from England, and who doesn't want to have a war. And meanwhile, do you see anything being done to the Americans who have shown themselves "slavish in their admiration of Hitlerism"? Don't be foolish! What word do you hear, let alone action, from high places against the anti-Semite Father Coughlin, who has been proved to have used in his radio chats word-for-word excerpts from Goebbels propaganda? What is done about the Ku Klux Klan which advocates and carries out a terror in no way differing from the Hitler terror in Germany? Klansmen even parade openly in their nightshirts through the streets of Los Angeles! And a character like General John F. O'Ryan struts about like a cocksparrow telling us about "Americanism" and about the violent things we ought to do to the "agents of Moscow." Imagine the gall of such a man, calling early this year for "Fighting Funds for Finland" to provide "realistic" aid against what he called a "conspiracy against Christian civilization"—when in July he was compelled to register himself under the Alien Registration Act as a Japanese agent! It was found and reported in *The New York Times* of July 14, 1940, that he was getting from Japan a "retainer or fee" of $5,000 a month, but this he airily waved aside with the statement: "I do not believe I can be classified as an agent of any principal because the relation of principal and agent implies some measure of control by the principal of the agent. However, the question is academic."

As for the French at the beginning of their war, they might well wonder whether there had not been a typographical error in the papers —whether the country France had really declared war on was not Russia. The principles and symbols of Fascism were shamelessly gloried in by the war Fuehrers of France, and by the wealthy Two Hundred families. In November an advertisement appeared in *The New York*

Times for the newest Paris fashion, a humble tribute to the Cagoulards
or Hooded Men, French equivalent of the Ku Klux Klan:

> Just Arrived from Paris via Yankee Clipper—
>
> THE CAGOULE HOOD
>
> Arresting . . . Flattering . . . with a distinctly
> military flavor that emphasizes its chic—
> Have it lined in one of the newest colors
> proclaimed by Paris . . . "Air Force" Red, "Vol
> de Nuit" Blue, Baby Blue . . .

That is what the Parisian set were doing as France settled down to
fight Hitlerism—glorifying the *chic* of Fascism! Does it recall anything
to you? Marie Antoinette, for instance, and a certain remark about
cake for which history remembers her?

Oh, yes, very thoughtless and stupid of them. But France and England had gone to war because of Hitler's attack on Poland. Presumably
the French soldiers tried to persuade themselves that at the eleventh
hour their government was repenting, was really trying to stop the
Nazi tide from rolling any farther. It had refused aid to the real democracies of Spain and Czechoslovakia, yes. But the invasion of Poland, a
country just one degree more democratic than Germany, was too much
and called for war.

If any of the soldiers did so persuade themselves, it was not for long.
Not a single thing was done either by France or by England to help
defend Poland. Poland's leaders fled while their armies were still fighting. Later, in France, Poland's refugee parliament passed a resolution
demanding impeachment of Marshal Smigly-Ridz, former Foreign
Minister Beck, and former Premier Skladkowski, for betraying their
country. But the French rulers could not allow that to be published, for
it was precisely what they were about to do for France. Only later did
an English reporter smuggle the story out.

So the French soldiers, wondering whether their families were keeping alive on the pitiful government allowances, sat in the Maginot Line
—or were transported, several hundred thousand of them, to sit in the
parched deserts of Syria. They were not told what they were going to

Syria for, but many of them must have guessed. France was officially at war with Germany, but the country France's rulers wanted to fight was Russia. For years they had been egging Hitler on to fight Russia for them; they had thought and hoped that Czechoslovakia was his first step in that direction, and they were so confident he would do as they wanted—so sure he would realize they were his ideological friends and respect them accordingly—that they hadn't thought it necessary to prepare for any other contingency. Hitler wouldn't play—not because he had any love for Russia but because he knew how well prepared Russia was and what a pushover France was. But for the rulers of France, Russia remained the real enemy. Even after the hope of attacking Russia through Finland was smashed, the Los Angeles *Daily News* reported that "the majority opinion in both allied countries is that war against Germany can still be advantageously developed into war against Russia, and that vigorous military action is a prerequisite to ultimate success. In France there seems to be virtual unanimity, on the part of the general staff and the most influential leaders of the government, in the belief that any vigorous military action should be taken elsewhere than on the western front."

Meanwhile, what of the men in the Maginot Line? Nothing to do, and a lot of time to think. And here is one of the things they had to think about—for there are leaks in the most ironclad censorship. Just as in the 1914–1918 war, the merchant princes of France and Germany were continuing to line their pockets by trading with each other in war materials across Belgium. (This was first reported here in a story in *Iron Age* which, despite French denials, was confirmed by later dispatches from Belgium.) Millions of tons of French iron ore were being sent to Germany so that when the fighting started the French soldiers could be slaughtered with their own iron.

And then the German break-through—and the final and ghastly disillusionment of the French soldiers. Hundreds of German planes, and hardly any French planes to fight them, hardly any anti-aircraft guns. A tidal wave of tanks, and nothing to stop them with. Fifteen generals including their commander-in-chief removed or arrested—and, supreme mockery of all, Weygand brought from Syria to take command of the fight against Hitler. Weygand, a man whose open Fascist connections had forced his resignation from the French Army in 1936!

Why were there no planes? France had 2,600 first-line aircraft: where were they? Well, there were hundreds of them in Morocco in case of an attack on the imperial sources of tribute; hundreds more in Syria waiting for the chance that would never come to attack Russia. The ones in Morocco were the best and latest type planes imported from America, sent over in response to Ambassador Bullitt's hysterical appeals, but still unassembled. As M. W. Fodor cabled to *The New York Post* in June: "Hundreds of American airplanes which for months before the invasion of Belgium had been stored at Casablanca in French Morocco" were given over, after the collapse, to Hitler. They had lain there unassembled because, said Fodor, "French manufacturers sought more advantageous business arrangements with the French government." The wonderful result of this is that now, as I write, Hitler probably has more first-line American planes than America has.

And why couldn't the tanks be stopped? One thing that might have helped to stop them would have been to let the veteran fighters from the Spanish war out of the concentration camps in the south of France. These men, to the number of over 100,000 (there had been more than twice as many but others had been shipped back to Franco's slaughter-houses), had had two years' of hard experience of stopping exactly the tanks which were advancing in a wave across France, of dodging exactly the dive-bombers which worked in co-operation with the tanks. But they had to stay in the camps and rot, under conditions described as even worse than the camps of Germany. They would have been useful only in a war against Fascism—and there was nothing like that about this war.

So it was the Communists and the parties of the left who betrayed France. Is not that as clear as a Los Angeles *Times* editorial? France is (I quote from that learned publication) a "tragic lesson" in "pushing political experiments to the point of jeopardizing national defense." And from the equally learned San Francisco *News:* "The lesson of France" is against "rapid social progress."

Again pause and try to figure this out. Just who and what *are* these Communists? Why can't our press liars decide that and stick to it?

We are forever being told that the Communists are *against* progress and want to hurl us back into dictatorship and disaster. And yet when they become part—a very small part—of a legal government, they immediately commit the crime of *"rapid social progress"* which, as it now develops, is the thing we must at all costs avoid.

The Communists of all countries hold certain views. Anyone is at liberty to disagree with them in a democracy, and explain why. The views they hold are not Russian, nor developed mainly in Russia, any more than the Catholic religion is Italian. The Communists in France— as elsewhere—merely "hold the same views about the social and economic reconstitution of France as the country with which France herself was in alliance" (to re-quote Lloyd George).

France was not at war with Russia; it was at war with Germany. Yet the people who held the same views as Russia were jailed; those who held the same views as Germany went free. As Sir Charles Trevelyan, former English Minister of Education, said: "The French government has suppressed the largest political party in France and is trying the French Communist deputies for treason for expressing their honest opinions. This is fascism. This is tyranny. This is the reverse of democracy."

Mark that well. This *is* Fascism.

The best place to find the truth of this kind of thing is in one of those tactless moments of the English aristocracy. After the French collapse Lord Elibank rose in his majesty in the House of Lords and said that the Communist party was responsible for it. He went on to say that the French leaders "went over to the Fascist side to save from the Communists what property they still possessed."

Correct, My Lord. All the evidence—and there are mountains more to the same effect—shows it to be the truth. The French leaders were never defending France; they were defending their property and their right to hang on to it by forcibly perpetuating scarcity.

France was sold out to the enemy by its wealthy class, just as Poland was, just as Spain was, because they saw the people organizing themselves to end artificial scarcity, to organize the production of wealth efficiently, to divide it equably. The same thing in essence that we saw operating all through the turbulent history of Europe since the Congress of Vienna.

And that is happening now in America. The same group is busily carrying out the same betrayal.

This is no time, we are told, for "rapid social progress." And what do they mean by "rapid social progress"? They mean such ludicrously inadequate legislation as the Wages and Hours Act which, while our warehouses are stuffed with rotting surplus food and nine millions are unemployed, calls for a minimum of $12.50 a week and a forty-two-hour work week. Such "Communism" must go—and it would be fatal to our national security to have, for example, a law against lynching.

This Fifth Column of vested wealth, which curses every nation, is not a disease of democracy. If we had real democracy it could not exist. It is a disease of undemocracy.

It must inevitably end, unless we take action against it, by plunging us, like France, into a war the people do not want, a war for which we are improperly prepared. And its great enemy from first to last will not be the country we fight but the democratic people of our own country.

Unless we learn at this eleventh hour the true lesson of France, our fate can be no happier than the fate of France. The traitors are not difficult to identify. Whenever you hear talk of "hardship, sacrifice, and suffering," you need no further clue.

CHAPTER EIGHTEEN

A Few Kind Words for Your Uncle Samuel

THERE IS so much wrong with America at the present moment, that it is a source of constant amazement to me that room remains for so much that is right.

A person of normal intelligence reading a 1940 newspaper in the year 1950 could be pardoned for concluding that the period it represented was the all-time low of homo called sapiens. It is very doubtful whether the worst Bourbon or Hapsburg ever so blandly disregarded the wishes of his people as Roosevelt has done with regard to the draft and his pro-English policy. It is certain that nothing so manifestly ludicrous—the word "undemocratic" hopelessly understates it—as the Dies Committee's "investigation" of everyone trying to live up to the United States Constitution, has ever been solemnly accepted and reported since the King and Queen of Hearts tried the knave for stealing the tarts in *Alice in Wonderland,* and the King cried: "Consider your verdict!" before any evidence was heard.

Only if he knew what was revealed in the 1936 elections—that the press of America represents at most 5 per cent of American opinion—would this hypothetical researcher of A.D. 1950 be able to understand how this generation of Americans managed not to die laughing at itself.

The fact is that there lives on in the American people a spirit which is separate from and greater than any of the official acts and statements of America: a resilient spirit, a determined and independent yet kindly spirit, an intensely healthy spirit of humor and skepticism.

Americans owe this spirit to the kind of people their ancestors had to be to do what they did; to the kind of country they found, and the way it molded them; and to the process of mixing racial strains from all over the world, a revitalizing process both physically, from the standpoint of improving human stock, and mentally, from the standpoint of breaking down walls of prejudice based on insular ignorance and building a new and broader social understanding.

That is something which is easy to say and which in consequence every political hack says in words of seven syllables. Like all truth, it is true in relation to external conditions. Like all truth, it is seized upon and mummified by mountebanks to make it a source of deception. We find, for instance, Senator McNary, as 1940 vice-presidential candidate, making speeches about the "pioneer virtues" of America and calling for a revival of those "pioneer virtues" to solve our present problems. That is in the best tradition of vice-presidential intelligence and on the basis of precedent made McNary eminently eligible for the post. To state that McNary was talking through his hat is not to cast aspersions on the American pioneer virtues, which all of us rightly admire. One merely wishes to ask McNary whether he has ever tried practicing pioneer virtues on a Detroit assembly line, and just how he suggests that Joe Doakes in the General Motors plant should apply pioneer virtue to the tightening of his particular nut as it goes by. One might also ask Mr. McNary how a farmer applies pioneer virtue to the task of plowing under his crop of cotton, or what is the correct pioneer-virtuous expression for him to wear as he and his family watch tractors smashing down his farm.

The same applies to the oceans of verbiage poured out daily about the "Founding Fathers." Not only Americans, but men of good will all over the world, venerate the memory of Washington and Jefferson and Tom Paine, for the beacon they lit was an inspiration to humble folk everywhere who saw the dawn-glow of the Good Life in the sky. But when Senator Burke drags out George Washington's remarks in the year 1783 about military service at that time, in order to sanctify the demand for conscription of men from 18 to 65 in 1940 to help America's historic enemy out of a hole, it is time for a sensible American like Senator Norris to say: "Mr. President, it seems to me that in a civilized age we should be able to do some thinking for ourselves . . . The responsibility for action is not on George Washington. It is on us."

Unfortunately it was ever thus. When we realize—as we almost never

do until after he is dead—that a great man has been on the earth with
some of the stuff of eternal truth in his make-up, we tend to seize
upon every word he ever uttered and sanctify it as eternal truth; entirely
forgetting that the greatest of men had to deal most of the time with
particular problems relating to their own period, so that what they said
about those problems is in no way pertinent to the problems of a later
time. That is the human way of distorting the basic truths taught by
a Jesus or a Buddha on the one hand, or by a Jefferson or a Lincoln
on the other. What Washington thought about military service in 1783
has nothing to do with conscription in 1940. Washington was a slave-
owner but we do not consider that a justification for slavery today.
Pioneer virtues, in so far as daily material life is concerned, were for
the pioneers who had entirely different conditions to face from those
we face now.

But if we only take the trouble to sort out what Washington and the
pioneers did and said about immediate problems from the *spirit* of
Washington and the pioneers—that is, from the aspects of eternal
truth which they were able to reveal—we immediately come out into
the open and see where we are. And we find in this spirit the real and
solid treasure which America possesses. The task is not to try and
imitate the lives of the pioneers but to apply their spirit and their
common sense to the entirely new problems of an age of potential
plenty. They were pioneers in a new and untouched world. We have
to be pioneers in a mechanized world wherein, whether we like it or
not, we must solve the problem of making the machines our slaves—
the only possible alternative being that we shall be their slaves.

The people of America have not become slaves yet. The spirit that is
in them is so strong that they absolutely refuse to accept a submissive
slave mentality, despite all the violent attempts by the millionaire
fringe to make them accept it. That is the great hope of America, as I
see it. That is what distinguishes America from the old and decaying
civilization of Europe.

Advocates of things-as-they-are—that is, the small minority who make
a good thing out of the present social organization—continually point
to the high standard of living in America in reply to the attacks of
the discontented. When they do this, they carefully turn their faces
away from the South, where some thirteen million Americans live on

a standard no better than that of the poorest Polish peasants. But leaving the South and Puerto Rico and the Philippines and the migrants of California out of the picture, it is perfectly true as we all know that Americans by and large get more material good out of life than any other peoples. That is something to be thankful for, and most of us are thankful. Statistically we have the highest per capita ownership of wealth in the world, 60 per cent of the world's total of life insurance, an automobile for every 4.3 persons, about the same number of radio sets, 50 per cent of the world's telephones, almost one-third of the world's total highway mileage. Of course those figures are deceptive in that they do not show how these things are divided among the people, which is the real test of democracy. And how many of them are bought and used "on time" and repossessed by the owners and resold to others "on time" ad infinitum. So too with most other of their utilities—ice boxes, washing machines, electric heaters, etc., etc. But beyond a doubt the average American regards himself as fortunate to be an American, and has reason to do so. I asked various average Americans who have crossed my path in the past few days why they so regarded themselves, and here are some examples:

(1) A workman who came here from Canada: "Here there is greater unity among the people." Returning to Canada after some years here, he disliked the religious bigotry of French Canadians and the arrogance of the English. He found that Canada mimics America, but like most mere mimics they do a good thing badly. The speed-up is used more stringently there than here, employers requiring no better work but wanting it done faster. But above all there is mutual resentment between French and English Canadians, with both resenting even more strongly the Englishman who comes in with the attitude that the place belongs to him.

(2) A gardener, born in Germany: "If I didn't like the government in Germany, I couldn't say so. My relatives write me it is fine, but I don't think so. If they had ever lived in America they wouldn't say so either. Here they let people draw all kinds of cartoons making the President look ridiculous. It's a good government that lets people say whatever they like about it; it's not afraid."

(3) A Swedish cabinet-maker: "I like America because the people—the mass of people who have small incomes—are so friendly. I read things in the newspapers about the menace of aliens, and sometimes by very wealthy people I am made to feel alien, but the people as a whole aren't like that. I

think the newspapers misrepresent the picture. Once I heard a lawyer telling some friends that the reason things are so bad here is that there are so many aliens. It turned out that the lawyer's own parent was born in Russia. All the other men laughed at him. Why should he talk about aliens? Hadn't aliens made this country?"

(4) A French chef, who has owned and worked in restaurants both here and in Paris: "One thing is that here it isn't as far between me and the banker as it was in France. And here I have worked for men who have underpaid or cheated me, and I have served rude and unreasonable people, but I felt I was being cheated or abused by my equals and so could retaliate. Americans are more ready to accept criticism of their habits and customs than are the French. I have just bought a used car on the instalment plan and I am unable to convince my relatives in France that this has not put me in a new and higher social class and that I am not rolling in money. Once, at the beginning of the depression, I lost my restaurant and was very frightened. But I learned something about America then that made me want to live here always. Americans are never really afraid. They are droll about their financial ups and downs and are extremely sympathetic about other people's troubles. Seeing their confidence, I was no longer afraid."

(5) An Englishman, member of a typographical union, wrote a letter to his union paper telling about his trip to England. He said he was unable to join the union in England because he had been away so long, and nearly starved to death looking for work. Here in the United States qualified foreigners can join the union and make a living. The unions are more a closed order in England, and all sorts of clauses make it impossible for a foreigner or a native who has been outside the country some time to join. He urged British subjects working here not to return to England. Also the wages in the United States were higher for the same work.

(6) The son of a naturalized Scotsman tells this story: His father came here from Glasgow in 1899. He was a die maker and belonged in Scotland to a very definite class. His wife lived all her early years in an orphanage, and the class to which he belonged looked down on her for this reason. He came to America and went to work for a small industrialist as a die maker. He got better wages and could live better. His wife began taking voice lessons. She became part of the social group to which her husband's employer belonged. The two families became very close. Despite different economic levels, they went for trips together on the employer's yacht and their children went to the same parties, went to the same university and joined the same fraternities and sororities. The wife sang in choirs and was once chosen to sing before the Governor.

Relatives in Scotland are very definitely held into one class, which they leave only to enter another. The children of these Scotch people cruise from one level to another. Their outlook is geared to America.

One of the sons, in England on a scholarship, went to see his relatives in Scotland. They were well off, but none of their children had a higher education. They owned their own homes but did not have cars. They were overcome when he mentioned something of his mother's background. That was a subject they had supposed his mother would have the decency to hide from him. They didn't quite believe him when he said that all his mother's friends in America knew she had lived in an orphanage.

The son found that his mother and father had a much broader and saner and casual outlook on life than relatives who had remained in Scotland. They concluded that his father must have become very grasping and made a great deal more money than he said, otherwise he could not have sent his children to college, owned a home, a car and a summer cottage. Or—God forbid!—he was setting nothing by for a rainy day.

His cousins were all intelligent people, but they had a healthy suspicion of higher education. It belonged to a class of which they were not a part.

Of the four children of the Scotch immigrant, one son is a college professor and one owns a filling station; one daughter married a publicity man in her father's employer's company, and the other is a nurse.

(7) A Negro girl from Arkansas, visiting London in 1939 as a white child's nurse, wrote this letter to her mother in Texarkana:

"I can never be able to tell you the weird things this people do. Every child must have completed its schooling (unless rich) at fifteen. He then gets a job and works until he is seventeen or eighteen; then he is old enough to be paid adult wages—as he demands—so they fire him and get another child.

"Child's labor to my conception is just the same as white slavery. If the child craves more knowledge he pays out of his few shillings for an advanced education. Now, can you imagine paying for what he deserves free? . . . The English child cannot go back to its second childhood, if he lives that long, because he has never had his first. . . .

"The unemployment is not as great as in America, but the wages are far below standard. The people work. Yes madame, no madame, they say with that feeling of lord and master of old days. . . . They still have the feeling that if you are born a scullerymaid, then all your life you are a scullerymaid, and don't try being anything else. . . . What was good enough for the England great-great-great-grand parents seems good enough for this young England. . . .

"I hope you won't get the wrong impression of dear old England. Please try to remember that Rome wasn't built in a day. When England gets where America is today America will have gone on and will still be that much ahead."

This letter contains, for me, the essence of the American spirit which I find so hopeful. Consider that it was written by a girl of a subject race in America, born and raised in a part of the country where no attempt has even been made to live up to the specific laws of the Constitution. But the girl had gotten a few dollars from somewhere and left the South, and found a job in a part of the country where her people are at least allowed to vote. She had been grounded in the Constitution, and even if she knew it had no reality at all in her own State she knew it was there and that in other States the people were struggling toward making it come true. She had been grounded in the idea that America was a land where people of the humblest origin could better themselves, and even though her station in life might still be called humble, she had achieved her independence and self-respect and a wage higher than many skilled workers get in England—and she did not feel she had reached the summit. She had refused to submit and be made abject. Her philosophy was based on the conviction that, if she was willing to do her part, life owed her something better than toiling in cotton fields for a ration of sowbelly and turnip greens.

The full force of the contrast can be brought out by a glance at the little colony of British "nannies," or children's nurses, that take care of rich English children in Beverly Hills. These women of the poorer—but not the poorest, and of this distinction they are extremely jealous—English class would not think of exploring behind the scenes of American society, as the Negro girl did the moment she got to England. Their attitude toward America is, in general, slightly patronizing, on the basis that Americans are too crude and vulgar to appreciate as any English person can the subtle distinctions between social classes. They keep themselves to themselves and "know their place" just as much in relation to those below as to those above them in the social hierarchy. The measure of their abjectness is that when speaking of and to each other they do not use their real names but say "Nanny Brown" for the nurse employed by the Browns, "Nanny Smith" for the nurse employed by the Smiths. This feudal attitude, which is so deeply rooted in them that they regard it as the most natural thing in the world, of course delights wealthy Americans who will pay premiums to get such a retainer into their service.

To the ordinary American it seems almost unbelievable, but it is true. Americans cannot conceive of such an attitude because they have not lost their sense of privilege and distinction as Americans. Things are far from perfect for them, but they have a tangible Bill of Rights to work for and faith that it can be won. They do believe—and though the wealthy belittle them for it, it is what they should believe as Americans—that society owes them a job and food and a decent room or home of their own. America is their country; those things are here; and they know that no miracle—merely a sincere application of democracy—is needed to get them those things. Fifty million Wall Street aristocrats could not make them accept the idea, which most of the English people accept, that one man is born any better than another, that is with any more rights than another. They will not accept that because a man condescends to let them work for him, that entitles him to expect them to cringe. This is their heritage from the pioneers, and as long as they don't lose it they can dare to look upward toward the sun.

If today they enjoy, as a whole, more material good than any other people, it is because of that spirit. The statistics on average American incomes are to that extent deceptive. If Americans don't get what they feel they have a right to get, they will go out and take it—and every intelligent citizen of this world of potential plenty will say, more power to them.

A man in the public eye who stands honestly and firmly for this idea is Harry Bridges, of the CIO in the West. Considering the way Bridges has been hounded and misrepresented by all the power of the great corporations—for no reason at all except that he is a labor leader and an honest man—his attitude toward America is remarkable.

"What," I asked him, "is the best you can say for this country? Do you still like it?"

He said: "Sure. Take it as you say—it's pretty hard to find a country that is better. First of all, the people in this country are generally very fair, honest and decent. Take my own case just for example. In spite of six years of pounding by the organized press all over the nation, we are still alive and going and gaining ground as far as organizing is concerned, which proves that if you can get to the American people and present both sides to them they will always decide right. I have never seen it fail. Of course that may be true in a general sense anywhere you go, but here you have to add to that the fact that Americans will stand by, prepared to fight to back up their decision. They will go all the way. They will give their lives if necessary.

"We have here that basic and traditional thing on which this country is built—the Bill of Rights. The Constitution is not a corporation document. It is a people's and worker's document. There is a constant struggle to keep the American people from getting even a glimmer of the truth. And yet every time we can give them a glimmer of the truth and facts with what little facilities we have, we have won—they swing around and go down the line with us a hundred per cent. In our strikes in '34 and '36, we went to the people who supported us. They are for good wages and good working conditions, shorter hours, the right of workers to have vacations and enjoy themselves, for the protection and advancement of civil liberties.

"Besides the American temperament is very good and very healthy. They never get so low down, so beaten, as the English—at least not yet. They haven't that defeatism, so that they can't slough off their ills and miseries for a while and see the good side of things, or humorous things, or the decent side."

To me that is a very fair, perhaps a surprisingly fair, statement. It is a blessed relief from all the newspaper drum-banging, which is based on nothing really but pure mysticism, about "Americanism"—as if everything America ever does must be right and sacred just because it is American. We get, for instance, the following psalm of praise from Sidney Hollaender, "a successful New York business man," listing the benefits of American citizenship as follows:

"I can go to any church I please.

"I read, and see, and hear, what I choose.

"I can express my opinions openly.

"My mail reaches me as it was sent, uncensored.

"My telephone is untapped.

"I can join any political party I wish.

"I can vote for what and whom I please.

"I have a constitutional right to trial by jury.

"I am protected against unlawful search and seizure.

"Neither my life nor my property can be forfeited without due process of law."

Of course that is what the Constitution guarantees, as we all know. But submit these ten points to critical examination in the light of realities today, and just see how much truth there is in them, when we have such things going on as the direct governmental interference with religious belief, the domination of press and radio and movies by small financial interests, the wholesale interference with telephones and mail, the denial of the ballot to certain parties, and underprivileged groups, and the completely unlawful searches and seizures of the FBI as evidenced recently in Detroit.

I clip from a newspaper column the following:

"We hear a lot about the totalitarian way of life being more 'efficient' than democracies. I challenge any one to point to a more efficient 150 years in the history of any people who have ever lived on earth than that of the American people since 1789."

Of course this is full of confusions of thought. The truth is that America in the past 150 years has been extraordinarily efficient—in so far as it has been democratic. It has been inefficient—and today is increasingly so as we destroy and restrict production by deliberate intent and finally gear production to purely destructive ends—in so far as it has been and is undemocratic (the word "totalitarian" as used in such remarks has no real meaning). It will become fully efficient only as and when we become fully democratic as the Constitution says. For it is the people as a whole who want efficiency for the benefit of the nation as a whole, while the monopolists who more and more control America are only interested in efficiency for their own benefit. If it pays them more profit to produce a thousand bushels of wheat than to produce ten thousand—as may be the case when prices can be artificially raised—then the fact that the people need ten thousand is of no interest to them whatsoever: they will produce a thousand and the people be damned. Is that democracy? Is that your notion of democracy? It isn't mine.

The greatest difficulty which I have to face in trying to make my point

clear is the confusion existing in millions of minds about efficiency in
the past and efficiency now and in the future. If one attacks the
monopolists of our present day one is immediately accused of attacking
"the competitive system," which is often called—though not necessarily
with any justification if you read our Constitution—"the American
way." The successes of the competitive system in the past are pointed
out in order to prove its indubitable merit: "this has brought us what
we have—it must be good."

But certainly—it has been good in building up the America we have
and know. The great enterprisers of America have built up the country
under the incentive of personal profit. No argument at all about that.
We owe, if you like, a great debt to the business leaders and great
capitalists of our country. Let us by all means pay it with heartfelt
sincerity. But I would like to say, right here, that it isn't only the
country that owes a debt to the great capitalists: the great capitalists
also owe a debt to the country which has made their success and wealth
possible. And that is the debt I do not see being paid. It cannot be repeated too often that if the American people have a comparatively
high living standard today they have had to fight for every inch of it.
Nor should we forget that European industries, which pay so much
lower wages, have been able to do so because they possessed twice as
big a reservoir of labor as they needed—whereas American industries,
until quite recently, had a shortage of labor and had to make concessions to fill the need.

But, most important of all, we started off this book by pointing out
that the world moves. There is no "yesterday, today and tomorrow"
eternally the same. What started out as a free-for-all competitive system
is one no longer because a small group has effectively monopolized all
the important industries. We have granted the advantages of a competitive system, as proved by our national history and development.
But it is idle to go on banging the drum for the virtues of competition
when in fact there is no effective competition left. Show us where
effective competition exists and then you have the right to bang the
drum.

And yet we are living in a hysterical period where any such statements as the above have to be endorsed by the most respectable sources
to dodge the "red" labels. So I will now proceed to quote from that

most respectable of publications, *Fortune*—an article published two years ago when the deadening effect of monopoly control was already plain to those who could see:

American business was founded upon the principle of free competition maintained through free markets. But during the era of bigness the units of business became so big that they developed a fear of price wars; they dared not compete against themselves, and no one dared to compete against them. There consequently emerged the super units—well defined industrial groups whose members act in concert and whose aim is not price competition but, on the contrary, price stabilization.

Now this technique of bigness, involving the artificial control of prices and other basic factors, is a collectivist technique. And the operation of the collectivist technique has created for business a precarious situation. Business has carried collectivism so far in its private affairs that its affairs are no longer private but, by the bigness of their impact, public.

It is untenable, for example, to suppose that the policies of the steel industry with regard to prices, production and employment are strictly "private" matters. These policies involve directly 570,000 employes, $976,000,000 of annual pay rolls, and a $5,000,000,000 investment. They have repercussions throughout most of Business, affecting at least remotely millions of people and eventually the entire economy.

But inasmuch as these policies impinge upon and invade the sphere of public welfare, they impinge upon and invade the functions of government. By its very office, government must intervene. And the method of intervention which is easiest and most obvious, and which was encouraged during NIRA days by business men themselves, is the method of direct regulation—of price, for instance, of production, of profit, itself.

Thus collectivism in industry begets collectivism in government. And if this is not collectivism as practiced in the so-called collectivist states, it is only a couple of theoretical steps removed from it. Carried to its extreme it means the downfall of the economy upon which American business has been reared; the perversion of the democratic order; the destruction of the right to risk and profit; and—all too easily—the loss of those civil liberties that are at present based upon the principle of the limitation of governmental power. . . .

. . . It is safe to say that if American business wanted to move in this direction it could move in this direction (back toward truly competitive competition). And it is safe to say that, if accomplished by private initiative, the unbuilding might be highly profitable and might indeed stimulate an actual expansion of business and an increase in the national income, comparable to the expansions and increases of the past . . .

. . . But if neither business nor government makes any moves whatever in the direction of breaking down industry into smaller, more compact, more mobile and better earning units; if *bigness* is allowed to remain as the standard concept of the economy: then, the American businessman, and the American politico and, in short, all American citizens, must prepare themselves for a different order of things; an order in which the powers of government are NOT limited; in which the right to risk and profit is NOT clear, and in which the making, the selling and even the buying of the products of the biggest show in history are all mysteriously directed from above.

So there you have it plain—the admission, more than two years ago, from the innermost shrines of the monopolies themselves (yes, the article was endorsed by Walter Lippmann and other Wall Street high priests, and reprints of it were distributed in tens of thousands by New York's National Industrial Conference Board whose executive includes a duPont and a Kohler)—the admission that our "competitive" system has ceased to be competitive and is therefore not functioning.

So I ask you to digest the fact now, before we go any further, that I am not a long-haired anarchist advocating the downfall of the competitive system. I have paid my respects with complete sincerity to the achievements of the competitive system. What I do advocate, in common as I understand it with *Fortune,* is the downfall of the monopoly system into which what started out as free competition has finally landed us. If we are to continue the competitive system, then it must be competitive. If it does not succeed in so being, then as *Fortune* justly says it means the eclipse of the democratic forms of society and the substitution in one way or another of force and compulsion.

CHAPTER NINETEEN

What Should Be the Objectives of the American People?

WE ARE being rushed into war because the economic monopoly system has riveted in its belly the germs of war and because it cannot solve the problems—the really very simple problems—of peace. "Whom the gods would destroy, they first make mad." Nature will not for long allow the monopolizing of wealth and production by and in the interests of a few, any more than she has allowed other systems to continue when they coagulated and became out-of-date; and not one of us, billionaire or pauper, will be consulted. In the end there is nothing left as a final fling for this anomalous and anarchic thing the monopolists call civilization except the madness of war.

The end is always violence unless men can make themselves think and show themselves to be the intellectual peers of the ant. "When the rich plunder the poor of his rights," as Tom Paine said, "it becomes an example to the poor to plunder the rich of his property."

This is not a point of view, but a fact. Only look at the mechanism we call a man. Countless billions of cells have to co-operate to make it work, and if they co-operate and each fulfills its function in relation to the whole the mechanism can last several score of years. If even one of the billions is not co-operating properly the mechanism becomes diseased and it dies. And the function of the cells becomes different as the body grows: they must learn to adapt themselves to changing circumstances and perform new tasks.

So in our social mechanism. If the present economic unbalance were

272

transferred to the human body you would see the anarchy of the cells which we know as cancer, in which a cellular growth, living at the expense of the whole cellular structure, appropriates for itself benefits and privileges which eventually destroy both host and parasite. If we cannot co-operate by a conscious effort to rid ourselves of the cancer, and if we cannot within the present structure learn our new kinds of tasks as the conditions change, the mechanism must die in protracted agony and give place to a new one which will do nature's job. "We must be born again," as Jesus put it. In blood—birth is like that.

All we are now doing is dismissing the idea of co-operation by adorning co-operation with a red label—as if a mere label sufficed to defeat nature. Co-operative working of the land by farmers is called "destroying initiative and the pioneer spirit." Giving relief to the starving and pensions to the aged is "robbing the worthwhile to maintain the worthless." Public work programs, reforestation, socially-owned power plants, a national offensive on the soil erosion problem mean "crushing business with taxes." Taxing the new labor-saving machines according to the number of laborers displaced, or shortening working hours to adjust our economy to them, is "destroying democracy."

How infinitely childish, how unworthy even of so lowly a family as the sowbugs, are these labels! "Call it un-American," and presto! It vanishes—Or does it?

Two hundred billion dollars is the loss to. the national income in the past decade—the cost to the American people of the idleness of men and machines. Industry offers no answer. The government offers none. The National Resources Committee, that calculated the loss, suggested no solution for getting the machinery going and the men to work. The one brilliant idea always appears to be to have a gigantic war and destroy everything we have and kill off millions of innocents.

Between 1930 and 1940, in the depression years, twenty-three million Americans became 21 and went out looking for jobs.

What did they find? Just look! National American Legion Commander Kelly criticizes the Youth Congress for holding out hands for aid "before they sought new frontiers to conquer." Where, oh where, are the new frontiers? There is no land to be had though millions of acres lie idle under the grip of banks and corporations. New inventions are not wanted. Small businesses are born only to be crushed or swallowed up. There is a "surplus" of everything. There are clerking jobs for the lucky ones, but available only on the condition of complete subservience and bootlicking of the sixty families in control. "The more abundant life," banker Spinney of San Francisco tells our young people, can only be had through the system of private enterprise with its "rewards for the diligent, the efficient and the ambitious." The young people wonder how the devil to make this tally with the fact that William Rockefeller's great grandchildren, for example, inherit a $50,000,000 fortune which by 1950 will have grown to $100,000,000. Where have the grandchildren of William Rockefeller shown their diligence, efficiency and ambition? In the womb?

"Roll up your sleeves," publisher Roy Howard advises them. "This is no time to advocate or consider labor reforms and social progress." Not even to consider them! Or they turn, perhaps, to that other great cerebellum, Roger W. Babson, humorously known as a "leading economist." Says Babson: "If we take the correct but difficult road, it will mean longer hours and a return to hard work, thrift and self-reliance." Work where? Thrift with what? Reliance on self in a society where even an ordinary millionaire cannot compete against the monopolies?

Thrift, indeed! In 1937 the needy of America owed loan sharks a million dollars, and were paying them an average interest of 271% and as high as 1131 per cent. Hospitalization and doctor bills bring most of the victims to the government-protected shark. Tuberculosis is seven times more prevalent among people having less than $1,000 a year than among those earning more than that. Pneumonia kills off 3½ times as many of the poor as the rich, cancer 50 per cent more. Life expectancy of Negroes, whose living conditions are the worst in the country, is 47 years compared with 59 for all white persons. In the Tri-State mining area the tuberculosis rate—an immediate result of silicosis contracted at the work people have to do to live—is four times higher than for any other area in the country. Even in a city like Los Angeles the Housing Authority found four thousand dwellings unfit for habitation, 40,000 substandard, and nearly 21 per cent of the 133,000 units covered by their investigation lacked toilet and bathing facilities. In the South each January thousands of families are evicted from their "homes"—to be charged with "trespassing" on the public highways. In California hundreds of thousands of families are homeless, starving and disfranchised. In Cleveland, while Roosevelt and Hoover and the other Fuehrers were calling for food for Finland, two thousand families were literally without any food at all except what they could scrounge from their relatives. And all the while hundreds of millions of pounds of food rotting in storehouses; the streams of California running gold—and black—with creosote-sprayed oranges; three million tons of sugar cane left standing at the close of the 1939 season in Puerto Rico. Entirely preventable disease caused by bad housing and undernourishment driving the poor to the loan sharks—and the American Medical Association surveying the whole beautiful scene and reporting:

"In these times when the maintenance of the American democracy seems to be the most important objective for all the people in the country"—not a word, mark you, about a little thing called food—"the people may well consider whether some of the plans and programs that have been offered for changing the nature of medical service are not in effect the first step toward an abandonment of the self-reliance, free will and personal responsibility that must be the basis of a democratic government."

How simple! Making medical care available to the sick is an anti-democratic blow at "self reliance, free will and personal responsibility" —but conscripting young Americans against their will to fight a war that is none of their business is apparently perfectly democratic! One may well ask, do simple words in our language any longer have any meaning? Or one may refer for a breath of air to Major General Gorgas, the great sanitarian who cleaned up the Panama Canal, who said: "The preventable mortality in this country is greater than that caused by the European war. Science knows that the chief cause of disease is poverty."

So our 23 million young Americans emerge into this strange sort of "democracy" and try their damnedest to be self-reliant and diligent and efficient, and what happens? Here are a few examples: In New York City Edward W. Talbert, 29, skilled Negro electrical worker, unable to find a job after two years' search, kills himself by electrocution. In Brooklyn Joseph Rinaldi, 16, hurls himself to destruction leaving a note: "My life is a failure. I tried to get work but I was unable to do so. Life has become unbearable." In Kansas City Harry Larsen, 11, cries out "I'm tired of living on corn meal mush!" and hangs himself.

In San Francisco Phyllis Rodgers, 21, a model, unable to find $35 for room rent and board, throws herself off Golden Gate Bridge. At Dedham, Miss., two 16-year-old boys commit a murder in stealing 45¢ to get food and are sent to prison for life.

And they tell us that Europe is where there's a war on! Isn't the human brain wonderful?

For heaven's sake let us go back to those eminently sane and marvelous documents on which our country is supposed to be based, the Declaration of Independence and the Constitution.

In 1861 Abraham Lincoln said: "I have often inquired of myself what great principle or idea it was, that kept this Confederacy so long together. It was not the mere separation of the colonies from the Motherland—but that sentiment in the Declaration of Independence which gave LIBERTY, not alone to the people of this country, but HOPE to all the world, for all future time. It was that which gave promise that in due time the weights would be lifted from the shoulders of ALL—and that ALL should have an equal chance. This is the sentiment embodied in the Declaration of Independence."

From that—in eighty years of "progress"—to the eleven-year-old boy driven by lack of nourishment to hang himself while the grandchildren of William Rockefeller inherit $50,000,000.

Lincoln is certainly correct in his interpretation of the import of the Declaration of Independence. Before that document there is no evidence in the history of men of any document or agreement that gave promise of any such thing, let alone the right to life, liberty and the pursuit of happiness. The sum and substance of Macchiavelli's *The Prince* is to keep power without doing a thing for anyone. Yet what would the prince have without his Leonardos, and without the mass where could he get them? It is the argument of a fool. A weak man or woman, like a weak animal, male or female, has ever been the rightful prey of a stronger. Yet in certain "societies" of ants and baboons, bees and beavers, one finds arresting illustrations of friendly social economies that seem to house, feed, and protect their members as well as and even better than many states and nations do theirs—our own era of plenty as against scarcity being no exception.

The thoughts and wishes of America's founders, for all the promise of the Declaration of Independence and the rules and laws of the Constitution, have never been implemented. The conception of equal chances for ALL has never come to life. There is no solution whatever in charity, in Community Chests and Red Crosses and such. If the government does not consider and reconsider the question of equal chances for ALL—and I mean ALL, and Lincoln meant ALL—under the conditions as they develop from decade to decade, then we have not even begun to build the America that the founders envisioned.

If you admit the claim of the mass to an equal chance, you have to give them work and in return for it a basic minimum share of the nation's products sufficient to end undernourishment, preventable diseases and bad housing. If you do not believe in the Declaration of Independence—if you believe that the mass are "worthless"—then presumably you must in the end resort to compulsory birth control or sterilization, or a gigantic human purge by war every few years. Do you know of any other alternative?

But "Americanism" as I understand it—with apologies to Mr. Dies, who has claimed an exclusive right to interpret the term for us lower mortals—means precisely giving equal chances to ALL, and nothing less. It means the recognition that the mass are *not* worthless.

The Americanism of the Declaration of Independence is a new concept representing a revolution from the assumption of all the ages of man—the assumption that, if you are one of the 3 per cent who are born clever or strong or born into a rich family, you are somehow the cause of it and deserve due reward at the expense of the mass, the 75 per cent. And that if you are born one of the mass, without money and without physical beauty and without special talent or strength, that is also your doing and you must live like a dog because of it.

This revolution in thought resulted from the discovery by thinking people that free-will is an illusion. Before that time the curious but useful fallacy that a man had somehow created himself—a weekday fallacy running in harness with the Sunday concept that God did the job— always existed. Plato could only suggest a society of free men based on slavery—the mass deserving nothing better than to be slaves.

Christianity was a useful religion for this idea because it could easily be twisted to demonstrate that God sanctified the fallacy provided that those who had the wealth were "charitable" to those less fortunate and had pity for them. Yet socially speaking pity never played any part at all. And truly, the concept of "pity" appears to be an unnatural one. Darwin noted this in connection with savage tribes, where the concept that an enemy or even a hurt child should be pitied was unknown. Darwin mentioned a friend who had seen a savage in South America pick up a child and brain it against a rock in a mere family tiff. Our billionaire Americans today would be horrified at such conduct but in actual fact that is what they are doing every minute of the day. That it is "indirectly" done is no consolation to the child. So we see the same idea running right through human society up to the present day, Declaration of Independence notwithstanding. We now have people seriously suggesting that sharecroppers, because they are "worthless" (no consideration at all of what made them so, if they are), should be castrated to solve the "surplus" labor problem in the South. And the more tactless English imperialists gloat openly about the "beneficent" effect of famines in India.

But nature, though it is not interested in "pity," says that the small tribe must ever be the prey of the larger and more unified tribe. In the animal world the big herd stands twice as good a chance of enduring as the small (though if the herd is too spread out and is not unified by any common denominator, like the British Empire, its chance of survival is negligible). So that there we have the obvious and basic objection to deliberate extinction of the mass.

But merely to make life interesting and livable and to provide that infinite contrast without which it cannot be livable, we must have the mass. Many of our wealthy class admit that, but produce another fallacy—that it is the very fantastic gulf between the richest and the poorest that provides this contrast. That is based on the supreme and most idiotic fallacy of our age, that money is the keystone of everything and the answer to everything and the only conceivable incentive for everything. In point of fact the continuance of a vast mass of slaves and a tiny class with all the wealth and power is just what robs life of the contrast and excitement it ought to have. The rich are rendered sterile by their wealth, and thousands among the mass who have the germ of creative greatness and individuality within them are struck down in childhood or youth by the hopelessness of their condition.

We often hear the accusation against America that it is "too materialistic," but what does this really mean? It means that by our ruthless and unfair monopoly system we hold up to our people the one and only ideal of making money for themselves at the expense of the next fellow. We have it dinned into our heads from earliest youth that the pursuit of money is the greatest thing in life, and the national "heroes" who are held up for our admiration are measured in terms of how much money, which they cannot use, they have succeeded in amassing. And because the mass try to get a few cents more a day it is they who are most roundly stigmatized for being "materialistic" and they who must "return to the pioneer virtues." But the objectives of the wealthy and the objectives of the poor are in fact opposites. The wealthy want more wealth for its own sake or for the power it gives them over others —since they cannot spend it—and the poor want food and clothing and houses and security for their children and their old age. It is the wealthy who are "materialistic" in the bad sense of that word. Ordinary wisdom, of which the very wealthy are as a rule no longer capable, tells you that money in so far as it brings undemocratic power, luxury, and social decay to the individual who has more than he and his family need is individually and socially destructive. It injures him and the state. It also tells you that the basic needs of life are here in great abundance, and that you want and should have your share of them in return for your share of the producing of them—and then that money should be forgotten so that you can react to more worthy and intelligent incentives.

This is not to say that the poor in America, as elsewhere, do not spend the great majority of their time thinking about money. For how can they forget it—how can money stop haunting them through every waking moment—as long as they suffer from lack of the basic needs while those same are being destroyed or the people who could produce them are forcibly denied the right to possess them? Actually money is not the love of the poor man's life but the curse of his life. Extreme need distorts all his other values and exaggerates the value of the wealth possessed by others. Poverty is like the 2,000 diameter power of a microscope. When your pocket is empty the sight of a man going into an automat for a two-bit dinner makes you wildly envious. I know too well from my own experience how belittled and humiliated the poor man feels. To subject any willing citizen to such hunger and want is social dynamite, not only when the man is poor but later when and if he begins to get money by some means or other. For when he has a little wealth in his hands and sees what he can do with it—when he sees the almost lunatic gratitude with which his handouts are received by the less fortunate—it gives him a wholly unnatural and unsocial and so undemocratic sense of grandeur and power, in fact turns him into a ten-cent lord, a ward-heeler, an aristocrat of the alley, a Mayor Hague. And then let those who have not fared so well in the jungle we call civilization watch out!

Most Americans, including the poor, because of the above facts are capitalistically minded. Also we inherit this idea from the early wealth of the country, the one-time privilege of pioneering, plus the tradition of being able to get a very great deal for very little—a gold mine, for instance, by finding it. Today, although most of us have nothing and the pioneering opportunity of our forefathers is over, we still think that if it weren't for the rich man and his "capital"—his figures on pieces of paper—everyone would starve to death; and if anything is said against exploitation, we the ordinary poor Americans are likely to get angry! Not only that, but the majority of poor people as well as the rich are mean and cruel—rendered so by the brutality of the standards we set up, and by the ignorance of realities in which they are deliberately kept. For instance, everyone who has a small job or owns a little farm or runs a two-by-four filling station imagines even today that he is a buddy to Pierpont Morgan—and instead of sympathizing with his less fortunate fellow-workers, he turns up his nose at them and says that if they were of any account they too would have a little job or farm or filling station. Imagine this, today, when 90 per cent of all are clerks and will stay so under our present monopoly contract!

The so-called "lazy WPA worker" who leans on his shovel handle has become a national joke. We do not pause to consider that while the standard work week is forty, fifty or more hours, and while production is deliberately restricted as it must be under a monopoly system, there is nothing for millions to do except lean on shovels. Nor do those who joke about the shovel-leaner ever have anything to say about the wealthy with their breakfasts served in bed every morning and their maids and butlers and valets to wait on them and wash and dress them and comb their hair, and their resorts and smart districts such as Park Avenue, Newport, East Long Island, Florida, Bar Harbor, and where not else.

Not the billionaire thieves who are robbing them by means of a complicated and unnatural system, but other poor persons or slightly richer ones nearer home are blamed: the "lazy WPA worker," or the unemployed, or those on relief. There is even talk by the cheated millions of Americans—lied to as they are by the press, the radio, the pulpit, the movies—about "too much relief!"—although they are so near the need of it themselves that if they had any understanding they would favor more of it, not less. Certainly if they had endured the hardships the Russians did at the hands of their Tsar tyrants, they would be thinking in the same terms about the billionaires as the Russians did about the Tsars: they would be forced to see the need of limiting wealth and power, the need, that is, of keeping it in such bounds as would maintain America as a true democracy, the kind of democracy outlined by our Constitution which contemplated neither enormous riches for any nor grinding poverty for the mass. So far we have not had to suffer to anywhere near the extent that the Russians under the Tsars suffered. We think that such misery and want as that are impossible here. I am not so sure that they are impossible. If nature gives us a chance to learn her lesson with our brains and we don't take it, she will end by teaching it to us through our stomachs in the old, hard way.

But here is what I would like to ask of the millions of the underprivileged. Can we not do just a little thinking right now and start off by realizing how small a thing is that Money which we have inflated into a national pneumatic god? And can't we—can't our monopolists above all, who so far have pursued in vain the phantom of happiness— think a little and realize what are the really worth while things in life?

Surely what is really worth while is art, or culture, or call it what you will: all those things which can only be pursued in leisure and which without leisure are barred off; all those things by development of which man has made himself superior, or at least potentially superior, to the ape. Money is not really anything in itself. It does not reproduce itself. It does not provide thought or taste or wisdom or humor or kindness or a sense of beauty. Nor does it even by love or beauty reach distinction such as the thinker, the scientist, the poet, the musician, the inventor, or the philosopher achieves. It does not and it never has and it never will. If there is special virtue in Rockefellers and duPonts—and certainly there is strength in them, strength to climb to the top of the human heap and sit on the weaker slaves below—it does not by any alchemy of theirs pass on to their descendants. On the contrary, since the money they "made" passes on, the descendants are nine times out of ten corrupted by it and are actually subnormal in any contribution they may have to make to society. There is not and never has been any such thing as a continued dynasty of superior mortals.

Where do the really great people who have made America come from? From the mass. Where did Rockefeller himself come from? He was just a farmer's son. But there will never again under the monopoly be any Farmer Rockefellers, unless they are Associated Farmers who cannot distinguish between a barn and the rear end of a cow. The great writers and thinkers of America come from the mass: the Fenimore Coopers, the Melvilles, the Poes, the Whitmans, the Thoreaus, the Emersons. America's great contribution to architecture has come from the mass. Great American symphonies and paintings and sculptures are beginning to come out of the mass. Art is beginning to come very much alive in America, because of the mass: it is more essentially than any other a mass art. If you cleave to the theory that the masses are not worth anything—the theory on which all eugenics is based—you end up with just what England has today: a gang of decadents at the top and nothing to show for England except their lunacies; no art and no creation that does not smell of decay.

Ever since the abolition of slavery the wealthy class in America would have liked to chase the Negro into the sea. The Constitutional amendments which resulted from the fratricide and destruction of the Civil War never became anything but words on paper. But the Negro has as you know insisted on struggling into the upper air and is now at last succeeding to a remarkable degree considering his disadvantages. He has given us artists and writers and musicians of importance; plus his humor, his rhythm, his durability and his world-pervading spiritual. Go on and castrate the Negroes now, and see how much healthy life you will have left in American art. If the wealthy drain the life out of art, what then remains for them to do with their money? How much good will it have done them? For everything we have in America comes out of the spirit of the Declaration of Independence—the hope, at least, if it is so far little more, that equal opportunities for ALL are to be the American people's heritage.

If to keep up the private monopoly system, the system of artificial scarcity, you must cut out everything else—and in the end you seemingly must, supposing that the system can be kept up—then there is only one intelligent answer: cut out the private monopoly system and let's have the other thing. Let's go back to the Constitution. More explicitly, let's make the Constitution come true and you will have democracy. Easy to say perhaps, but how to do it? How does the lowly individual citizen set about it?

Well, here is the broad general approach as I see it. Let us, the ordinary people of America, stop fixing an envious eye on our next-door neighbor who owns a corner filling station (or in reality, is told just how he can run it by the oil monopoly)—and fix our eye instead on the potentates of wealth who are taking away from all, all that is rightfully theirs. And in order to get things done we must concern ourselves more, not less, with *local* politics about which we can have more knowledge and over which we can more easily exercise control. We must stop voting for a Mayor because the machine he is in gives us a ton of coal at Christmas. We must stop expecting those who have great power and official eminence to carry out our democratic will, and look to our neighbors who are as poor and as worried as we are ourselves—combine with them to make various of such ordinary mortals our representatives, and support those who do something practical in the matters immediately concerning us. We must watch what they do about our street car fares and taxes and sewerage system and water supply; protest about what is left undone in *these* fields about which we have daily knowledge. This is where democracy must start—at the bottom; and if it starts on the right foot it has some chance of reaching the top without a broken leg.

And doubt as you please, as to that, the reasons our American Constitution is a dead letter today are two:

First, that the people are not properly informed about the real working of their country, because the sources of information are controlled in its own interests by the tiny minority to which the monopolies and their profits belong. And second, because our democracy does not have as its main objective the feeding and clothing and housing of the people, the exploitation and distribution to the limit of the wealth we possess. It is impossible for any order which fails in that to have the people's respect and approval.

So that the first big essentials to make the Constitution come true are to free the sources of information from giant-corporation control—if necessary, by subsidizing newspapers and radio stations which do not accept advertising. And to take away the power which the monopoly system places in the hands of a few lunatic individuals solely interested in piling up money they can't spend, but which they use to oppress the people to whom, truly, they owe their powers.

In saying this I am not necessarily attacking the competitive profit system. What I am saying is this: That we must have either .a real competitive system which would make it impossible for minority groups to establish monopolies and crush competition—or, if this cannot be done, then the people must take a hand in the running of the monopolies. Either a competitive system that is truly competitive, with the advantages to national progress which competition has in the past shown itself to possess—or a co-operative system of monopolies, with the power over them—their social control—coming from the bottom, not from the top, and with all the social advantages which are inherent in true co-operation flowing downward to the many.

Isn't that following out the fundamental American doctrine of forcing private selfish interests to be subservient to the people's life, liberty and pursuit of happiness?

Isn't that the Americanism of the Constitution and Declaration of Independence?

Isn't it just plain horse-sense? Are there any other ways of achieving that national unity of objective which alone can make America efficient for ALL of its people?

But the point is that, whatever the solution, and granting that only the people can bring it about. because the monopolists won't, it must provide a new basis for our whole social structure. The structure must be based on abundance instead of on scarcity.

"How do we know," you may ask, "that a society based on abundance would work—a society in which nobody went without the basic needs and in which all restraints were taken off production, so that none would need to labor more than a few hours a day? Everything we have today is built on scarcity and the incentive of actual physical need. Abundance as a basis for national life has never been tried."

Well, does that make it any the less worth trying? But anyhow, worth trying or not, your question is directed into the empty air. Because, for one thing, it is going to happen in the end and you can't stop it happening, for nature says so. And if you can realize that, you can see that it's better to start doing something about it now—this minute—so that it may not be ushered in with a bath of blood that will make the 1914–1918 war look like a Girl Guides' Field Day. Start doing something about your neglected Constitution, your tattered Bill of Rights, your forgotten Declaration of Independence. Make them come true. What better blueprints do you need?

And it isn't true that it has never been tried. They have been trying it, in their stumbling and error-strewn way if you like, in Russia these past twenty years. They have a Constitution based on the idea of abundance for all and they are trying to achieve their aim, despite the enormous natural obstacles and the unnatural ones placed in their path by monopoly-mad nations. They are trying abundance—trying the idea that the mass is worth while. I do not point at them as a model, for there is no comparison between the conditions they had to build from and the conditions we have to build from. Democracy was not even a word in their dictionary, and all the blueprints—unlike ours which have existed for 160 years—had to be worked out by costly trial and error.

We in America have no time to waste arguing about Russia's plan. We need an American plan; and we have it—in our Constitution and Declaration of Independence. We also need, to carry out our plan, a spirit—call it the "pioneer spirit" if you like. But the fallacy of all the present talk about the "pioneer spirit" is that this spirit and the private monopoly system are mutual contradictions. The pioneer spirit cannot be applied to *not* producing things, to restricting production, to destroying products. You cannot be a pioneer if you are a clerk, a mere cipher in a giant corporation controlled from above.

Yet with the dead hand of the private monopolies removed, with the brakes taken off creative effort and enterprise—and the brakes do not consist of taxes on the monopolists as our press tries to tell us, but simply and solely of the monopolies themselves—this spirit must automatically re-emerge in the people, and be just as vigorous as it was in the

America of a century ago or as it is today in those parts of the Russian "United States" which correspond to the America of a century ago in their material development.

Just come with me once more to the age-old desert wastes of Uzbekistan which we visited earlier in this book, and see for yourselves how this spirit can emerge in our time. A great cotton-growing country, if only it had water. A people who for generations have dreamed of harnessing the water, which the river emptied uselessly into an inland sea, to make their fields fertile. Never able to do anything about it because they were the poor by whose poverty the Tsar and his court became rich. And now look what they have done.

The farmers got together and asked if they might build a 270-kilometre canal with dams to store the water. It was a job that "normally" would take seven years. But the farmers, many thousands of them, were willing to go to work and do it in 45 days. The government told them to go ahead. Why not? What possible objection?

So they organized themselves into squads to compete one against the other, each taking a section of the digging. In July of last year they marched out to the job, bringing their own spades and crowbars and mattocks, tents and sleeping rugs—160,000 of them. And the government did this: it sent all the steam shovels it could spare, it sent three thousand irrigation engineers, over 700 doctors and nurses, a movie crew under Eisenstein, teachers and journalists, over 1,000 telegraph and telephone workers—and what else do you think? Eighteen hundred actors, singers and dancers to entertain the canal-diggers in the evenings and at the lunch intervals! But again, why not? The actors wanted to act, the singers wanted to sing, and there was their audience —in the middle of the Uzbek desert. Why not get together? In all, 2,686 midday and evening concerts, 39 plays and 1,500 movie performances were given there in that desert while the canal was being dug— and complete operas were given in the Uzbek language which before the revolution was not even written.

What do you think of that? Un-American? On the contrary, here is exactly the pioneer spirit of the great days in America, the spirit we are now asked to apply to the non-production of the things we need. Of course the basic urge behind the whole thing was the need for the material benefits the canal would bring. The farmers didn't do it for any mystical reason, even though—as the dozens of photographs I have seen of the episode show—they had so much pleasure in doing it. But money as money never entered into their incentive in any way. The incentives were the urge to create and build and progress—and also the healthy incentive of competition between groups on a common project. They were not mere personal incentives but social incentives. And their faces as they worked, making those old desert sands fly as the big ditch took shape, showed that everything we call drama and excitement was in them, everything that touches and stirs the heart deeply. What a contrast to the mean, sluggish, uncreative chain-drug-store mentality which the monopolists in America seek to force upon our people while prating about the "pioneer spirit"! But what other mentality can we have when our people, nearly half of whom are undernourished and wretchedly clothed and housed, are told they are already producing too much?

Seeking to sum up, I look back over what I have written in this chapter and find that I have mentioned our Constitution and Declaration of Independence nearly a score of times. And now I return again to those marvelous national documents of ours, because they and they alone can and must be the summation of a book such as this which attempts to look at American problems and to find an American way forward.

Those documents alone are Americanism—they alone distinguish our country and our problems from others.

Let us, please, avoid the ridiculous notion seemingly harbored by so many Americans that Rockefeller and Morgan and Ford and duPont and Mellon and Hoover and Roosevelt invented capitalism. Capitalism as an economic system is no more American than it is Siamese. Nor is there anything American about monopolies. The Constitution and Declaration of Independence do not say anything about capitalism and monopolies. They do not call for economic hardening of the arteries. The spirit that is in those documents is that if any system or any group stand in the way of liberty and the pursuit of happiness for the mass, then the mass have the right and the duty to change them or kick them out. If under these circumstances we do not change them or kick them out, then we are not good Americans. The test of Americanism is just that.

It is the existence of these documents, as I have tried to show, that makes America still a country of hope. Only compare America with England and you will see what I mean. England is officially also a democracy but it has no written democratic constitution—and the result of that is that the rights of the people can be taken away piece by piece, as they have been during the past two decades with increasing momentum, and the people have no weapon at hand with which to fight. What is "constitutional" can be twisted at will by the monopolists and their butlers and footmen and the people cannot see, as we can, where a clear breach of constitutionality has been made. The election of representatives to do the fighting for the people by remote control becomes more and more dominated by huge corrupted political machines; there as here the control becomes increasingly remote. But if here there is hope still of comparatively peaceful change and progress, that hope lies in the people themselves, in the leaders of the people's organizations near home for whom the constitution remains an ever-potent weapon.

It is time now for every American to re-examine with the utmost care his Constitution and Declaration of Independence in order that he may understand those weapons to the last detail and use them to the utmost of their power. He should read them and read them tonight. Only the ordinary men and women of America can make the fight that has to be made. Leaving the job to Senators and Congressmen in Washington, surrounded as they are by lobbyists of the great monopolies and largely cut off from the voice of the electing mass, is futile. The Senators and Congressmen, nine out of ten of them, have shown that they will ignore the Constitution and the will of the people to the utmost that they can so long as their $10,000-a-year jobs and their perquisites are not endangered.

What is the Declaration of Independence? Just what it says it is—a manifesto declaring America independent of the selfish and predatory squabbles of Europe and imperialists everywhere. Specifically and particularly declaring us independent of England, once and for all. Yet, what are our President and Congress doing? Wearing themselves out, competing strenuously with one another, to get us embroiled in these very squabbles and specifically and particularly with imperial England.

We know what this kind of embroilment means. We have had some. We know—surely we know, surely the lesson must have been learned—

that there is nothing in it for us but headaches, to put it very mildly.

Look what has happened already. We were informed by the President—with the most bland disregard of the people's ideas on the subject—that we were in favor of the "Allies," of the "democracies"; that we wanted to aid them in every way short of war. From the start there was not as much democracy in imperial France and imperial England as you could shake a twig at. And already there are no "Allies." There is just England, the imperialist monster from which we specifically declared ourselves independent.

The French government made a solemn promise to their "Ally" that they would not make a separate peace. That government is gone, its leaders are on trial before a new group of dictators who have made a separate peace and are ready to become "Allies" of Germany.

Suppose America enters the war on England's side, as we have already almost done. England would make an equally solemn pledge not to declare a separate peace—and what greater assurance have we that the pledge would be kept supposing the government making it were overthrown? We have no assurance whatever and could have none. Yet, if that happened, we would be left holding the bag just as England has been by the defection of France.

We are forever saving the world and certainly in the last war we were left holding the bag. We went in too late (by military standards—too soon by any standard of common sense); our monopolists made big war profits. Afterward we were Shylocks—yet we gaily renounced all the war debts owing to the American people, and still more gaily lent new money which of course was likewise not repaid.

Our sympathies are so easily roused. Back in the early part of the century we were dutifully in our pews cheering the little men of Japan in Japan's war against great big horrible China, which was nothing but a country of opium-eaters (a habit spread and encouraged by England for profit). In the Russo-Japanese war our sympathies were with Japan and there we were again cheering Admiral Togo's great naval victory.

And now we see the recriminations flying back and forth between the two late "Allies," France and England, when both countries—or rather, the great monopolists in both countries—had been backing and supporting Hitler for years because they thought he was the bulwark against Communism.

If we should get into this war, no matter who wins we will be hated
by the winners and reviled by the losers. We would not make the world
any safer for democracy than we did last time. We would merely
ensure that everyone hated us.

Consider again the background of our national identity. The whole
meaning of the Revolutionary War was independence from England
and her empire. Washington's advice is a true expression of this historic meaning—but it is so forgotten now that this year many Americans were actually ashamed of celebrating the Fourth of July!

Our country has developed not in co-operation but in competition
with Europe and England. England has put every possible barrier in
our way and has never co-operated with us except when its own interests were solely concerned. We have, it is true, received cultural, scientific, and technical impetus from Europe—but at the same time we have
been burdened with the heritage of Europe's divergent history. All
through our history the main factor holding us back has been the fatal
disease of our masochistic love for England.

Why can't we get an American slant on affairs just for a change?
Why can't we face the facts squarely and put aside the surge of our
unnatural passion for our worst enemy? Why can't we formulate a
solid, realistic national doctrine with regard to foreign relations which
will become traditional—which every citizen will know in detail and
understand—and by which all our defense policies will be guided as
new conditions arise? Events are moving and changing so fast, and if
we don't get ourselves an American doctrine concerning our relation
with other countries, and let it be known and stick to it, we can only
end by finding ourselves alone in a war-mad, hate-filled world with no
compass to guide us, not even the compass of internal democracy.

Frazier Hunt, who for years lived in England and who actually
called himself an Anglophile, returned recently from Europe after several months covering the war for International News Service. He is
starting a one-man fight to keep us out of the present mess. He says
it is too late to save Europe—that we must save America first.

He hits it right on the head. The only place where we can fight
effectively for democracy is here at home—and there is plenty of fighting to be done. The fight for democracy is the fight to meet the challenge of new conditions, the challenge of the industrial machine and

of the machine itself. It is the fight to put the machine to work for man and for America, not man and America for the machine. Here we are coolly raising billions for destruction—$15,000,000,000 at this writing—and how easy it is, how almost comically easy when you think of the "bankruptcy" which was to ensue if one paltry billion was spent on relief projects last year! And yet over the last decade we have had from ten to fifteen million people unemployed. We could have had a system of marvelous highways built across this country. We could have done for the country as a whole—for that huge backward slum which is most of the South—what Robert Moses has done for New York with the West Side Highway and the new East River drive. We could have rehabilitated our parks, harnessed millions more units of water power, taken electricity to the uttermost parts, enlarged and beautified our beaches, reclaimed our slums. Think what these billions would do if they were put to work for education, for research, for invention, for the conquest of disease! And think what real greatness would lie ahead for America if we concentrated on these things instead of dirtying our hands with the filth and insanity of Europe's destruction orgies! And not alone Europe's, but Asia's too. "Our interests," we are now told, must be protected by force in the Orient. What are those interests? A $400,000,000 investment in Japan, a $200,000,000 investment in China, the profits to be made from coolie-produced tin and rubber in the Malay States, Rockefeller's oil sources in the Dutch East Indies. What concern are these of the American people who want the decent living conditions our own country could easily provide for all?

Wherever we look, we come back to the Declaration of Independence and the Constitution as the anchors of our democracy and welfare. We do not want an empire, we want democracy. The ideal of democracy is the highest humanity ever developed. It will withstand any propaganda from within or without if the people can only be satisfied that the ideal of the benefit of ALL, including the under-privileged, is fixed on the horizon. To speak of democracy flourishing and being saved or advanced in war is like speaking of a fish flourishing out of water. The only air in which democracy can breathe is peace, and it must be free air and abundant air, in which all ideas regardless of labels and origin can be expressed. Fighting "isms" is merely fighting symptoms, not the cause. Give the "isms" rein and they will stand or fall by what common sense there may be in them for America. The Constitution is not concerned with "isms" but with the right for every man to speak his mind together with his neighbor's right to disprove his contentions if he can.

We must get a little sense in our heads at this late date and use our perfectly specific Constitution and Declaration of Independence as the only acid test of a man's loyalty to democracy, instead of persecuting, as we are now doing, the very people who stand up for those national charters.

We must make an end, however ruthless the means that have to be employed, to the possibility of individuals and small groups accumulating and inheriting huge sums of money, which they inevitably use to suborn the government and to get us into foreign wars by the eternal search for more profit.

We must make this the criterion regarding what should and should not be done in the exploitation of our own land: Does it or doesn't it add to the general wealth of the whole community? We must stop courting scarcity as if it were the most desirable of bedfellows.

We must make the Constitution work—all of the Constitution—or we will never have democracy. We must do it in a fully conscious and methodical and speedy way because if we don't it will come to fighting in our streets between brother and brother.

For as Tom Paine pointed out, what an old sage, Archimedes, said in the dawn of civilization about the mechanical powers may be applied to reason and liberty: "Had we a place to stand upon, we might raise the world." America plus our Constitution is certainly a place to stand on to raise democracy into being. Let us save America and democracy by not joining in this foreign blood-bath, but rather by showing the world in our own example how democracy can work.

Only the mass can get America out of the mess. Not a small group of a few thousand crusaders. America will be on the road forward, solidly and unmovably on the road, when a great throng of people comes out on the streets of our cities with the Constitution and Declaration of Independence as their banners and the un-American monopolists will see them and will say: "That's America."